'Layla is right that the challenges to opportunit
communities – I am thrilled that she's not only highlighting these disparities for the LGBTQ+
community but is providing insights and solutions to overcome these challenges.'

John Amaechi OBE, author of the New York Times *and* Sunday Times
bestselling leadership book, The Promises of Giants

'This much-needed and engaging book will resonate with LGBTQ+ people on every step
of the career ladder and leave everyone who reads it with a little extra knowledge, insight,
inspiration and a sense of hope.'

Dame Inga Beale, Former CEO of Lloyd's of London

'As CEO of the premier non-profit organization working exclusively on LGBTQ+ workplace
equity, inclusion, and belonging, it is such a pleasure to find a book so full of personal insights,
research and practical actions on these topics. This book makes it clear how the rainbow ceiling
was built, and how to break it down, with anecdotes from people all over the world that make
it funny, sad, surprising, and real. Required reading for LGBTQ+ people pursuing their careers
as well as for anyone seeking to build a more inclusive workplace.'

Erin Uritus, CEO of Out & Equal

'Employers can ignore the rainbow ceiling or deny its existence altogether as self-identification
and representation estimates remain rare. Consequently, LGBTQ+ people are often not part of
the decisions that shape their lives. Through fascinating interviews with business, diplomatic,
and administrative senior professionals, Layla McCay has pinpointed the subtle mechanisms
of exclusion behind this phenomenon and how to mitigate them. Her book honours the
experience of a generation of resilient and exemplary LGBTQ+ leaders who often had to
overcome significant hurdles and do twice the work for half the recognition. But perhaps more
importantly, it provides a guide to overcoming these obstacles for LGBTQ+ people and their
employers today. Breaking the rainbow ceiling is crucial in filling the representation gap – Layla
McCay's book brings us one step closer to this goal.'

Fabrice Houdart, Founder and Executive Director, Association of LGBTQ+ Corporate Directors

'For many people, being openly LGBTQ in the workplace still presents a challenge. The
rainbow ceiling loomed large in my professional career and was one of the reasons I remained
in the closet for so long. I was outed by a tabloid newspaper in 2007, resigned as CEO of BP,
and began to build a new life in the world I had feared since my youth. After the initial pain, I
found it to be life-giving. Coming out enabled me to think bigger and aim higher.

'Layla McCay's *Breaking the Rainbow Ceiling* picks up where I left off. Much has changed
for the better in the decade since I told my own story in *The Glass Closet*, but we are still not
where we should be. This book is essential reading for those who are building up the courage
to bring their authentic self into the workplace, for those who have already taken that leap, and
for those who stand ready to support them. No one should be held back on the grounds of their
sexual orientation or imprisoned by their own fear. This book is a reminder that the rainbow
ceiling can and will be broken."

Lord Browne of Madingley, Group CEO of BP (1995–2007) and author of
The Glass Closet: Why Coming Out Is Good Business

'A brilliantly researched book packed full of insight, advice and inspiration for those who want
to be able to live, work and succeed as their authentic and fabulous LGBTQ+ selves.'

Suki Sandhu OBE, Founder & CEO of Involve and Audeliss, and author of
How To Get Your Act Together: A Judgement-Free Guide
to Diversity and Inclusion for Straight White Men

'At last we have a view from the top from LGBTQ+ leaders in business and other sectors. Layla
McCay convincingly shows that these pioneers did not have an easy path. But even as the stakes
grew higher on the way up, this impressive group of leaders managed to break through the

rainbow ceiling. LGBTQ+ readers of this fascinating book will have an easier time on their own journeys thanks to the wonderful advice that McCay has distilled from her research.'

M. V. Lee Badgett, Economist and author of The Economic Case for LGBT Equality: Why Fair and Equal Treatment Benefits Us All

'Layla McCay has deftly brought together clear facts and compelling stories to shine a light on the realities of being LGBTQ+ in today's world. This compulsively readable work celebrates the progress that has been made and illuminates the challenges that still lie ahead. It is an important prompt for questions we all must ask ourselves – whether gay or straight – about our shared commitment to busting through the rainbow ceiling on the way to a more inclusive and compassionate society.'

Marjorie Chorlins, Senior Vice President for Europe at the US Chamber of Commerce

'Enough of talking about inequity! It's time to start doing, to help create change, and in this brilliant, and useful book, Layla McCay gives us a manual of how to create inclusion infrastructures for LGBTQ+ people to thrive and rise to the top. It is time for us, along with help from our allies to break that rainbow ceiling, and to "lift as we climb". Layla's interviewees come from different professions and from all over the world, and they offer a wealth of perspectives that support her extraordinary data-driven research. For instance, I was fascinated to read about the barriers to LGBTQ+ progression that Layla outlined, like "unmooring", or simply the fact that so many queer leaders may have been lost due to the AIDS pandemic! I teared up when I read the "advice to my younger self" section and I think that you will too.'

Parmesh Shahani, Head of Godrej DEI Lab, and author of Queeristan: LGBTQ Inclusion in the Indian Workplace

'Profound research, inspiring stories, a clear message: Why are LGBTQ+ people under-represented at the most senior levels in global workplaces? What can be done to change this – by employers, lawmakers, managers, the queer workforce? And why is this so important – for all of us? Layla McCay has written a very important book, essential for every leader at all levels.'

Jens Schadendorf, Economist and author of GaYme Changer: How the LGBT+ community and their allies are changing the global economy

'An important look at ways to combat the impacts of prejudice in the workplace so that everyone can thrive at work.'

Matthew Todd, author of Straight Jacket: Overcoming Society's Legacy of Gay Shame *and previous editor of* Attitude *magazine*

'McCay is spot on. In this new era for LGBTQ+ equality, it's imperative that we continue to break down the structural barriers to LGBTQ+ equality. In our global advocacy work – from developing emerging LGBTQ+ talent to empowering senior LGBTQ+ leaders – Out Leadership has seen time and again that the lift-as-you-climb approach is our best hammer to break the rainbow ceiling.'

Todd Sears, Founder and CEO of Out Leadership

'In the decade since Lord Browne published *The Glass Closet* it's disheartening to see LGBTQ+ folks on both sides of the Atlantic enjoy fewer protections than they did 10 years ago and still encounter inequalities in the hiring process and in the workplace. Layla's research is therefore both important and timely: more than ever we're relying on corporations to step into issues of social justice, and today's managers need more guidance than ever before. My hope is that this book will help more LGBTQ+ folks rise to positions of leadership, and in turn inspire the next generation.'

James Hudson, British HR executive working in the US for brands including Levi's and Nike

'It's unacceptable to feel excluded and disadvantaged because of who you are. It's still too common. Layla's book describes vividly how this feels, where its roots lie, and what can be done about it. A good read for anyone who wants the world to be a better place.'

Sue Unerman, CTO of EssenceMediacomX, author of The Glass Wall *and* Belonging

'A powerful, inspiring and critically important read for HR professionals and for LGBTQ+ people developing their careers.'

Lutfur Ali, Senior Policy Advisor (Equality, Diversity, Inclusion and Transformation), Chartered Institute of Personnel and Development (CIPD) and Non-Executive Director, Business Continuity Institute

Breaking the Rainbow Ceiling

How LGBTQ+ people can thrive and succeed at work

LAYLA McCAY

BLOOMSBURY BUSINESS
LONDON · OXFORD · NEW YORK · NEW DELHI · SYDNEY

BLOOMSBURY BUSINESS
Bloomsbury Publishing Plc
50 Bedford Square, London, WC1B 3DP, UK
29 Earlsfort Terrace, Dublin 2, Ireland

BLOOMSBURY, BLOOMSBURY BUSINESS and the Diana logo are trademarks of
Bloomsbury Publishing Plc

First published in Great Britain 2024

A catalogue record for this book is available from the British Library

Library of Congress Cataloguing-in-Publication data has been applied for

ISBN: 978-1-3994-1076-2; eBook: 978-1-3994-1075-5

2 4 6 8 10 9 7 5 3 1

Typeset by Deanta Global Publishing Services, Chennai, India
Printed and bound in Great Britain by CPI Group (UK) Ltd, Croydon CR0 4YY

To find out more about our authors and books visit www.bloomsbury.com
and sign up for our newsletters

For my parents and my wife, whose support has been
so important to me.

And for everyone who has looked up and seen
a rainbow ceiling.

Contents

Foreword by Lord Michael Cashman

I think this book is really timely – actually, I think it is urgent. For me, it's a reminder that the rainbow ceiling has always existed for LGBTQ+ people, affecting our ability to get on in life and work. Some of us ignore it – it's our way of coping. Some of us have crashed through, causing damage to ourselves (and hopefully not damage to others). And some of us manage to pass through, though we still get stuck in places.

I will probably always be remembered for being part of the first gay kiss on a British soap opera on television, on *EastEnders* on the BBC, back in 1985. I played their first gay character at a time when to be gay or bisexual was synonymous in the public eye with HIV and death. When I left *EastEnders*, my agent spoke to me about taking over a role in a musical in the West End, but the casting director said: 'Oh, we couldn't have Michael – it's a family show.' I have had this happen on other occasions and these are just the rainbow ceilings that I know about. I can only imagine I have come up against many more.

Some things are changing. Shortly after my introduction into the House of Lords in 2014, Baroness Barker said to me: 'Once upon a time the only way we could get in here was by abseiling from the public gallery. Now, we walk in through the front door.' She was referring to a group of lesbians who protested after a vote that discriminated against LGBTQ+ people in 1988. After that vote we campaigned for equality, people exited from the closets we thought we had to live in and we defied the stereotypes, showing that we don't have two heads, that we have the same hopes, dreams and aspirations as anyone else, and now we are breaking through.

But some things aren't changing, which is why I see this book as so urgent. Right now, people are still trying to impose that ceiling, to push us back. I see my job in the House of Lords as giving a voice to people who otherwise might not be heard. LGBTQ+ people are still being misrepresented, stereotyped, dehumanized. There seems to be a well-organized attempt in several countries to send us back underground, where our love 'dare not speak its name'. It reminds me that the enemies of equality never go away.

Layla McCay has written an important book at an important moment. A leader in the health sector and recently recognized as one of the top 100 LGBTQ+ executives internationally, she has combined research with her own experiences plus insights from fascinating LGBTQ+ people in senior roles around the world to examine the rainbow ceiling as it applies to the workplace and see how these leaders broke through. The result is this gripping book that should inspire and empower LGBTQ+ people, our colleagues and our employers.

We haven't achieved equality until we have difference removed from the equation and everyone has the chance to succeed. We're still not there. But young people are not going back to how it was. They show us how amazing, diverse, wonderful and at times threatening the world can be. They like being who they are, taking the totality of who they are into work. Workplaces and society will be better and richer for it. Eventually I hope we'll no longer have a rainbow ceiling, we'll just have an amazing view of sky.

Lord Michael Cashman

July 2023

A note

In this book, I refer to the many people who are affected by the rainbow ceiling by primarily using the term LGBTQ+. The letters stand for lesbian, gay, bisexual, transgender, queer and questioning. The plus includes other sexual orientations and gender identities, such as intersex, asexual, non-binary, gender-fluid, pansexual, omnisexual and two-spirit. Different versions of the abbreviation are commonly used. For example, people and research quoted in this book also use the terms LGBT, LGBTQI+ and LGBTQIA+. I sometimes use the word queer to refer to this complex group of identities; however, while some people embrace the word queer as their preferred way of identifying, and many use it as an umbrella term, not all LGBTQ+ people identify with the word queer – and though it has largely been reclaimed from its history as a slur, some people still find it insulting. It is always best to ask people how they identify as individuals.

I also refer to people who are not LGBTQ+ and for this purpose I use the terms cisgender (or cis, pronounced 'sis', for short) and heterosexual and straight. The word cisgender is often used to describe a person whose gender identity corresponds with the sex on their birth certificate. And the words heterosexual and straight both mean a woman who is primarily sexually attracted to men, or a man who is primarily sexually attracted to women. Sometimes these words are brought together and abbreviated to cis-het.

These terms are widely accepted at the time of writing, but may evolve.

The people interviewed

As well as my own, the following people's personal experiences feature in this book. I have indicated their job role and location at the time of our interview – some will have proceeded to new roles by the time you read this book.

Name	Job role at the time of our discussion	Location at the time of our discussion
Rosanna Andrews	Programme Manager at NHS Employers	UK
Dame Inga Beale	Former CEO of Lloyd's of London and now a portfolio director	UK
Dinesh Bhugra	Psychiatrist; Past president of Royal College of Psychiatrists, World Psychiatric Association and British Medical Association	UK
Annie Bliss	Policy Adviser at NHS Confederation	UK
Ralph Breuer	Partner at McKinsey & Company	Germany
Becks Buckingham	Head of Mission in Caracas, British Government	Venezuela
Pips Bunce	Director and head of investment banking technology strategic programs at Credit Suisse	UK

Matt Burney	China Country Director, British Council; since then, His Majesty's Consul General in Shanghai, British Government	China
Rosalind Campion	Director of the Office for Life Sciences, British Government (and the author's wife)	UK
Marjorie Chorlins	Senior Vice President for Europe, US Chamber of Commerce	USA
Darryl Clough	Senior Policy Adviser, Innovation and Growth at the Office for Life Sciences, British Government	UK
Omar Daair	British High Commissioner to Rwanda and Non-resident Ambassador to Burundi	Rwanda
Matt Dabrowski	Founder and Director of OutBritain LGBTQ+ Chamber of Commerce	UK
Dame Jackie Daniel	CEO of Newcastle upon Tyne NHS Foundation Trust	UK
James Devine	Director for Health and Care Workforce at a professional services consultancy	UK
Alim Dhanji	President of Adidas Canada; since then, Chief People Officer and Executive Vice-President, Equinox Group in New York City	Canada
Dan Farrell	Company Director at Sparks Film Schools	UK
Jim Fitterling	Chairman and CEO of Dow (Fortune 500 company)	USA
Loren Fykes	President and Co-Founder of Fruits in Suits Japan and Pride Business Alliance Japan	Japan

Peter Gordon	Chef, often described as 'the godfather of fusion cooking'	New Zealand
Judith Gough	British Ambassador to Sweden	Sweden
Jim Harra	Chief Executive and First Permanent Secretary of HM Revenue and Customs, British Government	UK
Sivan Kaniel	CEO of LGBTech	Israel
Eva Kreienkamp	CEO of Berliner Verkehrsbetriebe (BVG)	Germany
Nesta Lloyd–Jones	Assistant Director at Welsh NHS Confederation	UK
John Lotherington	Former teacher, now freelance thinktank convener and Director of 21st Century Trust	UK
Allegra McEvedy	Chef, writer and television presenter	UK
Mitch Mitchinson	Managing Director of Mitchinson Associates Ltd	Venezuela
Peter Molyneux	Chair of Sussex Partnership NHS Foundation Trust, England liaison for the International Initiative for Mental Health Leadership and Co-Chair of the LGBTQ+ Health and Care Leadership Network	UK
Leng Montgomery	Senior diversity and inclusion consultant	UK
Ken Ohashi	CEO of Brooks Brothers	USA
Pedro Pina	Vice President, Head of YouTube in Europe, Middle East and Africa, Lead for Google's LGBT+ chapter and member of Google's Diversity Council in EMEA	UK

Simon Pollard	Theatre Director	UK
David Quarrey	British Ambassador to NATO	Belgium
Gautam Raghavan	Assistant to the President for Presidential Personnel at the White House	USA
Nancy Schlichting	Retired President and CEO of the Henry Ford Health System	USA
Tammy Smith	Major General (retired), US Army	USA
Rick Suarez	President of AstraZeneca Spain	Spain
Keshav Suri	Executive Director at The Lalit Suri Hospitality Group	India
Karen Teo	Vice President of Sales at Meta	Singapore
Rosemary Tickle	Digital content officer at the NHS Confederation	UK
Sarah Weaver	Associate Director, Accenture	Australia

Introduction

'The concept of a Rainbow Ceiling completely resonates…
It's like you've run the race, you've made it, but then you
collapse at the finish line' – a senior business leader based in
the United Kingdom

If asked to name a prominent LGBTQ+ CEO, you would probably
be able to do it. But as your brain runs through the list of options,
be aware: you are quite possibly thinking of the same handful of
people as everyone else. Tim Cook from Apple, maybe? When
he came out as gay in 2014, he was the first openly LGBTQ+
CEO in the Fortune 500, the list of the 500 biggest corporations
in America. At the time, his decision was considered daring and
maybe even transformative. There was a feeling that this would
herald the start of far more out-and-proud LGBTQ+ people in
top jobs around the world. That has not happened. A decade later,
at the time of writing, there were still only four openly gay, lesbian
or bisexual CEOs on that list – and no trans or non-binary people.
Delve into the almost 5,500 board seats held by these companies,
and at a recent count, only 41 of these seats, fewer than 0.8 per
cent, were held by LGBTQ+ people (worse, some were held by
the same person sitting on multiple boards, meaning the actual
number of individuals is even lower.)[1] On the other side of the
Atlantic, it may be helpful to look at the CEOs in the Financial
Times Stock Exchange 100 Index, otherwise known as the FTSE
100, the 100 biggest companies on the London Stock Exchange.
Or perhaps it's not that useful. At the time of writing, not a single

one of these 100 CEOs was publicly known to be LGBTQ+
– nobody lesbian, gay, bisexual, transgender, non-binary, queer,
pansexual, intersex, asexual or any of the other identities that
make up part of the LGBTQ+ rainbow.

Why should we care? Because the tiny proportion of
LGBTQ+ people who have reached the upper echelons of
the business world gives us insight into some of the differences
in opportunity that are playing out across the world – even in
countries that pride themselves on their anti-discrimination
laws and inclusion policies. Most people have heard of the 'glass
ceiling', a metaphor typically used to describe how women are
prevented from reaching the top jobs. But there is also a rainbow
ceiling. The discrimination and other barriers that contribute to
inequality for LGBTQ+ people in our careers have largely been
flying under the radar on board papers and on managers' priority
lists for some time. When I raise the topic, people have routinely
responded: 'Oh, that was in the old days – it's fixed now.' The
evidence tells us that it is not. And making the assumption that it's
fine now doesn't help at all. The barrier does not affect everyone
equally, but data tells us, as do personal stories, that there is a
rainbow ceiling that holds LGBTQ+ people back as we progress
up the career ladder. Looking at it properly will help improve
equality – a laudable aim in itself – but also potentially improve
the performance of individuals and the overall performance of
the organization. There is a compelling link between diversity
in the workplace, including on executive teams, and better
recruitment and retention; problem solving and innovation; and
ultimately, financial performance, including revenue and market
share. If LGBTQ+ people are given a fairer chance to succeed
in our careers, it makes things better for everyone.

Awareness of the rainbow ceiling

Even some LGBTQ+ people do not like to acknowledge the
existence of a rainbow ceiling, or at least, not one that affects us

personally. Some have been lucky not to see it, or more often, have been able to largely get around it by using other types of privilege. But according to Rosalind Campion, Director of the UK Government's Office for Life Sciences, 'I think of the hope we all have that we are accepted and wanted, and then it turns out that's a lie. We know it's a lie because we've not had an out prime minister (in the UK); we've not had many leaders in other sectors that are out. We should call it a rainbow ceiling because it might look pretty to see a rainbow, but actually, sometimes you're stuck.'

That said, despite some people's instinctive denial or lack of awareness that LGBTQ+ people can still get stuck on the basis of their sexual orientation or gender identity, it's hardly a secret. Around the world today, LGBTQ+ people in their millions stay quiet at work for fear that publicly acknowledging this part of themselves could come with career repercussions. This is by no means a problem that only affects older LGBTQ+ people. There has undoubtedly been much more representation, support and social acceptability for LGBTQ+ people in recent years and more focus on inclusion in many workplaces. Yet senior leaders who participate in staff groups and employee resource groups, or ERGs, reflected that the concerns of their young LGBTQ+ colleagues today are uncannily similar to their own. Prejudice and discrimination persist and in some cases, it is getting worse, not better. My own father, upon hearing I was writing this book, panicked and instinctively tried to talk me out of it. Even though I came out at the age of 17, he feared that talking in public about LGBTQ+ matters – and identifying myself not just as a lesbian but one who is willing to point out equality gaps – would disadvantage me. And maybe he's right. As we will see, it absolutely could. But it doesn't have to.

Let's look at how LGBTQ+ people fare in different leadership contexts beyond the lens of business. Only seven of the thousands of heads of state in the world, past and present, have ever publicly identified as LGBTQ+ (in Andorra, Belgium, Iceland, Ireland, Luxembourg, San Marino and Serbia). The first of these leaders was not appointed until 2009. In the US, a recent study found that just 0.19 per cent of elected officials were LGBTQ+ and this proportion was such a significant increase that it was felt to be cause for celebration.[2] That said, the trend of LGBTQ+ people in elected positions is confusing. For example, there's a much higher proportion of LGBTQ+ Members of Parliament in the UK. In October 2021, around 60 of the 650 Members of Parliament in the UK publicly identified as LGBTQ+, 9 per cent of all MPs at the time. But tellingly, none was selected to be in the Cabinet, that most senior cadre of parliamentarians below the Prime Minister.

History and the rainbow ceiling

Perhaps the story of LGBTQ+ inequalities in professional life can be most easily traced back to the recent history of unelected government officials. Consider what's been happening in the US and the UK. In both countries the rights of LGBTQ+ people to live their lives and not be rejected for jobs, denied promotion or fired due to their sexual orientation or gender identity are surprisingly recent and quite precarious. Many people who might have been senior leaders today were until recently not allowed to get on to the career ladder, or were pushed off. This is one reason that the rungs are still slippery beneath our feet as we try to climb.

In 1953, the US decided to ban anyone who was gay or lesbian from serving in the federal government and then added in state and local governments, under President Dwight D Eisenhower's Executive Order 10450. A presidentially endorsed witch hunt was set up to investigate every government employee, interrogate 'suspects', detect LGBTQ+ people, then fire any they could find, deeming them a national security risk. According to historian David K. Johnson, between 5,000 and 10,000 LGBTQ+ people lost their jobs as a result; many more were probably deterred from applying in the first place.

This period, known as the 'Lavender Scare', persisted until 1975 when people who were fired successfully framed this as a violation of their civil rights and the rules were finally changed. Unless you required security clearance, of course, in which case the discrimination didn't officially end until 1998, after which there were still checks on a case-by-case basis. The reason was that being LGBTQ+ was still considered shameful or scandalous enough to be a potential blackmail risk. The result of this is that many people remember when discrimination against LGBTQ+ people was officially endorsed and indeed required in workplaces. Marjorie Chorlins, Senior Vice President for Europe at the US Chamber of Commerce, recalled: 'In the earliest years of my career I was closeted and that was a challenge for me. Getting my first security clearance in the 1990s, I remember vividly the agent asked if I was dating. I said I was not, and she asked why and started to probe – I was scared at that point. But it all worked out... Do I think I might not have been offered a job if it was known at the time? Yes.'

Bans on LGBTQ+ people in the workplace were even more rigorous within the US armed forces, where the outright ban evolved in 1994 into a 'Don't Ask, Don't Tell' law passed by the US Congress to allow gay and lesbian people to serve in the military as long as they didn't ever mention their sexual orientation on pain of being discharged (and about 13,000 people were indeed discharged after it became known). According to Major General Tammy Smith, now retired, who was the first general to come out in the US military: 'Before Don't Ask, Don't Tell, the policy was much stricter – there were actual witch hunts and sting operations to try to identify the gays and lesbians in a military unit so they could kick them out. We would share among the community if a local witch hunt was going on, saying: "Be careful – we've seen folks at the gay bar. Don't go down there for a while". We tried to protect each other. But people got caught. The fear increased as I got more invested that this was going to be my career – then you're thinking of grown-up things like healthcare, your pension, what home loan you can get. My aversion to risk increased as I grew in rank. I was hiding like lots of other people who were gay and had jobs.' Don't Ask, Don't Tell lasted until 2011. In fact, consensual same-sex sexual activity was only made legal across the whole US by a Supreme Court ruling in 2003. And the Executive Order that originally banned gay and lesbian people from government service in the US wasn't fully repealed until 2017. More widely in the US, it was only in the year 2020 that the Supreme Court ruled that workers cannot be fired for being gay or transgender; prior to that, only about half the country was protected by local laws to that effect.

As for the United Kingdom of Great Britain and Northern Ireland, the first law making homosexuality illegal came in 1533 and involved the death penalty, downgraded in 1861 to 10 years in prison for sodomy, but promptly upgraded in 1885 so that even a mere romantic letter between two men could be sufficient evidence for imprisonment. Women were never included in these laws, first because the lawmakers inaccurately assumed this didn't affect many women, and also for fear of giving women the idea of becoming homosexual. Sadly, these British laws were propagated across the world during colonization. The British Empire codified homophobia and transphobia into the laws, policies and culture of many countries in Africa, Asia and the Pacific from 1860; some of these countries had not previously had anything against gay, bisexual or trans people; others had not formalized existing prejudice into legislation. The majority of these laws and attitudes remain in place to this day, long after Britain's own laws have evolved to be less discriminatory. More than half of the countries where being LGBTQ+ is against the law today are a legacy of British colonization. At the time of writing, it was illegal to be gay in 64 countries; in some of these, prosecution is unlikely but LGBTQ+ people are subject to severe punishment, including the death penalty in Brunei, Iran, Mauritania, Saudi Arabia, Yemen and some northern states in Nigeria in 2023 – plus potential death penalty in about five other countries. Currently, some countries are reducing penalties and decriminalizing homosexuality; for example, India repealed their Colonial-era law banning sex between men in 2018, Botswana in 2019 and Singapore in 2022. But other countries are doubling down and increasing the penalties, often instrumentalizing homophobia, biphobia and transphobia as a backlash against globalization. Nigeria and Uganda have recently made their laws criminalizing and punishing LGBTQ+ people more severe.

Progress does not flow in one direction

Even when discriminatory laws are repealed, LGBTQ+ people cannot relax – there is no guarantee that progress will continue to flow in the direction of inclusion. Sir Chris Bryant is a gay Member of Parliament in England. He made the point in a House of Commons Debate for LGBT+ History Month 2023: 'In the 20th century, the most liberal place in the world for gay men was Berlin, from 1928 to 1931. By 1936, gay men were being carted off to concentration camps and we do not even know how many lost their lives under the Nazis.'[3] These about-turns take place regularly and are not a thing of the past. The same year that the US law allowing discrimination against LGBTQ+ people in the US workplace was repealed, there was an election; the new President immediately issued an Executive Order that revoked parts of that repeal, bringing back the ability to discriminate in some cases. And during the first quarter of 2023, more than 400 bills seeking to reduce the rights and visibility of LGBTQ+ people at state level in the US were introduced – more than were put forward in the whole of 2022. Meanwhile, having annulled its Anti-Homosexuality Act a decade ago, in 2023 Uganda passed an even harsher new Act that introduces life imprisonment for LGBTQ+ people and the death penalty in certain circumstances. The Act even threatens jail sentences for some landlords renting a home to a gay couple.

In the UK, sex between two men in private was eventually decriminalized in 1967 in England and Wales (1980 in Scotland, 1982 in Northern Ireland), more than 100 years after France repealed a similar law. But British LGBTQ+ people were not out of the woods as the police actually intensified their persecution of LGBTQ+ people: in 1966, 420 men had been convicted of gross indecency; in 1974, four times as many were convicted. A further homophobic wave swept the country in the 1980s, where a range of other old laws, and some new ones, continued to be used. Gay and bisexual men and lesbians were still being arrested for 'gross indecency' deep into the 1990s and when I was at school, the introduction of Section 28 made it unlawful for a teacher to even talk to me about my emerging realization that I was gay.

Clearly these laws impact on work. Legal protection against being denied employment or being fired for being LGBTQ+ didn't arrive in the UK until the 2000s. Gay and lesbian people have only been allowed to serve openly in the UK's Foreign, Commonwealth and Development Office since 1991 and in the UK's armed forces since the year 2000, after two people who were investigated and fired took their case to the European Court of Human Rights. Many people have been not hired, or have been fired, thanks to these laws. In 2015, a senior civil servant was quoted in a government report, saying: 'I'm certain I wouldn't be as senior as I am now if I'd been openly gay at work during the last 15 years. That makes me slightly sad, almost every day.'[4]

Today, there are no formal restrictions and plenty of LGBTQ+ people in the UK government's civil and foreign service, but it is telling that at the time of writing there were only two out LGBTQ+ permanent secretaries of the almost 50 people at this top level of the Civil Service who run or help run departments such as the Home Office or the Treasury. And there are very few LGBTQ+ people at the director general level just below. For those who get there, it has sometimes been suggested that they are held to higher standards.

A personal rainbow ceiling

And then I think about my own, comparatively privileged professional life. I started out as a junior doctor in Scotland and I believed myself to be the only LGBTQ+ staff member in the whole hospital. Clearly there must have been many more, but I had no way of knowing that, as they certainly weren't broadcasting it. Which meant I looked up and I saw nobody like me in the top positions, and I worried that being gay could hold me back from those jobs. It hasn't changed as much as you might think. With every role I've had since, I have seen LGBTQ+ people represented at the highest levels only as notable exceptions. I've repeatedly been the only out LGBTQ+ person on my management teams and looking up, I have continued to lack role models in my organizations who are gay like me. A recent influx of not one but two LGBTQ+ board members to my current organization has felt thrilling, important – and confusingly transgressive: a token one gay person, perhaps, but two feels somehow greedy. In unpacking these bizarre feelings, I realized I am so unused to seeing senior diversity that reflects my own diverse characteristics that it feels disorientating. I'm confident that no cisgender, heterosexual person has been impressed to realize there are two people who share these characteristics on a board.

My awareness of the risk of being LGBTQ+ to my own career progression felt only theoretical for a long time. Then a few years ago, I ran into someone who had been on my interview panel for a prestigious fellowship. He quite casually mentioned that other members of the panel had argued against selecting me because I had mentioned my wife in the interview and at least one panel member did not want to appoint a lesbian. I thought he was joking. He was not. Had the panel not known I was LGBTQ+, my chance of getting that fellowship would have been far better. If I had put any clues in my application form, like how I run a national LGBTQ+ Health and Care Leaders Network or that I authored this book, I might not have even made it to interview.

It made me stop and think. I found it chilling. It's not as though homophobia (or biphobia or transphobia) was a foreign concept to me. It was just galling to see it being quite so overtly applied to myself in a professional context, and so recently. I had falsely imagined that this didn't happen anymore, or that by now perhaps I have enough privilege to rise above it. It does, and I do not.

But at least I knew what had happened on that occasion. I can't help now wondering about the many, many other interviews and other potential opportunities I didn't get over my lifetime so far – did my sexual orientation play a part? In most of the locations where I have lived and worked, few interviewers could overtly cite my lesbianism as a disqualifier thanks to laws prohibiting that... but even so, how many of them might have secretly or subconsciously been thinking it? How many of these interviewers might have tended to think just a little less well of me because they weren't entirely comfortable with the knowledge that I'm gay? And might that have affected their instinct as they chose how to rate me on an interview form, considered whether to give me the benefit of the doubt, or decided how strongly to advocate for me for an opportunity? I can't help but wonder if my career might have gone in a different direction, if I might have been more rapidly promoted, or had different opportunities if I'd been straight, or was able to wave a magic wand to eliminate all LGBTQ+ bias. It's obviously unknowable – but it's disconcerting to think about. When that person casually mentioned my fellowship interview over a convivial lunch, I realized I had caught a glimpse of the rainbow ceiling above me. And now I know it's really there, I can't help seeing it.

How the rainbow ceiling relates to the glass ceiling

Of course, it's well recognized that minority groups face obstacles to professional success that have nothing to do with their personal competence. Rather, the barrier is created by bias from people at the top who subconsciously, or sometimes consciously, like to see themselves reflected in the cohorts they choose to commend, support and champion, which means they express positive prejudice towards these people. Which leads to prejudice against others they judge to be less like them, who in turn get fewer opportunities, are judged more harshly, and as a result, have a harder time ascending the career ladder. This effect is often described as the 'glass ceiling'.

I have mentioned the glass ceiling as a popular metaphor for the almost invisible barrier of discrimination that stands between women and minorities and their progress to increasingly senior management positions. The term was first coined in 1978 by an HR professional and management consultant called Marilyn Loden.[5] Sitting on a panel discussion at an event one day, she listened to her fellow speakers framing the likelihood of women's career success beyond middle management in terms of their professional attributes: they had to be more effective, more confident, more assertive, more... something. Loden articulated the issue that many women knew all too well: it wasn't just about their competence. In the words of Professor Henry Higgins in *My Fair Lady*: 'Why can't a woman be more like a man?'

Let's consider the glass ceiling as it applies to women, because it helps us understand the similarities and differences that constitute the rainbow ceiling. Despite all the anti-discrimination initiatives that have been introduced to empower the entry and thriving of women in the workplace, the glass ceiling has not yet been smashed. More qualified, talented women than ever have entered the labour market, but we remain markedly under-represented in senior management roles across all sectors.

Why? Umpteen research papers, reports, books, panel discussions and HR presentations have laid out the facts.[6,7] Males and females are treated differently from the moment of their birth, with boys more likely to be encouraged to excel at mathematics and science, and girls at art and literature; boys praised for the same leadership skills that are described disapprovingly as 'bossy' in girls. We know this affects people's career aspirations, opportunities, experiences, as well as self-belief in what we can achieve.

Once out in the world and progressing professionally, these differences solidify into the glass ceiling. Women are more likely to assume caring responsibilities and are less likely to have consistent access to senior role models and informal networks of senior managers, mentors and champions. Women tend to be assigned positions with lower visibility, constraining their career opportunities. We face HR decisions that disadvantage us based on gender: our workplace skills are less likely to be positively perceived by senior managers; we're still likely to be tarred with the 'bossy' brush if we try to lead. Stereotypes of expectations about where men and women excel often influence conscious and subconscious bias in hiring decisions, and women are more likely to face more stringent promotion criteria.[8] Hence, the glass ceiling metaphor. As we climb the career ladder, at some point many women's heads bash into a glass ceiling, and while we can see the next step, even if we are ready for it and we want it, we can't quite get there. Which leaves the most senior opportunities for those people whose various types of privilege enable them to move upwards without that constraint.

This glass ceiling is well recognized as affecting women's opportunity for professional progression. The concept has been extended to describe the experiences of people from ethnic minority groups and people who are disabled. There are many stories attesting to the impact of the glass ceiling on people being unfairly kept away from the top jobs on the unspoken basis of being perceived as different and therefore less suitable than those who resemble the people who historically held those jobs. But when it comes to LGBTQ+ people, the ceiling effect is rarely recognized. And yet the premise holds – in fact, in some cases, the effect can be multiplied many times over. People who are already held down by a glass ceiling due to their gender or race or disability or other diverse characteristics face an extra barrier if they are also LGBTQ+.

Breaking the rainbow ceiling

I hope everyone is starting from the premise that a person's sexual orientation or gender identity should not affect whether they get a job or are promoted or get fired. But numerous analyses find that they do. As an LGBTQ+ person, the research tells us I am less likely to thrive at work and less likely to reach the upper echelons of my profession. This is bad news for all LGBTQ+ people who are not flourishing and not getting promoted alongside our heterosexual or cisgender peers – and for those who are getting promoted but in return feel obliged to conceal that key part of ourselves. It's also damaging for the organizations that would benefit from having people able to be their authentic selves at work and bring valuable diversity to the organization. This is the rainbow ceiling: it is holding LGBTQ+ people down in the workplace, it is holding companies back, and it is clearly unacceptable.

What is this rainbow ceiling made of? It's built from historical and current societally endorsed prejudice and discrimination in different forms that start affecting LGBTQ+ people before we even realize we're different, undermining our self-esteem, pulling rungs from our ladders of social support and security and achievements, and making us feel like we do not belong, or we do not deserve to succeed. It's built from hiring and firing decisions that are subtly or overtly influenced by someone's sexual orientation or gender identity. Opportunities not offered. Connections not made. Doors not opened. The rainbow ceiling is holding people down and pushing us out by excluding us, overlooking us, badmouthing us, bullying or harassing us, disrespecting us, writing policies that don't work for our particular needs, scrutinizing us more deeply and judging our performance more harshly. By making us feel the need to disguise our authentic selves over and over again, apologize for ourselves and second-guess ourselves and struggle to picture people like us in senior roles. All these experiences, which are very common across the world, conspire to build the rainbow ceiling that holds back LGBTQ+ people in the workplace. Some people can see it more clearly than others. Many don't think it exists until they hit it. And if you think of the rainbow as an arc, some people hit that ceiling sooner than others, because lesbians, gay people, bisexual people, trans people, queer people and others within the LGBTQ+ population do not have the same experience. We experience different types and levels of prejudice according to all sorts of variables, often compounded by additional prejudices from intersections with other diverse parts of our identities that cause disadvantages in the workplace, like being a woman or being of an ethnic or racial minority. Consider the glass ceiling we just explored – glass and rainbow can combine to bring that ceiling lower and reinforce its robustness.

But the rainbow ceiling is also beautiful because it is coloured by differences and commonalities and talent and hopes and dreams and effort. And robust though it might be, it is not impermeable. Plenty of LGBTQ+ leaders have shown that it is very possible to break through the rainbow ceiling and reach the most senior positions in their careers despite the challenges in their paths, and organizations have shown how they can evolve to make things fairer.

The question is: how to break through the rainbow ceiling? To answer that question, I asked LGBTQ+ people who have achieved career success at the upper echelons of their professions around the world. They generously offered insight from their own experiences of how being LGBTQ+ affected their climb up the career ladder – and crucially, what helped. I also spoke to young people at earlier stages of their career. I refer to everyone using their job title at the time of interview; some have since moved to new roles, but this approach should provide helpful context. These people's personal insights shed light on the many, often unrecognized ways that being LGBTQ+ affects people's careers today, for better and for worse. And by identifying what helped others thrive and succeed, LGBTQ+ people coming next can find wisdom and inspiration. Meanwhile, CEOs, managers, HR professionals and others whose remit includes equality, diversity and inclusion, career counsellors, teachers, parents and guardians and the general public, can gain a better understanding of how this inequality plays out within the workplace and society and harness those insights to improve inclusion. There are lots of talented people out there who aren't being given a fair chance simply because they are gay, or lesbian, or bisexual, or transgender or non-binary, or queer, or fit somewhere else within that LGBTQ+ spectrum of sexual orientation and gender identity. That's not morally right. Nor, in many places, is it legally right. Nor does it make good business sense. Breaking the rainbow ceiling is an opportunity to get the best from people, from teams and from organizations.

In this book, we will examine the equality and opportunity gap that exists for LGBTQ+ people climbing the career ladder. The focus on leadership and role models at the top does not diminish the problems LGBTQ+ people face at less senior levels – but that would be a whole other book. Here, we'll seek to understand the true nature of the rainbow ceiling, why it exists and how to break it, with insights from people who have successfully done just that – LGBTQ+ professionals who have become CEOs, vice presidents, directors, ambassadors, senior government officials, senior military officers, chairs and others at the upper echelons of their professions, across the United States, Canada, the United Kingdom, Germany, Singapore, Spain, Portugal, Israel, India, Australia, New Zealand and other countries, as well as hearing from some at the start of their careers who are already catching glimpses of the rainbow ceiling. We'll also see how employers are making their workplaces more inclusive in ways that really matter to LGBTQ+ people. This book will explore how they all did it, and how you can too.

2

Mapping the rainbow ceiling

'I've heard of people who have constantly proven themselves, have risen through the ranks but when push comes to shove, when the question is who a company wants to represent them in the public sphere, sometimes the LGBT person misses out on that. Right now it feels like the world is only truly comfortable with the cisgender happily married family man or woman' – Karen Teo, Vice President of Sales at Meta, Singapore

So far, attempts to understand the rainbow ceiling and its effects have been largely confined to academic research, plus reports and surveys commissioned by LGBTQ+ organizations and some workplaces, but the issue has not quite made it into mainstream discussion. This means that LGBTQ+ exclusion is not always systematically recognized and addressed. Why not, when the barriers facing women, people of minority ethnicities and other minority groups have been well defined and are being actively addressed by national and organizational policies and practices?

Four key reasons for dismissing or downplaying career barriers affecting LGBTQ+ people

I have identified four key reasons: stigma and prejudice; political currents; reputational anxiety and simple lack of awareness about the extent of this equality gap.

First, let's consider stigma and prejudice. History, public narrative and cultural prejudices have led many people to feel uncomfortable talking about people's sexual orientation or gender identity, especially in the workplace, as it feels somehow more personal and potentially more political than asking about a person's sex or marital status or race and ethnicity. The box is often missing from workplace forms or left blank. Many professionals who are happy to ask about other diverse characteristics feel less comfortable asking about sexual orientation and gender identity. Some worry that this is private, perhaps somehow lewd information; some think that by asking they might offend the person being asked; and some heterosexual, cisgender people worry that if they say anything about LGBTQ+ matters, assumptions might be made about their own sexual orientation or gender identity. It's worth thinking about whether that last one worries you – fearing someone thinking you could be gay or lesbian, or bisexual or trans, as if this is a bad thing, can be a sign of internalized homophobia, biphobia or transphobia. Others may be LGBTQ+ but not ready to be public about that. Barriers like these can put people off venturing anywhere near the topic. And all this discomfort combines to create an impression that being LGBTQ+ is somehow shameful and secret.

Of course, this concern is entwined with political currents. It's very important for organizations to have information about the diversity of staff and their experiences to understand inequalities and drive improvements. But the concept of such a list even existing in a world that continues to have high levels of prejudice, volatility and unpredictable politics may be unsettling to people who know from distant and recent history that there is no guarantee of the direction in which LGBTQ+ rights will flow. Even now these rights exist in only about half of the world, and where they do, political rhetoric is such that many LGBTQ+ people fear these rights could be temporary, revoked on a political whim. Even where there are strong laws protecting against discrimination, lawmakers, leaders and future leaders make public statements that diminish LGBTQ+ people and socialize the benefits of constraining our rights. We discussed the US's recent anti-discrimination law being partly reversed following a change of president; we see this happening in other countries too. Laws that reduce LGBTQ+ people's rights are currently being introduced across the world from the US to Europe to Africa, often providing a convenient populist distraction from other political challenges.

All this creates a precarious and vulnerable situation for LGBTQ+ people, conscious that we could lose various rights at any time. In this context, you can see that when an LGBTQ+ person is asked to tick that box identifying themselves in a survey or a form, even if that person is generally open about their sexual orientation or gender identity, they may have qualms. It's an act of courage and faith to tick the box because the reality is that safety cannot be guaranteed.

Then there's reputational risk. In this complex world of political correctness, wokeness, identity politics, social media pile-ons and cancel culture, just talking about LGBTQ+ equality and inclusion can feel like a minefield. Leaders may fear personal criticism as well as reputational risk and practical repercussions for their organizations as a result of speaking up for LGBTQ+ people or instigating inclusive policies. For example, the state of Florida in the US has sought to end Disney's self-governing privileges in what has been described as retaliation following the company's opposition to a new law aiming to largely prevent discussion of LGBTQ+ matters in schools. Repercussions can happen either because some people disapprove of a person or organization's approaches to inclusion, or because navigating the 'right' way to talk about LGBTQ+ issues can be tricky, is continually evolving and has the potential to cause inadvertent offence even as leaders seek to be inclusive.

Many leaders who want to support LGBTQ+ people worry that they could do it 'wrong'. It's a valid concern. While there are many benefits to improving LGBTQ+ visibility and inclusion, plenty of cisgender and heterosexual leaders I have spoken to around the world have received death threats just for publicly affirming their support for LGBTQ+ people and have received complaints from the public about inclusive policies or actions their organizations have taken. This sometimes leads to damaging stories in the press and across social media, protests and calls to boycott or otherwise harm their organization, all of which have the intended effect of making many people anxious about publicly and visibly being an ally to LGBTQ+ people. That said, slapping a rainbow onto a company's logo during Pride month when that act is largely without risk has been similarly criticized as 'rainbow washing' rather than leaders choosing to do anything more meaningful that month or year-round to reduce LGBTQ+ inequalities. It is undeniably a fraught time, and arguably, being actively, visibly pro-LGBTQ+ inclusion currently requires more courage than supporting people's other diverse characteristics like sex, race, religion, disability or age. But that is obviously not a reason not to try.

There is a fourth important reason for not recognizing and addressing the rainbow ceiling: not being entirely sure it exists, or what it looks like. And in some ways, that's even more challenging. In mid-2023, a mere four out of the top 500 CEO jobs in America were held by LGBTQ+ people; none of the top 100 in the UK. But what should we make of that? Is it under-representation, and if so, by how much? Figuring out whether LGBTQ+ people are disproportionately missing out on the most senior jobs means answering three big questions: What proportion of the population (and specifically the working population) is LGBTQ+? What proportion of your organization's staff? And what would a representative proportion of the most senior positions held by LGBTQ+ people look like? These are surprisingly hard questions to answer.

How much of the population is actually LGBTQ+?

Seizing the biggest question first: how many people are actually LGBTQ+ in the world, or in a particular country or state? It's hard to believe, but we genuinely don't know. No objective measurement exists. With the exception of some intersex people, this isn't the kind of information that can be recorded on birth certificates or based on external observation. It relies on self-reporting, a process which is fraught with inaccuracy at the best of times, and as we've seen, even more so when it comes to sexual orientation and gender identity. There are all sorts of reasons people might not yet know how they identify or feel unable or unwilling to share that information honestly in census data, surveys, employment or other official contexts. Which makes it pretty hard to understand the extent to which LGBTQ+ people are under-represented or over-represented in various aspects of life. Hard, but not impossible.

There is a popular and much-quoted adage that one in 10 people are gay. This ballpark figure was calculated by Alfred Kinsey, the American sexologist who is famed for having developed the Kinsey Scale in 1948. He popularized the concept that sexual orientation exists on a continuum from exclusively heterosexual to exclusively homosexual, and that many people fall into the middle.[9] His seven-point scale is considered a little old-fashioned these days. But even now, with more than 200 different surveys and scales and almost as many terms dedicated to describing people's sexual orientation and gender identity, it is fiendishly hard to answer that one simple question. How many people are LGBTQ+? The one-in-10 figure may not be the most modern estimate, but nothing decisive has replaced it.

The research company Ipsos interviewed 19,000 people in 27 countries around the world in 2021[10] and found that only four out of every five people described themselves as heterosexual: 3 per cent reported being gay, lesbian or homosexual, 4 per cent bisexual, 1 per cent pansexual or omnisexual, 1 per cent asexual, 1 per cent 'other' and 11 per cent 'don't know or won't say'. When the survey channelled Kinsey and asked specifically about sexual attraction, just 83 per cent said they were exclusively attracted to the opposite sex. (7 per cent said they were only or mostly attracted to the same sex, 4 per cent were equally attracted to both sexes and the others didn't know or preferred not to say). So could the Kinsey figure be updated to 1 in 5? Perhaps.

The proportion of LGBTQ+ people identified in that international survey is significantly higher than lots of in-country surveys – but of course they all use different methods and select their respondents in different ways, which can skew the results. In the UK in 2021, the national census sought to get a true and unbiased answer by asking the entire population about their sexual orientation for the first time and found that about 3.2 per cent of people identified as gay, lesbian, bisexual or 'other orientation' and about 0.5 per cent reported that the gender they identify with is different than their sex registered at birth, very similar to the UK's Annual Population Survey in 2020, which found 3.1 per cent of adults identified as gay, lesbian or bisexual (this number has been steadily increasing over the years – it jumped from 2.7 per cent the previous year). The British percentage is in line with the lower end of proportions found in US surveys in which around 3.5 per cent of people identify themselves as LGBTQ+, but other surveys are finding higher numbers; for instance, a Gallup poll in 2020 found 5.9 per cent of Americans to be LGBTQ+. It's clear that people may answer differently depending on the context, or who's asking, or what they think the information will be used for.

Looking more closely at the international survey figures, a lot of differences emerge – and unsurprisingly, it varies according to local attitudes and laws. Far more people describe themselves as lesbian or gay in Brazil, Spain, Australia, Canada and the Netherlands compared to Hungary, Poland and Japan. But are there really five times as many gay people in Australia than in Poland? Doubtful. A more likely explanation is that the less socially or legally acceptable it is to be queer, the fewer people may choose to blithely declare their sexual orientation or gender identity on a survey. The researchers did not ask anyone in the 11 countries where the death penalty currently exists for LGBTQ+ people and they didn't approach many people in the around–70 countries where being gay is still illegal. But in the countries where they did ask people, the significant variation in responses according to social and cultural acceptability, and whether or not there are laws that prevent discrimination against LGBTQ+ people is telling.

For example, few people in Poland declared themselves to be LGBTQ+ in that survey, but at the time, LGBTQ+ rights in Poland were among the worst in Europe, with several Polish regions having declared themselves 'LGBT-free zones' (some backtracked following concerns about EU and other geopolitical consequences). National leaders in Poland were making statements that in their view LGBTQ+ people are unacceptable. In this context, where the repercussions of being publicly gay, bi or trans could be harmful at best and devastating at worst, it's not hard to see why you'd need to be feeling particularly brave to risk ticking the LGBTQ+ box on a survey.

How much of the workforce is LGBTQ+?

The same dilemma holds true in any company or organization and affects their ability to find out how many LGBTQ+ people they employ and how many are in senior positions because this means asking everyone about their sexual orientation and gender identity. Valuable information for any organization interested in improving inclusion. But as we have seen, sometimes employers do not feel comfortable asking that question due to anxieties often rooted in homophobia, biphobia and transphobia or reputational concerns. Sometimes it's not deemed a priority, especially if there is not a legal or other official requirement to ask. Sometimes organizations are constrained by the software they have procured, or other policies. And even when the questions are asked, some people don't respond accurately, because they feel it's too personal, inappropriate or intrusive for a work context, or not the organization's business, or they fear negative repercussions. Overcoming these barriers to get anything approaching an accurate response requires understanding why the barriers exist and creating a sufficiently trustworthy leadership team and a sufficiently supportive workplace culture that people feel safe and comfortable to share this information. This is definitely not always the case. Why not?

Some people may dislike the concept of even being asked the questions at work, find them too black and white or feel alienated because the response choices do not offer the option of their particular sexual orientation or gender identity. Some may be not out at work, or only out to a select number of trusted colleagues and worry that disclosing this information on a form could lead to them being more widely outed and bad things happening as a result. Colleagues who are still figuring themselves out may not feel ready to put their sexual orientation or gender identity in a box and may fear unwanted repercussions from making an 'official' pronouncement. For others, their reticence to disclose the information might be a philosophical view, or one rooted in history. Since the world is not a dependably safe place for LGBTQ+ people, ticking that box is not a neutral act. In 1930s Germany the Nazi Party famously compiled lists of known gay and trans people, tracked them down and sent them to police prisons and concentration camps; even after the war many continued to be imprisoned, this tragedy not fully recognized. In the US and UK in the 20th century, within living memory, lists of gay colleagues were compiled with the explicit intention of using the information against them at work. And far more recently, newspapers in some countries have published lists of people they believe to be gay, some of them alongside entreaties such as 'Hang Them', inciting public shame, vigilante violence, imprisonment, loss of jobs and death. Concern about sharing this information is therefore not paranoia.

Most LGBTQ+ people have had a lifetime of seeing information about our sexual orientation or gender identity being used against us, from the playground and our own families onwards. Decisions to tick that box at work aren't just about whether it could affect current and future career opportunities – it's also about the repercussions of colleagues finding out this information, leading to the potential of bullying, harassment and discrimination, which affect safety, happiness and success in the workplace. Surveys tell us that in America, a third of LGBTQ+ people have been harassed at work and more than a quarter have been fired or not hired at some point in their lives because of their sexual orientation or gender identity – and that's just the jobs they know about. We know that a decision to voluntarily come out, even by means of a form, means taking an element of risk which some people may feel outweighs the benefits. Many LGBTQ+ people I spoke to at every level of seniority said they took years to work up the courage to tick that box on staff surveys.

Improving the data

To get more accurate responses that can drive actions and better inclusion outcomes in the workplace means building trust. Data privacy and security are incredibly important. But just as important is the context in which an employer is asking staff to share this information. Some workplaces have clear policies that protect LGBTQ+ people's rights and condemn discrimination – but others do not. Some talk the talk, but do not walk the walk, and regardless of policies, discrimination can be rife, in many cases ignored, endorsed or even perpetrated by senior managers. This culture will be reflected in how confident staff feel in sharing that information and therefore the accuracy of survey responses. Responses can be improved, but given the number of personal, professional and political variables, any survey is likely to underestimate the proportion of LGBTQ+ people in a population or in a workplace.

There may be further clues in the people who tick the 'prefer not to say' box on surveys that ask about sexual orientation or gender identity; at least some of this cohort will likely be

LGBTQ+. In countries with significant deterrents to disclosing queerness like Malaysia and Russia, more people tick 'prefer not to say'. But again, we can't make assumptions: the reasons people might select that option are myriad. Plus, plenty of LGBTQ+ people who are anxious about the repercussions of ticking a certain box might just as well choose 'heterosexual' as 'prefer not to say', to be on the safe side. This is an imperfect science and yet, self-report surveys are what we've got for the task.

Unsurprisingly, this all makes it hard to draw conclusions. In the international study, we can surmise that at *least* one in five people in the cohorts surveyed across 27 countries seem to be something other than heterosexual. In Britain, at *least* 3.1 per cent of people are gay, lesbian or bisexual.

There are even fewer reliable data points available for trans and non-binary people. In the UK, the Government Equalities Office estimates up to 0.7 per cent of the population is trans or non-binary and the census found 0.5 per cent; in the US, figures are around 0.3 per cent. All are considered significant underestimates. The 27-country survey found that one in every 100 adults identified as a different gender to that assigned at their birth, but the researchers have reason to suspect that's an underestimate too: if you separate out 'Generation Z' (born from around 1997 to the early 2010s), a cohort that tends to be more conscious and comfortable with the concept of gender differences than previous generations, the proportion quadruples. In that survey, four in every 100 young people described themselves as trans, non-binary, gender non-conforming, gender-fluid or 'other'. Similarly, in a Pew survey in 2022, 1.6 per cent of all Americans reported being trans or non-binary, but if you separate out people under 30, this percentage more than tripled (5.1 per cent).[11] Notably, people with a trans or non-binary identity vary widely in their sexual orientation within these surveys, with a fairly even spread reporting that they are heterosexual, gay, pansexual/omnisexual, bisexual and other. These results highlight some of the intersectionality that exists within this minority population.

So what do we know?

These surveys tell us that somewhere between one in five and one in 25 people have a LGBTQ+ identity they feel able to report on a form; younger people tend to feel more able to commit this information to paper. To get a true figure of how many LGBTQ+ people are in our workplace, we need to add the unknown extra proportion who have chosen not to disclose it. This range – of a minimum 4 per cent to probably more than 20 per cent – is an imperfect denominator but it helps us understand more about who is in our workforce.

What else do we know? Overall, lesbians tend to be particularly active in the workforce – the limited data available tells us that we are more likely to have achieved a higher academic degree, and over 8 per cent more likely to work full time than straight women; for those who have a partner, that goes up to 15.4 per cent more likely. Part of this is linked to lesbians historically being slightly less likely to take time out of work to have children, and when we do, only one woman within a couple tends to be off at any one time, plus both women tend to share caring duties; in heterosexual couples, the woman typically takes more parental leave than the man then continues to provide disproportionately more care. Meanwhile, gay men are slightly less likely to be in the workforce than straight men. It may be that the reduced likelihood of having children in a household and more equal sharing of childcare duties empowers women to work more, and men to work less.[12] Intriguingly, bisexual, pansexual and queer men and women fare badly – they're less likely to be in work and more likely to have an income below the poverty line compared to any other group.[13] It's been speculated that this could be linked to experiencing stigma from every angle, including from gay and lesbian people, and having less access to supportive communities.[14] Transgender people probably fare worst of all – they are twice as likely as their cisgender peers to be unemployed and to live in low-income households;[15] the very limited information tells us that this disparity is even wider for non-binary people.[13] Of course, all this information tells us about the overall workforce, but what of the most senior professional roles?

Quantifying LGBTQ+ representation in senior roles

The C-suite is a term used to describe the most senior management positions in a company or other organization. It includes the chief executive officer (CEO), chief operating officer (COO) and chief finance officer (CFO) among other relevant roles. If LGBTQ+ people were proportionally promoted to senior roles, at least 4–20 per cent of each of the C-suite members would be LGBTQ+. This is not the case. The fact that at the time of writing only 0.8 per cent of the Fortune 500 CEOs were LGBTQ+ people serves as a spoiler for this unsurprising conclusion. But what's interesting is that not only are LGBTQ+ people less likely to be in senior positions than heterosexual, cisgender people, it also varies by gender. And it won't be a surprise to learn that being a woman confers an extra disadvantage.

A fascinating survey done by the Williams Institute at UCLA along with McKinsey[16] identified that by their count, 3.9 per cent of men in the US population are LGBTQ+, but only about 3 per cent of C-suite roles and senior management positions are filled by gay and bisexual men. The population figure is likely to be a significant underestimate, but even then, the researchers found gay and bisexual men are under-represented compared to their heterosexual and cisgender male colleagues in the top jobs. Things are worse for LGBTQ+ women, where the rainbow ceiling abuts the glass ceiling. That same survey found that 5.1 per cent of women in the US population were LGBTQ+, so all things being equal, we would expect to see them filling 5.1 per cent of C-suite roles. It will be no surprise to hear that they did not. But it is galling that lesbian and bisexual women filled only 0.6 per cent of C-suite roles. And it gets worse. The research found that with every step up the career ladder, the proportion of lesbian and bisexual women dropped. Another McKinsey report[17] showed further evidence of under-representation: of the more than 750 of America's largest corporations that participated in their study, only one CEO was an out queer woman; none were trans.

This shows us that being LGBTQ+ is associated with barriers to professional success – but not all LGBTQ+ people are affected equally. That's hardly a surprise. The abbreviation itself is a convenient way to define an immensely diverse group of people who face both common and separate challenges. As I touched on earlier, if you imagine the rainbow ceiling in the shape of the arc of a rainbow, everyone standing under it has their own personal ceiling height based on the combination of their LGBTQ+ identity and other minority identities. The rainbow ceiling has a multiplier effect on any other barriers holding people down and generally makes career success a bit harder for LGBTQ+ people. As we start to picture the rainbow ceiling, it rises up as an arc that is superimposed onto the glass ceilings that already exist. At its far ends, the data tells us that it's generally lowest for trans and non-binary people, especially those who also have other minority characteristics – they tend to encounter the ceiling first. As the arc of the rainbow rises up the career ladder, we see lesbian, bisexual and queer women hitting that ceiling. And as it soars further, bisexual and gay men hit its limits. And beyond that rainbow ceiling? It can be lonely for LGBTQ+ people who make it, it can be harder than it needs to be, and new ceilings keep appearing – or what Marjorie Chorlins from the US Chamber of Commerce referred to as 'rainbow clouds'.

Understanding disparities using the LGBTQ+ pay gap

Senior diversity and inclusion consultant Leng Montgomery said: 'As well as looking at the gender pay gap and the ethnic minority pay gap, I would like to see research on the coming out pay gap.' He is not wrong. Research repeatedly finds that there is a clear LGBTQ+ salary gap. If you are a LGBTQ+ person, chances are you're earning less than your heterosexual, cisgender colleagues.[18] Marc Folch from the University of Chicago looked at people who had received bachelor's degrees across the US. Just a year after graduation, the LGBTQ+ pay gap was 12 per cent, and 10 years after graduation, LGBTQ+ people were earning 22 per cent less than their peers.[19] Other analyses find similar gaps, though it varies by country.

But of course, it's not quite that simple. The LGBTQ+ pay gap is not evenly spread, as you might imagine. Being a gay man means you're likely to earn less than your straight peers. Research has found that gay men earn 4–5 per cent less than straight men in the UK, France, the Netherlands and Greece, but there are much wider gaps (12–22 per cent) in the US, Canada and Sweden.[20] Differences in household salary can give us further clues about what's going on. Men who live as part of a same-gender couple generally earn less than men in mixed-gender couples. This difference is not seen for single people.[12] Some of this might be abutting the gender pay gap because male couples with children take more time off to care for them than men in heterosexual relationships. Male couples are also less likely to be close in age and in academic achievement than mixed-gender couples;[21] these households may have income disparities simply by being at different stages of their careers. It may also be that older gay men are particularly affected by the LGBTQ+ pay gap compared to their straight peers because they were held back by more socially and legally acceptable (and sometimes mandated) discrimination at the start of their careers.

The impact of being LGBTQ+ on women's salaries is more of a mixed picture because of interactions with the gender pay gap. Lesbians earn an average 9 per cent more than heterosexual women around the world. This can be as high as 20 per cent more in the US and 15 per cent more in Canada; in the UK it's about 8 per cent, but then in Australia it's 20 per cent less, and in France and Sweden there is little difference.[20] Lesbians who are single, who have lower levels of education and who don't live in big cities fare worst. Research tells us that like all women, we are penalized in our salary for the mere fact of being women – plus extra discrimination for being LGBTQ+. But in some countries, we more than compensate. There are many theories. One is that some lesbians are more likely to be rewarded for having leadership traits that have historically been considered as stereotypically 'masculine' like achievement-orientation, dominance, autonomy and rationality, all of which managers tend to be predisposed to equate with competence and leadership potential – as long as these women exhibit gender-conforming traits too.[22] Another is that we tend to invest a little more in academics and pursue jobs with higher earning potential because of a recognition that we are more likely to be the primary breadwinner. But the main theory is that we are simply less likely to take time out of work to have children than our heterosexual peers. Women who live as part of a same-gender couple earn more than women in heterosexual couples – unless we have children. Ironically, by improving opportunities for LGBTQ+ people to have children, anti-discrimination laws have the effect of reducing lesbian women's salaries and workforce participation and doubling down on the impact of the gender salary gap.

Indeed, the wider LGBTQ+ pay gap does share a common root with the gender pay gap – although the influence of gender is complex. Mark Folch's research tells us LGBTQ+ people are more likely than the general population to opt for female-majority courses that tend to be associated with less lucrative careers. LGBTQ+ people are disproportionately unlikely to choose science, technology, engineering and mathematics (STEM) courses and those who do are more likely to drop out, mostly thanks to bias, discrimination and a sense that they don't belong.[23,24] In the US, LGBTQ+ people are up to a fifth less represented in STEM fields than they should be. The problem is a chicken and egg situation – partly due to the masculine, heterosexual ambience of many STEM settings, existing LGBTQ+ staff may not be open about their sexual orientation or gender identity, which means fewer visible LGBTQ+ role models who could mentor incoming cohorts, which helps with retention.[24] Some examples of existing role models in STEM? The mathematician Alan Turing, who was chemically castrated when found to be gay; the engineer Lynn Conway, who made huge leaps in computing but was fired when she revealed she was transgender; and the astronaut Sally Ride, who kept her lesbian identity secret throughout her career – when she died in 2012, *Scientific American* pointed out there had been no out LGBTQ+ astronauts in the history of the space programme, describing coming out as a likely 'career wrecker'.[25] More positive, visible LGBTQ+ role models in STEM are sorely needed.

On the other hand, there is a stereotype that there are certain 'gay jobs' and the research tells us that to an extent, this is true – for example, LGBTQ+ people are over-represented in psychology, law, social work and university teaching, plus gay men are more likely to be found in female-majority jobs, and to some extent, lesbians in male-majority jobs than their heterosexual peers.[26] The more we look at the research, the more we find evidence of LGBTQ+ segregation into particular jobs in the workplace. Why?

There are two main theories. The first is that LGBTQ+ people gravitate to jobs that have a certain level of 'task independence' (like a fire safety inspector) rather than operating as part of a team (like a fire fighter) because this makes it easier to conceal sexual orientation or gender identity at work, and by being less dependent on our co-workers, it reduces the likelihood of experiencing prejudice and discrimination. The other main theory is that LGBTQ+ people have particularly strong social perceptiveness – years of having to adapt to navigate people's complex reactions associated with our sexual orientation or gender identity makes many LGBTQ+ people particularly alert to social cues, so once we have developed this perceptiveness, we may be attracted to jobs where the skill is especially helpful, becoming – for example – psychologists or teachers.[27] Plus, gay and bisexual men may consider predominantly female colleagues to be more accepting of their differences.

The research seems to back up these theories: lesbians are under-represented in some female-majority jobs but those present tend to have roles that involve above-average task independence and social perceptiveness – the top five choices being psychologist, probation officer, training and development manager, sociologist and community service manager. When lesbians work in male-majority jobs, task independence takes on particular importance and we are over-represented among female workers in roles like bus and truck mechanic, elevator, heating, air conditioner, security alarm and home appliance installer and repairer. Gay men on the other hand tend to be over-represented in female-majority jobs including flight attendant, hairdresser, nurse practitioner and travel agent; in male-majority jobs they are most over-represented in the arts, including as actors, news reporters, artists, agents and producers or directors.[27]

Overall, there is a significant gay male, bisexual and trans salary penalty and a current but diminishing lesbian salary advantage. And black and ethnic minority LGBTQ+ people of all persuasions are likely to earn less. A survey published by the Human Rights Campaign in the US in 2022 found that for every dollar the average worker earns, LGBTQ+ workers earn 89 cents. Breaking it down further, they found white LGBTQ+ workers earn 97 cents, Latinx LGBTQ+ workers earn 90 cents and Black LGBTQ+ workers earn 80 cents. Trans men get 70 cents, trans women 60 cents.[28]

LGBTQ+ people are less likely to hold senior roles and more likely to find ourselves in jobs, settings and sectors that may limit our opportunity for promotion and high salaries. This tells us LGBTQ+ people's income is significantly affected by prejudice and discrimination in several different ways – from not making career choices that maximize our earning potential to having our applications and performance judged in a biased way, to having poor experiences at work, to not seeking a promotion because we are so relieved to be currently in an inclusive team. But Mark Folch's research in the US published in 2022 proposes that these factors only account for half of the LGBTQ+ pay gap; the rest is set in motion in our schooldays, where pre-work experiences of stress, bullying, isolation and rejection (or feared rejection) and gender stereotypes affect LGBTQ+ people's career potential and aspirations. Let's explore why.

3

Ten childhood factors that affect career success

'It felt like a very hard time and I'm very glad I came through it intact' – Dame Jackie Daniel, CEO of Newcastle upon Tyne NHS Foundation Trust, UK

When I asked senior leaders whether knowing they were LGBTQ+ at an early age had affected their achievements, opportunities or aspirations, some did not think so, but most spoke about the anxiety, fear, shame, stereotypes and false beliefs instilled in them by friends, family, school, media and society. They described prejudices manifesting into bullying and then discrimination in the opportunities they were able to access, all while they were going through adolescence and developing into adults. Many remembered feeling low self-esteem and self-confidence. Isolation. Confusion. The majority of leaders I interviewed realized that even if they had not previously considered it, being LGBTQ+ had an early impact on their career. Though these leaders had triumphed over any career adversity they experienced, others have not been so lucky.

It is odd that the fact of growing up LGBTQ+ impacting young people's future careers – for better and for worse – is so patchily understood and addressed by care givers and educators, because recognizing it means being able to provide support. Obviously, there is no one experience of growing up gay or lesbian or bisexual, transgender or non-binary, asexual, intersex or any other identity in the LGBTQ+ rainbow. There's not even a standard timeline. For some, the realization of difference comes when they are children or teenagers; for others, it becomes clear in adulthood. Everyone has their own personal story, shaped by the year, the place, the people around them and their attitudes, the media, even the law. Which means the impact of growing up LGBTQ+ on a person's career potential is as diverse as this population. But there are commonalities. Let's consider 10 key ways in which the experiences of young LGBTQ+ people can differ from those of our cisgender, heterosexual peers and manifest in career impact.

1. Growing up in a society that does not embrace LGBTQ+ people

Many LGBTQ+ people have experienced a lifetime of feeling different from our peers and being judged (often negatively) for that difference. That is because heterosexual and cisgender people continue to be seen as the standard, expected and socially endorsed model through which society operates. From the first moments of awareness, children tend to be faced with certain expectations of what a boy or a girl should be like through clothes, decoration, toys, books, television, film and advertising, school communications and peers, loved ones and role models. This is further shaped by all sorts of factors like location, politics, family culture and religion. By high school, almost every young person has to some extent been submerged in an overarching narrative that 'normal' people are heterosexual and cisgender and, even today, largely operate within stereotypical gender roles. For many LGBTQ+ people, realizing that we can't fulfil that narrative can be hugely stressful: deviation has long been discouraged and punished by society, which bombards LGBTQ+ people with messages that we are not good enough, that we are morally bad, that there is something wrong with us, that we are less important, less deserving, less acceptable, even less human.

This is evident in societal decisions that are playing out around the world right now, like LGBTQ+ people not being allowed to get married in some places, or countries not recognizing our marriages when we travel, or putting same-sex couples' right to marry at all to a public vote. Heated debates over which bathroom a trans person can use. Banning books that mention our existence. Firing people or locking us up or killing us for being LGBTQ+. Even if some of these things are not happening in a certain country right now, LGBTQ+ people continually live with the knowledge that across the world our basic rights continue to be a matter of public debate, with prominent and respected people from celebrities to politicians being allowed, or even incentivized, to say horrible things about people like us, which endorses that narrative for use by people in our personal life. We know that even if some of us feel fairly safe, for now, in the country in which we happen to live, we're only a plane ride from places where it would be deemed legitimate for the authorities to kill us or beat us or lock us up. Sometimes we're only a political election away from it. These are disconcerting truths for a person to come to terms with in their teenage years and they play havoc with self-esteem.

Digging into history only makes it worse. It is common practice to teach young people who are part of minority or oppressed groups about role models from the past who contributed great things to the world, or who stood up to their oppressors and advanced their rights. This helps instil pride and self-esteem and motivates young people to take their place in a tradition of pressing for positive change. It is harder to do this for LGBTQ+ young people because so many potential historical role models were not formally recognized as being LGBTQ+ and in today's ongoing homophobic, biphobic and transphobic society, many people's estates do not welcome so much as speculation about their ancestors' sexual orientation or gender identity. Rosemary Tickle, digital content officer at the NHS Confederation in the UK, reflected: 'Queer people's identities are often erased, hushed-up or kept private by the person in question. I love classical music, but only found out Tchaikovsky was probably gay in my 20s.'

Another episode in LGBTQ+ history that young people eventually encounter is the HIV/AIDS pandemic of the 1980s which led, for example, to the death of 10 per cent of all gay men born in America between 1951 and 1970 while for many years, the government, particularly the US government, seemed to look on impassively. This is a period that many adults remember vividly and one that does little to build young LGBTQ+ people's self-esteem. Fresh from witnessing the no-expense-spared, massive international mobilization to find a vaccine and cure for Covid-19, young people may be jarred by the realization that the authorities might not consider a virus that mainly affected LGBTQ+ people to be quite as worthy of such an effort.

These historical experiences, and many more, have built a prevailing narrative in most societies that LGBTQ+ people should deserve less and expect less than cisgender, heterosexual people. That we should be grateful for *any* rights. That's why the Stonewall Riots in 1969 are so important: when gay and trans people in New York City resisted the police when their bar was raided and demanded the right to live openly without constant fear of arrest, it empowered people all over the world and ignited an LGBTQ+ liberation movement that continues today.

But let's face it, today, even where the law is permissive, cisgender heterosexuality is widely enforced through policing by family, friends, school and messages in all sorts of media. Boys are still criticized for having 'girly' attributes and girls are criticized for failing to have sufficiently 'girly' attributes. Toys and clothes are codified into blue and pink. Toddlers watch TV programmes about the importance of princesses finding their prince. And people exploring their sexuality or gender still tend to be punished with a wide range of slurs, taunts, concealment and marginalization.

Matt Burney, previously the Country Director for China for the British Council at the British Embassy in Beijing and now His Majesty's Consul General in Shanghai, reflected back on his childhood in Blackpool: 'The so-called banter was horrible, homophobic. You'd hear homophobic slurs about anyone who came out. You'd hear: "Oh, I feel very sorry for gay people, they live a lonely life". Because it was so suppressed and it was so scary, it was lurking at a very subconscious level. We were obviously never encouraged to talk about it, we were encouraged to suppress it ourselves. I had fears that I was gay, but I shut them away.' Sarah Weaver, Associate Director at Accenture in Australia, said: 'I've always known since I was a child that I was different. When I was a child in the late 70s, there was no word that I had for what I was, for the feelings I was experiencing except: "I'm not a boy". I saw a current affairs programme about transgender people which was not in a positive light. While seeing it on television I thought: "That's what I am!" But I felt incredible shame because it was portrayed as a bad thing. I just repressed that part of me even more.'

Keeping things quiet was also the experience of Jim Harra, now First Permanent Secretary and Chief Executive of HM Revenue and Customs in the UK. He said: 'Coming from Northern Ireland, homosexuality was a criminal offence until about 1980. I was at university when it was decriminalized. There was no anonymity – everyone knows your business. I think that slowed me down... There was a lot of private, not-shared wondering and worrying about how this was all going to work out.' And with good reason. John Lotherington, a freelance thinktank convener and Director of 21st Century Trust, said: 'I was very much aware of gay people being sent to jail, of police being more brutal.'

The message that being queer is not acceptable and in some ways LGBTQ+ people are second-class citizens still features in legislation and its aftermath around the world. Many of the people I interviewed from the UK grew up during Section 28 of the Local Government Act, a 1988 law passed by Margaret Thatcher's Conservative government that prevented councils and schools from 'promoting the teaching of the acceptability of homosexuality as a pretended family relationship'. John

Lotherington, who was a high-school history teacher at the time, said: 'Section 28 was so regressive, it was such a chill factor for teachers.' It was also chilling for students. The clause essentially prevented any mention of LGBTQ+ matters by anyone employed in a school. The intent: to prevent young people from becoming gay. It is damaging enough to have your identity disparaged or rejected by your peers or your family, but making it illegal to even talk about it created shame and secrecy for a whole generation of LGBTQ+ people. As a teenager, I lived in fear of somehow being arrested, or getting a teacher fired, so I kept my sexual orientation secret and didn't kiss a girl until I was at university, by which point things had very slightly improved. Even then, I had to walk to my medical school classes each day past a giant 'Keep the Clause' billboard erected by supporters of Section 28. I felt ashamed and afraid. I also reflected it was odd that campaigners who didn't want young people to hear anything about LGBTQ+ matters thought it was fine to display hateful things about us in huge letters on billboards alongside busy roads on school routes. The Keep the Clause campaign eventually failed and the relevant law was removed in 2000 in Scotland and its equivalent in 2003 in the rest of Britain – but it kept affecting young people anyway. My mother told me that as a teacher, years later she was still afraid to talk about LGBTQ+ matters in the classroom and avoided any mention in case she got into trouble. And as a pupil, Rosemary Tickle remembered: 'Most of my secondary school was post-Section 28 but most people didn't talk about it and if they did, they talked about it with a sense of luridness.'

These days many cisgender, heterosexual people and even some LGBTQ+ people assume these experiences are historical and ask: is this really relevant to young people coming up through the ranks towards senior positions today? Yes. In 2019, years after Section 28 was repealed, there were weeks of protests in the UK when some adults realized that schools were talking to children about the existence of LGBTQ+ people as part of teaching about relationships and families – and mobilized to prevent this. Just as when I was young, these protesters exposed children to a lot of hateful rhetoric about themselves and their friends and families, amplified and legitimized by mainstream media. In 2022, Florida created their own form of Section 28, the Parental Rights in Education Bill, informally known as the 'Don't say gay' law, joining several other US states that already had restrictions in place to stop schools talking or reading about LGBTQ+ people; umpteen similar Bills are currently being debated in the US. LGBTQ+ discrimination in law is by no means a thing of the past.

Most young LGBTQ+ people soon realize they are living within an environment that contains at least some degree of homophobia, biphobia and transphobia at school, in friend groups, at home and in the media. Often long before we come out, we hear hateful jokes about gay people and snide comments by family members. We hear disparaging remarks about LGBTQ+ celebrities or storylines on TV. We see news coverage giving voice to people advocating for us to have fewer rights than our peers. And we notice that many of the words technically describing our identity double as insults. In high school, my bullies used to shout 'lesbian!' and I'd wonder: 'gosh, how do they know?' But they didn't know – they had simply repurposed a LGBTQ+ descriptor as a general slur, just as youthful parlance adopted the phrase 'this is gay' to imply something was bad. My mother once told me that in a school where she taught, a particular step in the building's staircase had been designated 'the gay step' by generations of children, who treated it with disgust and meticulously avoided standing on it. Message received: gay equals bad. Young people who are questioning their sexual orientation or gender identity know that being different from the majority will not be universally welcomed and may bring ridicule, abuse and rejection. This doesn't make for great self-esteem. In the UK, surveys tell us nearly half of young trans people (aged 11 to 19) and almost a quarter of cisgender LGB young people have tried to take their own life, compared to 5–13 per cent of their peers who are not LGBTQ+.

Overall, it is a matter of bad planning that our teenage years, famously a time of angst, confusion and trying to understand ourselves as individuals and fit in with peers, is also such a crucial moment to make decisions that may shape our future careers. It's hard for everyone. But young people who realize they may be LGBTQ+ often find themselves navigating this stage at an advanced level of difficulty.

2. Stress distracts from success

Every LGBTQ+ person has a different experience growing up. Some people I interviewed told me they loved school and had good friends, but more described a mixed experience made more complex by their sexual orientation or gender identity. As Dame Jackie Daniel reflected of her high school years: 'It was a particularly difficult time in my life. I was at that point of wondering who I was in the world, I felt different, a bit isolated.' Almost every leader I spoke to who felt different at high school or university described some level of anxiety and confusion about their emerging awareness of being LGBTQ+. Reactions (and feared reactions) from other people affected their academic work, concentration, motivation, decisions, behaviour and wellbeing. Now at the US Chamber of Commerce, Marjorie Chorlins reflected: 'I've always been kind of a tomboy – I felt very acutely self-conscious when I was in school. I didn't feel I was in a community that completely understood me or where I could be truly authentic.'

For some, this escalated into isolation and homophobic, biphobic and transphobic bullying, which remains a major problem in schools and, to an extent, in further and higher education. Some leaders emphasized that their schooldays had been largely happy, which may have contributed to their later career success, but even so, many experienced ostracism and bullying for their suspected or expressed non-conformity to sexuality or gender norms. Pedro Pina, now head of YouTube in Europe, the Middle East and Africa, said: 'I was bullied to the ground in school because I was a great student, loved classical music, loved playing with the girls, didn't play football.' And Karen Teo, a Meta Vice president at the time of our discussion, generally had happy schooldays but remembered the impact of her first non-platonic relationship: 'I was seen by my schoolmates being very close to another girl. Some girls told my peers to rein me in – this was not appropriate behaviour. I got ostracized from my extracurricular group.'

Such experiences are recognized by the UN's Human Rights Commission, which describes that a typical school day for many LGBTQ+ people can include teasing, name calling, public ridicule, rumours, intimidation, physical and sexual assault, social isolation, cyberbullying and even death threats.[29] Transgender students can encounter further dehumanizing behaviour like restrictions on their use of toilets and changing rooms, and people refusing to use their correct names, or referring to them by different genders.

Having been in the closet all through high school, I was largely free of bullying due to my sexual orientation, and since I had not yet summoned the courage to come out to my parents, I had not yet experienced rejection and (thankfully temporary) loss of the support and security I enjoyed throughout my school career. Although anxiety about these things did affect me daily, I was in the privileged position to largely be able to concentrate and do well academically. I contrast my experience with many people who were mercilessly bullied or punished and rejected by their peers and families, and with my discussions with trans people, who told me the constant feeling of being in the wrong body during high school, known as dysphoria, was such a distressing and confusing experience that it significantly distracted them from fulfilling their academic potential on the path to career success; for some, it was so hard to see a future that academic effort felt irrelevant.

Many people I interviewed described feelings of depression and anxiety, suicidal thoughts, low confidence and low self-esteem at school linked to being LGBTQ+. This affected their ability to concentrate, the quality of their schoolwork and exams, the decisions they made about their post-high school life, the opportunities they were able to access and ultimately, their career potential. These experiences are common for young LGBTQ+ people and can also include sleep disturbance, alcohol and drug use, homelessness and self-harm. LGBTQ+ people are more likely to feel unsafe, skip classes, avoid extracurricular activities and leave school as soon as possible. For example, Mitch Mitchinson, Managing Director of Mitchinson Associates, said: 'I was hated at school, people always picked on me for being queer. If people hadn't been so homophobic, I might have stayed in education longer.'

Of course, some people do not discuss their sexual orientation or gender identity at school and that constant censoring, hiding and sometimes lying also takes its toll, affecting people's ability to enjoy close, confiding friendships and be their true self. Omar Daair, now British High Commissioner to Rwanda and Non-resident Ambassador to Burundi, said: 'I think the worst time was at school, not being able to talk about it – I think it does long-term damage, just internalizing the shame.'

That said, there can also be positive career impacts arising out of that anxiety about sexual orientation or gender identity. Ken Ohashi, CEO of Brooks Brothers, said: 'For a long time I was in the closet. I poured all of my energy, my anxiety into work. I think the struggle LGBTQ+ people go through in their personal life, all of that fed into me working harder and harder and harder.'

3. Subverting gender roles comes at a price

A lot is understood about the differences in academic achievement between boys and girls, but less about LGBTQ+ young people compared to their heterosexual, cisgender peers. An American researcher called Joel Mittleman brought together the limited US data available and found that gay boys seem to do better academically than any other group, regardless of ethnicity or other minority characteristics. Gay girls tend to achieve similarly to their heterosexual peers, perhaps a little better. And bisexual boys and girls both tend to do worse than the average.[30] Why should this be?

It may all come down to queer people being less likely to adhere to gender stereotypes. In simple terms, Mittleman believes that high school society rewards the 'bad boy' persona socially as an admirable display of vigorous heterosexual masculinity. Unfortunately, this behaviour also brings distractions and negative assumptions that can affect these boys' academic achievements. (It's one of the mechanisms by which gender theorists think girls often overtake boys in academic attainment.) That same high-school society tends to socially penalize boys who contravene the masculinity pact by being too studious or conscientious, often branding these traits effeminate or gay with scornful intent. This can present a problem or an opportunity for gay, bisexual, non-binary and queer boys: if they are actively trying to conceal that part of themselves, they may feel obliged to overcompensate by being overtly less studious and more rebellious, compromising their academic potential. But if not, an opportunity exists for these boys to veer out of the confines of their gender lane, study any topic to their heart's content, as rigorously as they want, and ultimately do better academically. Overall, this may account for gay boys doing particularly well at school.

Gender theory tells us that things work differently for girls. Despite the gender revolution, girls are still socially rewarded for adhering to the 'good girl, good wife, good mother' stereotype, which prizes being compliant, well behaved and studious. Many LGBTQ+ girls already know that the heterosexual wife and mother stereotype cannot apply to them. Some may react by branching out from performing the requisite 'good girl' behaviours. Again, liberation comes with problems and opportunities. LGBTQ+ girls who look or act in ways that are perceived as tending away from feminine stereotypes are at risk of paying a 'bad girl penalty' at school, experiencing negative assumptions that can affect their achievement and opportunities. Chef, writer and television presenter Allegra McEvedy shared: 'The school didn't like the fact that I was having flings with quite a lot of the girls. From what I understand, I basically got expelled for threatening the status quo.' Research in America tells us that queer black girls are particularly likely to pay the 'bad girl penalty': they are more at risk of being disciplined, suspended and expelled than either heterosexual, cisgender black girls, or lesbian or bisexual white girls, probably because some of them are not only failing to adhere to the idea of a 'good girl', but also to the idea of a 'good white girl'.[30]

Today, across Europe, one in five LGBTQ+ people say they have felt discriminated against in educational settings. Educators need to be very aware of this bias so they can recognize when it is happening and avoid acting on it. Incidentally, so-called 'masculine traits' tend to be favoured within many job markets, so while subverting stereotypes about how a woman 'should' look or act at school might come with penalties at the time, it can reap rewards later in life.

4. Taking the emergency exit

Speaking to LGBTQ+ leaders across different sectors, I was surprised to learn how many of them had left school at a young age, sometimes without qualifications, and fled as far as possible at the earliest opportunity. Peter Molyneux, who is now Chair of Sussex Partnership NHS Foundation Trust, England liaison for the International Initiative for Mental Health Leadership and Co-Chair of the LGBTQ+ Health and Care Leaders Network, described the classic dilemma that dictated his own choices at the end of high school: 'I went to a very homophobic school and I also grew up in a very homophobic home. It's not surprising I wanted out of both as soon as possible.' James Devine, director at a professional services consultancy, said: 'I had a focus about what I wasn't going to do – I had no interest in working for the family painting business and I wanted to be away from family because of the reaction I thought I would get if I told them I was gay.' Some LGBTQ+ leaders described choosing higher education in a faraway big city. Others planned their escape directly into the workforce. The leaders I interviewed were able to make this work for them, but of course that has not been the case for everyone.

Sadly, this experience persists. I interviewed Darryl Clough, Senior Policy Adviser for Innovation and Growth in the British government's Office for Life Sciences, at an early stage of his career and he told me: 'I wanted to get to university, reinvent myself, start my new story – I didn't necessarily feel I could do that with the people I knew at secondary school who were all going to the same university. That feeling of not gelling, not finding my people.' This is important. Even though Keshav Suri, now Executive Director at the Lalit Suri Hospitality Group, moved from India to the UK for university, he did not feel able to come out at that time: 'It was a mini-India – there were a lot of students from India who knew me, knew my family, so I was still very nervous.'

This is one reason why many LGBTQ+ people don't successfully access escape routes right away. Matt Burney is one of them. He told me: 'I completed my degree at Oxford and got a place at the Royal College of Music to study performance, so I applied for the Japanese Exchange and Teaching programme to earn a bit of money to pay for it – what I thought was going to be a year; then I deferred my place… I never went back to music. I sometimes wonder on a deep subconscious level whether my going to Japan wasn't completely related to saving up money; whether it was some way to get away from the homophobic noise in the UK and come to terms with who I was, the opportunity to get away from the corrosive socialization I'd been exposed to, to really understand who I was. Had I been straight, I don't think I'd have ended up in Japan.'

5. Unmooring

Perhaps one of the biggest things that LGBTQ+ leaders have in common is a feeling of being unmoored from the standard life path of study, job near family, engagement, marriage, children, retirement and grandparenting. While this path is generally not a requirement, and technically has been disrupted by the gender revolution, expectations die hard. But Rosemary Tickle reflected that: 'Questioning, coming out and transitioning can often make you feel "unstuck" from the typical life path you're expected to follow.'

Pedro Pina concurred: 'When you're gay, you have a blank canvas in front of you of possibilities, you don't have pressures to do this or that, you're not expected to get married, have kids, settle down… that can show you a wealth of opportunities. It can also be a very lonely place as your sense of belonging starts dwindling. Your sense of identity becomes very important.'

Most of the LGBTQ+ leaders I interviewed grew up at a time when same-sex marriage and same-sex parenting were not available. Retired major general Tammy Smith remembered: 'I just felt there was more to the world than getting married, having a husband, raising sheep. Now I look back, I realize there was nothing that appealed to me about married life because I was gay. I didn't know that at the time, but I knew there was something else bigger out there.' And as a genderqueer person, Mitch Mitchinson reflected: 'I wasn't expecting to marry, but when I was growing up and at secondary school in the 90s, there was still an assumption that being married to a man would provide some kind of security or stability. It was never something I wanted, or something I considered. It was always: you're going to have to look after yourself.' In many countries, even where same-sex marriage is now available, society's expectations are probably less ingrained. Being LGBTQ+ breaks the rules: there is no centuries-trodden default life path. Pedro Pina felt liberated: 'Honestly, I spent a lot of my life free to explore, to try, to experiment, without the fear of meeting expectations of people I loved. I was prepared to reboot, and I did reboot my life a few times.' The opportunity to forge new, creative paths can be freeing and has the potential to help careers.

The leaders who realized they were LGBTQ+ when they were at high school told me two main stories about how they approached the first part of their career:

One story was a focus on getting away and starting the next phase of their life. Many people told me that after leaving school, they struggled to visualize and work towards long- or even medium-term plans. Instead, they just grabbed the first job that came their way, figuring it out as they went along. Some leaders I spoke to benefitted from the serendipity of those roles leading to further opportunities and eventually to the senior roles they hold today. For example, Dame Jackie Daniel said: 'I thought: "you know what, I'll just get a job"' – and this path eventually led to her becoming CEO. And Ken Ohashi reflected: 'I couldn't have imagined I'd be sitting in this chair. I think for me it wasn't about building a north star – I was about two to three years out, not 15 to 20. I was trying to figure out my sexuality, I was trying to date women. It's only been in the last 10 years I've been able to visualize a 10- to 15-year plan.' However, the short-term, random job approach is obviously not failsafe. As a trans and bisexual woman, Rosemary Tickle said: 'In order to reflect on where you see yourself in the future, you need to be *able* to see yourself in the future – I couldn't visualize that, because of gender dysphoria. It meant that when I was looking at opportunities for jobs, I was thinking: "did this pay the bills?" I wasn't thinking if it would advance my career or fulfil me as a person. It's left me at a weird place at this point in my career – my first few jobs were not very career-focused and I'm only really getting to the point when I can formulate a five-year career plan.'

The other story people told was the opposite: unusually strategic thinking from an early age about how to develop a meaningful career. Having deviated from the standard life path, these leaders had an early hunch that their career might be disproportionately important in their life compared to some of their peers, so they threw themselves into working very hard and climbing upwards. That was my experience. Realizing that I wouldn't be marrying a rich husband and settling down with multiple children anytime soon, as per my friends' fantasies, meant I had to put more thought into writing my own story: what would I do instead? Having never met another lesbian, I had no idea if I would ever have a partner or family. So, I concentrated on getting a good degree that would lead to a fulfilling, meaningful career that would support me well financially if I remained single. It's why I applied to medical school (a vocational degree leading to a clear and dependable career with good earning potential) rather than studying English or acting (my passions but not so clearly linked to a dependable job afterwards). This turns out to be a common feeling, particularly among lesbians. Knowing we are excluded from traditional assumptions about relying on a man to be the family breadwinner, we tend to feel the essential connection between academic achievement and earning potential quite strongly and may invest more in career decisions, like staying in school for longer and choosing degrees associated with higher salaries. As an added bonus, we are far less likely to have our academic journey derailed by unintended pregnancy. So, while it's a mixed picture, if we can overcome the challenges, LGBTQ+ people can have interesting opportunities.

Sure enough, the data tells us that when it comes to higher education, lesbians and gay men are disproportionately high achievers. Analysis from the National Health Information Survey in America finds that we are more likely to have a bachelor's degree or higher, compared to people who are bisexual or straight. That disparity increases at each level of academia. The American Community Survey tells us that 34 per cent of people in mixed-gender couples have a bachelor's degree; it's 43–52 per cent for partnered lesbians and nearly half of all partnered gay men. For higher degrees the difference is even bigger: 21 per cent of people in same-sex relationships in the survey had master's degrees and doctoral degrees compared to a mere 13 per cent for straight women and 14 per cent for straight men in relationships.[30]

I asked a lot of LGBTQ+ leaders if they felt they'd have had different careers if they'd been heterosexual or cisgender. Some said definitely; some said no way! But most of them were flummoxed by the idea. Mitch Mitchinson reflected a lot of people's thoughts: 'I think most queer people have made decisions about their life that heterosexual people simply don't have to. I don't think I could say opportunities have been more open or closed, but I have taken different types of risks, I have been motivated by slightly different things in life.' Personally, reflecting today, if I'd been heterosexual, I might have been an actress right now and never studied medicine.

6. Bracing for independence

Linked closely to unmooring is an awareness among many LGBTQ+ young people that as they move into higher education and adulthood, if they want to live as their authentic self, they might lose parts of their current support system and have to walk that path alone. Many LGBTQ+ people have grown up hearing family and carers saying things like: 'I'd kill myself if my son turned out gay'. Even the most apparently supportive of parents and carers cannot be depended upon to remain supportive once a young person comes out of the closet, which is part of the reason that so many still feel obliged to keep their authentic selves hidden while they are still dependent on their parents' financial, practical and emotional support. They know that some parents and carers, driven by their own prejudices, hopes and expectations, reject their children in different ways when they come out of the closet, so the support they currently experience could have to be forfeited at any point if they come out, either temporarily or longer-term. It is no coincidence that LGBTQ+ people are disproportionately represented within the young homeless population. In the UK, a full quarter of young homeless people are LGBTQ+, most of whom became homeless for that very reason.[31]

Most LGBTQ+ leaders I spoke to were both afraid of disappointing or worrying their family and all too aware that family support was no guarantee. Matt Burney shared: 'It does feel in that scary world where everyone and their cousin is homophobic, like it's you against the world. I was always really, really afraid of rejection and I never felt able to come out until I at least had a modicum of financial security, so I waited until I got my British Council job to come out to my parents. It just went down like a lead balloon.'

James Devine said: 'Because of my perception of my parents' and friends' likely reaction, it made me more independent in my career process, how I conducted myself. Even now I have a very strong independent streak which I struggle to let go of, which I believe comes from my childhood and fears.'

Dame Jackie Daniel shared: 'My mum took it really badly, so I left home at 17; it very much felt like I was making my own way in the world… It felt difficult. Everything felt like a struggle. I went on to do a first and second degree, and got a little bit of help financially, but it felt like I was really struggling.'

Eva Kreienkamp, CEO of BVG, the public transit company that manages the U-Bahn, the trams and the buses in Berlin, said: 'I always had this idea that I had to take care of myself in one way or another.' And Mitch Mitchinson reflected: 'There was no situation where I thought I wouldn't be looking after myself.' The impact is unpredictable. Several LGBTQ+ leaders told me that knowing they lacked a safety net made them feel more tentative about taking risks in their early careers; others felt liberated and emboldened to take more risks.

7. Imposter syndrome and the myth of compensation

Many LGBTQ+ people grow up all too aware that friends, family and society may judge us negatively for our sexual orientation or gender identity, which is outside our control. But we do have some control over academic effort and achievement. Overcompensation academically not only offers the opportunity to gain approval of grown-ups in the here and now, but going on to have a prestigious career enables a form of conformity that offers a different way to gain approval in society, especially for boys who grew up with all the patriarchal expectations and stereotypes of masculinity. In some ways it's a positive thing to be motivated to career success. But there is a more toxic effect of making people feel that they *need* to have career success to somehow compensate for being LGBTQ+. There is a lot of discussion about the problem of excellence and exceptionalism as a prerequisite for legitimacy in other minority groups, but it is less well recognized in LGBTQ+ populations. But many of us feel we need to work harder, prove ourselves and be exceptional to be recognized as a person of value, to earn the esteem and societal approval that is freely given to our peers.

Matt Burney reflected: 'When you're growing up, gay people are likened to failures. I didn't want to be one of those failures. It has spurred me on. I don't have an ambitious bone in my body, I don't have a career plan, but what's got me to where I am is the fear of being swept to one side because you're not accepted... It creates some kind of muscle, being othered, that I don't think I would have had otherwise. You can either give up or you can fight. It's resilience born out of a fear of failure.' And Darryl Clough said: 'I have a lot of imposter syndrome that comes from being gay – it's made me want to push myself.' Let's face it – all of this was a driver for me deciding to become a doctor.

8. You can't be what you can't see

A very common theme shared by LGBTQ+ leaders today is that when they were growing up, they lacked positive role models who were lesbian, gay, bisexual, trans, non-binary, queer, or any part of the rainbow spectrum; any visibility tended towards unrelatable and often negative caricature. Surrounded by seas of cisgender, heterosexual success, many young LGBTQ+ people have felt that certain career paths or levels of seniority were not open to us at all. Matt Burney remembered: 'When I started my career there was no role model. Absolutely zero.' At the time of our discussion, Alim Dhanji was President of Adidas Canada, about to move to be Chief People Officer and Executive Vice-President at Equinox Group. He said that when he was growing up: 'You didn't have the role models – you didn't have the Tim Cooks, and people in government – you really did feel that this is a dead end.'

Nancy Schlichting is the retired President and CEO of the Henry Ford Health System in the US and sits on the Boards of the Walgreen Boots Alliance, Duke University and numerous other organizations. But she told me that when she was young: 'In my head I thought I'd never be a CEO because I was gay. I didn't have the aspirations – I set the bar lower in my head because I was gay.' Pedro Pina concurred: 'I remember knowing I was gay, and looking, and thinking my options were either to be Freddie Mercury or my mum's hairdresser.' And Pips Bunce, Director and Head of Investment Banking Technology Strategic Programs at Credit Suisse at the time of interview, lamented that as a non-binary, gender-fluid person: 'I could never see any role models like me. That would have made things so much easier if I'd seen people who were out and visible, and that they and their identity were accepted, included and it was all fine.'

When I first met Simon Pollard, he was directing *Billy Elliot: The Musical* in Japan, having been Resident Director of the musical in London's West End. He is interested in the impact of visibility of LGBTQ+ people. He said: 'Continued visibility of queer people is always going to reaffirm that belief that we're as entitled to something as anyone else.' And reflected that: 'It's so brilliant seeing younger people coming out earlier. It's to be celebrated, but it makes me feel sad that I wasn't able to do that and makes me think about how different my life might have been if I wasn't hiding my true self.'

There has indisputably been a massive tradition of cisgender heterosexual people and their happy relationships depicted on stage, screen and literature over the years to encourage young people and provide role models, but until very recently, LGBTQ+ people have not been able to access a version of this that resonates. From the 19th century to the 1950s, LGBTQ+ people were rendered almost invisible in most countries, save for an occasional newspaper story reporting something bad or scandalous. Hollywood's Motion Picture Production Code, known as the Hays Code, in the 1930s, implicitly included homosexuality and trans people in its ban on showing 'sex perversion' on screen. And there were plenty of laws and rules making sure it didn't happen in the theatre, television, or in books. If any depiction was allowed to get through, it usually had to adhere to the now-infamous trope that the gay character must die tragically at the end or be locked up in an asylum – LGBTQ+ people were not allowed to have happy endings.

I remember when I was young and desperate to find evidence that I was going to be okay, the one and only depiction of a lesbian I managed to find in the library was in Joanna Trollope's A Village Affair, and it was thrilling, transformative, despite the fact that even then, the two women were not allowed to go happily off into the sunset. When the adaptation for television happened, I clipped a tiny black and white photo of the main characters out of the newspaper and stuck it to the wall next to my bed. It was an acknowledgement that people like me existed, which felt incredibly important. I couldn't have dreamed of the many books, television shows, plays and films depicting LGBTQ+ people today, much less that they might suggest people like me are not doomed to meet a sorry end. Although it cannot be denied that even now, storylines still tend to focus on coming out angst, homophobia, biphobia and transphobia, as though LGBTQ+ people couldn't just be living our lives.

9. Second adolescence

The concept of 'second adolescence' is one that many LGBTQ+ leaders describe to some extent. Adolescence is of course that period of physical and psychological development between being a child and being an adult where young people are generally given a little licence to experiment, test boundaries and figure out, often by trial and error, how best to interact with the world as they move towards becoming a grown-up. It's an important developmental stage, as everyone knows from umpteen coming-of-age stories in books, film and television. Gender expression and sexuality play a starring role in the transition.

But many LGBTQ+ people do not have the same adolescent experience as our cisgender, heterosexual peers, or we don't have it on the same timeline. Some are not yet aware that they are LGBTQ+ or do know but are trying to hide or suppress it and find themselves having their quintessential adolescent experiences like first kiss and first romantic relationship with a person to whom they are not sexually attracted. Others may be out and very much ready to explore romantic or sexual experiences, but as a minority, find themselves isolated in a sea of cisgender, heterosexual teenagers. While the internet may help, it can still be hard to find local contenders when most peers are not LGBTQ+ and of those who are, some are in the closet for any number of reasons, including for their own safety. John Lotherington, for example, articulated many people's experiences of: 'essentially suppressing my sexuality, thinking: "I can live the life of a monk".' Even if the stars do align for young LGBTQ+ people to find each other, and happen to be sexually attracted to each other, these first experiences can be tainted by anxiety about the implications of being LGBTQ+: how to feel about acting on this type of sexual attraction, the risks of telling people or being found out, the question of what happens now.

Plus, there is still an absence of role models for young romance. Amid an enthusiastic deluge of cisgender, heterosexual relationships playing out in almost every book, film and TV programme, it can be harder to find plots that reflect queer adolescence in a positive way, compounding the alienation that many young LGBTQ+ people feel, though this is improving. As a theatre director Simon Pollard reflected that: 'Working in the arts, the more queer stories being told on screen and stage is definitely important. It's moving to see your stories, like *Heartstopper*, or *It's a Sin*. But it's a complicated process – you think it's so brilliant that mainstream audiences are engaging with these stories and gaining some sort of understanding of what it means to be queer... but at the same time there's a mourning process – you think: "I didn't have that experience as a teenager."'

The result of not being fully able to engage in the experience of adolescent romance on a standard timeline can in some ways be helpful to young people trying to pass exams and pursue career success. For example, civil servant Rosalind Campion reflected ruefully that: 'Being different was super-helpful. I was so sad and so repressed that there was nothing to do but work. If I hadn't been different as a kid, I probably wouldn't have worked so hard at school. I'd have been out drinking, taking drugs, getting pregnant. In one way being gay saved me from a path of mediocrity.'

However, it's also convenient to experience the tumultuous emotions, angst, drama and experimental behaviours in your teens alongside your peers – and considerably less convenient later in life when you're trying to focus on work and make grown-up decisions. I didn't have my first kiss until I was 21. When I tried to come out as a teenager my parents were so traumatized, I found myself crammed back in the closet, chaste and tortured for years while my straight friends exuberantly explored their sexuality. When I finally got up the courage to start dating at medical school, it was new and exciting and dramatic. I felt as though I was 14 all over again. Frankly it was incredibly distracting – and quite incongruous for that age! I lost a lot of the academic focus I'd been able to take advantage of while my high school peers were running around experiencing their earlier romantic angst and drama. One person I interviewed described naively allowing her first romantic relationship with another woman to play out on a social media platform used by her colleagues, complete with salacious shenanigans. When colleagues figured out who she was in real life, she felt so humiliated she ultimately left not just that job but the whole sector.

10. Missing the window of opportunity

Pre-career and early-career opportunities like internships, scholarships, mentorships and other special programmes can be incredibly helpful for ambitious young people trying to get a foot on the ladder. But some LGBTQ+ people may not be in a position to access these on the specified timeline. Rosemary Tickle summed it up well: 'There's always the worry that as a queer person, you're too late for something – being who you are, getting the job...'

She described how figuring out who you are can be a consuming process that disadvantages some LGBTQ+ people: 'It's often difficult to obtain meaningful, timely experience without a life plan, or while navigating the early stages of coming out or transitioning... I'd say that many other trans people (particularly people who start transitioning earlier in life) experience challenges in academic contexts which would put opportunities like university internships out of reach... I compose music. I have done for a long time, but never had the wherewithal to explore getting pieces performed until I was out. Unfortunately, a lot of early-career development schemes for composers cap out at 25 – I'm sure there are similar age barriers in other fields too.'

Senior diversity and inclusion consultant Leng Montgomery wishes he had focused more on academic achievement, but dysphoria made him think it was less important at the time: 'I didn't think I was going to live past 27. Now I have, how do you now make sense of a world when what you were living on was borrowed time? Now it's my time.'

These 10 factors can deeply affect LGBTQ+ people as we are growing up and entering the workforce; they provide insight into particular decisions we make, approaches we take and challenges we face as we start to climb the career ladder. It's essential to recognize that factors which may at first glance appear to be historical affect young people even today and that many of these factors continue to affect LGBTQ+ people at every stage of our working life. Applying this knowledge in supporting LGBTQ+ young people has the potential to have significant positive impact for their careers.

4

The risks and rewards of coming out or transitioning at work

'I knew it was one of these things I had to hide in order to keep my scholarship, keep my job' – Major General (retired) Tammy Smith, US

Some leaders have been out of the closet from the early days of their career. Younger LGBTQ+ people today may not fully recognize this as the bold and transgressive choice that it was when many of today's senior leaders were young. Homophobia, biphobia and transphobia were rife in the workplace, often with less societal acceptance and fewer legal protections. Peter Molyneux, now chair of a mental health organization, felt that as an activist for LGBTQ+ rights in his twenties, many people knew he was gay so he had to be out, saying: 'I've never felt that was really an option to hide because I was camp as a row of tents.' But it came with repercussions: 'Because I was out, I remember someone saying: "oh you've obviously decided you don't want a career" and I realized I hadn't thought about that.' He expressed frustration that others did not feel able to take that leap, saying: 'You see some of the Chairs [of organizations today] saying "you really couldn't come out in 1990" and I think: "no – you could have, but you would have suffered. You wanted a career and that's your choice. You needed the activists to make it possible."'

Coming out is perhaps the quintessential shared experience that unites the very diverse members of the LGBTQ+ population. It also causes some of the biggest challenges we face. Chef Allegra McEvedy reflected: 'My dad said to me when I came out to him: "That's fine, but just be aware your life will be slightly harder now." He said: "Don't talk about it, don't confirm it." But I couldn't be that person.' The act of coming out can be freeing and empowering… but it can also be unpredictable and unsafe and repeatedly puts us in a vulnerable position. So, what does it mean, and how does it affect career progression?

The term 'coming out' as it relates to revealing oneself to be LGBTQ+ originated in the early 20th century. It is based on the concept of debutantes 'coming out', in other words certain young women who have attained marriageable age being formally presented to enter society, usually via attending a debutante ball, with a view to finding a suitable male suitor. In the early 20th century, the LGBTQ+ concept of coming out was inspired by this tradition – it referred mostly to gay men being introduced to gay society. In some parts of the US like New York and Chicago, this was just as ceremonial and glamorous as the heterosexual version, taking the form of elaborate drag balls that started as far back as the 1860s; in time some were even covered in the society pages of newspapers. Beyond those balls, 'coming out' came to mean any sort of presentation of a LGBTQ+ person to others in that community and didn't initially have a particular association with hiding or shame.

Then in the 1960s, the 'coming out' concept expanded to mean a person revealing their identity not just to other LGBTQ+ people, but also to friends, family and colleagues. And around the same time, probably not unrelatedly, it merged with another phrase to become 'coming out of the closet', derived from the concept of having a 'skeleton in the closet', in other words publicly revealing something that had been hidden because it was shameful. And sure enough, coming out became a rather less festive experience. I've heard some people say 'coming out' is a Western concept, but regardless of how it happens, or how it's described, most LGBTQ+ people find it necessary to reveal this information about themselves to other people at some point in their lives, and it can be an anxiety-provoking, high-risk endeavour because every time, you never quite know whether the reaction will be supportive, neutral, distressing or disastrous. That's a lot of emotional and practical risk, especially in the workplace context. Nobody should be rushed on that journey.

What some cisgender, heterosexual people get wrong is thinking of coming out as a dramatic one-time event. The reality is a lot more repetitive. Certainly, most LGBTQ+ people remember the anxiety and impact of the very first time we told someone about being gay, lesbian, bisexual, trans, non-binary, asexual, queer or another LGBTQ+ identity. But that moment is just the start of our journey of coming out literally thousands of times over the years, navigating the unpredictable responses of close family, extended family, friends, acquaintances, educators, taxi drivers, hotel receptionists, the plumber, random people in the street who spot us holding hands… and of course, interview panels, colleagues, managers and clients at work. The responses we receive when we first come out colour our anxiety about future occasions. Just as coming out can lead to sudden rejection by family and friends and religions and other communities, so too might it lead to various forms of rejection in the workplace. Any one of the people we tell may have a negative reaction that can range from ruining our day to ruining our lives.

That's why it's not an inconsequential decision to come out at work and the impact shouldn't be underestimated. Feeling able to be open about being an LGBTQ+ person at work varies according to factors such as a country's laws and culture, an organization's policies and culture, relationships within a team and with managers, and of course the mix of an individual person's personality, preferences, support systems and past experiences. There are LGBTQ+ anti-discrimination laws for the workplace in only about 20 per cent of the countries in the world and are sometimes applied inconsistently; in places without these laws and policies, people are far more likely to be at risk if they come out, not least those who live in the nearly 70 countries (including large parts of Africa, Asia and the Middle East) where it is illegal to be LGBTQ+. But even in countries like Australia, Canada, the US, the UK and vast swathes of Europe where it's technically accepted and there are plenty of legal protections, LGBTQ+ people are still very likely to experience harassment, abuse and discrimination in the workplace. In my own sector, the National Health Service (NHS) in England is one of the biggest employers in the world, and the 2022 staff survey told us that more than a quarter of LGBTQ+ staff experienced bullying, harassment and abuse from their managers or colleagues, far higher than their cisgender, heterosexual colleagues. In the US, a fifth of LGBTQ+ workers in one survey said they have stayed home from work because of homophobia, biphobia or transphobia. Some have left their jobs altogether.[32]

Not coming out

The result is that in the US and across Europe only about half of LGBTQ+ people are out at work;[32] bisexual people are the least likely to be out.[33] In China, where many workplaces have no anti-discrimination policies, only about 5 per cent of all LGBTQ+ people have taken the plunge.[34] Part of the challenge is a double standard. In a US survey, 80 per cent of cisgender, heterosexual people said that LGBTQ+ people should not have to hide who they are at work... but in that same survey, 59 per cent of respondents also thought it was unprofessional for colleagues to even mention their sexual orientation or gender identity in the workplace – presumably while comfortably mentioning their own opposite-gender spouses or partners and their own gender identity.[32] Even worse, 46 per cent of cisgender, heterosexual workers in the survey said they are not very comfortable working with an LGBTQ+ co-worker. Of those who have come out to some of their colleagues, one in eight LGBTQ+ people, including one in four trans people and one in five disabled LGBTQ+ people, have been encouraged by colleagues to hide or disguise their sexual orientation or gender identity at work.[32] Director of the British government's Office for Life Sciences, Rosalind Campion, reminisced that: 'When I was first coming out, someone at work advised me: "You just don't need to talk about it – there are other people who are gay and they don't say anything".'

Many LGBTQ+ people face this workplace dilemma – overtly lie, lie by omission, or participate in work life as your authentic self and risk potentially negative repercussions to your wellbeing and career. Diplomat Omar Daair remembered: 'I'd been out at university but I sort of went back in when I started work – there was still this worry at the back of my mind – is it going to limit me?'

There is often an assumption that younger people today are better able to come out at work due to the social changes towards inclusion, but I was struck by a comment from Sivan Kaniel, the CEO of LGBTech in Israel, an organization that works towards LGBTQ+ inclusion in the workplace. She said: 'I always kind of felt Gen Z grew up in a very different world; they had it better, they're able to be out of the closet. But our research discovered almost 70 per cent of young people stay in the closet in the workplace. We asked them why – the word "fear" constantly popped up. It's fear of their manager, their colleagues, that it will affect the rest of their career.'

Every day, people take active steps to disguise that they are LGBTQ+. The stakes are so high that no matter where you live in the world, a special kind of braveness is still required to come out at work. Rosalind Campion reflected: 'People say being gay is not different, but I think it is, I think it makes it harder to succeed. A colleague said to me: "what's in it for anyone to come out?"'

Why come out?

Given the risks, why come out at all? There are three big reasons: first, the impact of hiding yourself can be a huge emotional and practical burden. Second, being your authentic self helps you to excel in the workplace, gain the trust of colleagues and clients, and grow into leadership roles. Being unable to be your best self can hold back career progression. And lastly, altruism – LGBTQ+ people tend to be very conscious from their own experience that in most sectors, there is a paucity of role models for the next generation. Tim Cook, CEO of Apple, reportedly came out publicly in 2014, the first ever Fortune 500 CEO to do so, to show young LGBTQ+ people that they too could achieve senior positions in their careers. Many of us feel that personal responsibility to be visible to help support and inspire the next generations, and drive inclusion across our organization and sector, especially because we know how helpful it would have been if we had been able to see LGBTQ+ role models in our own youth. So we do it. Despite the risks.

Many leaders did not feel able to come out when they entered the workplace and had to expend significant emotional energy staying alert and keeping up a façade, sustaining the ongoing moral injury of having to lie passively and sometimes actively. Diplomat Matt Burney said of the time he was in the closet at work: 'I almost had two lives. I was very fearful of anybody at work knowing my true identity.' Retired President and CEO of the Henry Ford Health System, Nancy Schlichting, concurred: 'Early in my career, I'd have fake boyfriends, I'd go to social events and bring a boy.' Alim Dhanji, President of Adidas Canada when we spoke, explained how it felt for him: 'You often have frontstage/backstage behaviour and you know how to turn it on – when you're trying to survive in these years, it was an important skill. I think my frontstage/backstage behaviour took a huge toll on me – on one hand it built a capability that was useful to me, but the mental toll it takes – you feel guilty, you feel disingenuous.' It's an experience shared by many LGBTQ+

people at work. Pedro Pina remembered how a typical office ritual felt before he was out: 'I had that Monday syndrome where everyone asked what I did over the weekend and I'd have to lie, pretend something else. I'd be terrified that someone asked me that, I'd be terrified to be found during the weekend.' That concept of 'Monday syndrome' to describe the barrier of not being able to participate in casual, convivial discussion with colleagues about your life is something that resonates with a lot of LGBTQ+ people. Surveys tell us that discussions about spouses, relationships, dating, children, weekend plans and feelings about celebrities and TV shows come up in people's workplaces weekly. Taking part in these conversations is an important part of building workplace rapport.[32] Becks Buckingham, Head of Mission for the UK Government in Caracas, said: 'It's that general conversation: what you did at the weekend, if you have a funny date story – if you can't bring any of that into the workplace, which we all do, your work suffers because you're hiding a bit of yourself.'

Judith Gough, British Ambassador to Sweden, was aware of the impact hiding had on her wellbeing. She said: 'I went through a couple of years of terror and trying to skirt over it, skirt around it. Hiding is pretty toxic, it's pretty tiring.' Karen Teo, who was Vice President of Sales at Meta at the time of interview, had a similar experience in an early job: 'I found myself slinking and hiding into myself more than I ever had. People would ask me about my boyfriend, and I'd be lying. Someone said: "you're a lesbian, right?" and I straight out lied.'

Hiding an LGBTQ+ identity at work doesn't just affect people during the working day, it imposes on home life. Nancy Schlichting remembers the impact of hiding: 'I was scared to death of coming out. I was so afraid of being found out, my partner and I for many years didn't live in the same apartment. It was challenging – it's not the way you want to live. It was a lot of lies, a lot of deception. It's like this constant shadow or cloud over everything, it's tough.' And Dame Jackie Daniel said: 'I didn't feel safe to say I was living with a woman – we'd bought a house near the hospital. Members of the team later told me they'd driven on to the drive and looked through the windows to figure out what sort of life I might be leading. I remember feeling really shocked and that made me feel even more insecure and unsafe and less likely to share that I was gay. I didn't actually come out with that team until I left that job. It did feel really hard.'

Even if someone is out to a select number of trusted colleagues, they may still feel the need to be in the closet to others. Dame Jackie Daniel had in fact been out to some people she worked with who were also LGBTQ+ but during the early part of her career she did not feel able to share beyond that supportive group. Of that time, she said: 'Do you know what's the worst thing? Making up a story. I've spent at least ten years trying to pretend I was somebody I wasn't. It's awful because you know you're doing it, you know you shouldn't be doing it, you don't know what to do. You just feel you're being so judged. We need people's mindset, their brain, their physiology to be creative and not in defence mode. I was always waiting for that question, so I wasn't able to be my creative self. If you've got someone in the team who is just waiting to be outed, it just must be the most horrendous place.'

Why does this matter? Coming out is a key opportunity that can empower people to thrive at work – and not being out can inhibit our potential. People excel at work when they are being their authentic self. When people are not out, concealing an intrinsic part of themselves can have negative effects on their wellbeing and their career. Being in the closet takes up mental headspace, distracts from work, obliges people to lie about their personal life, reduces opportunities for building relationships and networks, and often adds stress to LGBTQ+ people's day so we can't always perform at our best. We are too busy being careful never to mention our partner, to screen our conversations about what we did at the weekend, or for holidays; to self-police our clothing, hairstyles, gestures, communication and personality, and generally keep up a constant state of alert, always worrying about being outed. Loren Fykes, President and Co-Founder of Fruits in Suits Japan and Pride Business Alliance, reflected: 'I don't go around saying "I'm gay, I'm gay, I'm gay" around the office but I've not made an effort to hide myself – people can sense when someone feels shame, is hiding themselves or being inauthentic and it just makes things worse.' Peter Molyneux said: 'I always remember someone saying about gay men "there's something shifty about them, isn't there?" And I thought: "maybe, because they're being asked to hide their true selves". You're being accused of something caused by their prejudice.'

Associate Director at Accenture Sarah Weaver reflected on the time before she came out as a trans woman: 'Career progression is harder for people who managed to get this far. Having a career, overcoming that crushing anxiety and depression knowing you're not living authentically. It's affected my work for my entire life.' She added: 'When I came out at work, people were trying to be supportive: "What do I have to do for you? Is this going to affect your work?" The answer was: this has always affected my work. What you've had is a version of me that's been held back, that's suffered from anxiety and depression. Yes, it's going to affect my work – it's going to make me better.'

The benefits of coming out

More than half of the people I interviewed used exactly the same phrase about their experience of coming out at work: 'It felt like a weight was lifted off my shoulders.' Pips Bunce explained the impact of ceasing to hide being non-binary: 'It affects how I interact with people and how I am perceived – I've noticed before I was out, I was a lot less assertive, proud and confident. A lot of people commented on the shift within me when I became authentic. When you're concealing a part of your identity, you're never entirely genuine. Once you're being open, honest and authentic, people respect you so much more. And because you interact with them in a more honest and open way.' Karen Teo also experienced a transformation in her workplace performance when she started work at Facebook, as the company was then called, and finally felt safe to come out. 'By embracing myself fully I started to find my voice, I started to feel more comfortable speaking up, I started to hone that voice in a way that became more collaborative, I started to get better, more well-liked. I attribute my success to Meta as it was the first place to take me to the roots of who I am and grow me in the company. I became a director in less than a year. Uncovering and embracing and showing who I am to everyone helped me build relationships with people at work I never could have, and they lifted me up, supported me, helped me grow. These are not just my peers and managers, but my team.'

Dame Inga Beale is the former CEO of Lloyd's of London and now a portfolio director. She also reflected on the impact of not being out at work: 'Well, you don't network in the same way. When you're in the closet you're hiding your real self all the time, which takes a lot of energy away. Through doing that it makes you have a bit of a veneer or surface to you – people think you're unapproachable or they don't trust you as they sense you're not quite open. You cannot perform your best because you're so busy trying to be something you're not. It becomes so ingrained in the way you behave because you're trying to be something different – I think back at times and think, gosh, I was limiting myself as to what I can do. Even though I was out I was still a little embarrassed, it's not easy to unravel or even understand.'

Nancy Schlichting had a similar experience: 'It's like this constant shadow or cloud over everything, it's tough. I felt like I was an imposter, I felt like people didn't know who I was. I always worked hard, but in terms of enjoying it, I enjoyed it way more when I could be myself, put a picture of my family on my desk, bring my spouse to events.' Dame Inga Beale also felt this: 'At work it affected me big time. You're not hiding things, you've got more energy somehow, it changes your life. I encourage people to come out. I say: "it's invigorating, you should do it".' There are also clear practical advantages to being out at work.

She remembers: 'I'd been in the closet for many years. Moving countries, my girlfriend came everywhere with me. It was a secret – even though my company moved me around, they thought I was single – it affects your housing allowance. And if you were going as a couple, they'd assist you in getting a visa – we had to do that by ourselves.'

Another important consideration is that some people feel unsafe to be out in their private life – or they may have come out and faced rejection. For some of these people, the workplace has the potential to provide a safe haven, offering inclusive corporate culture and policy and legal protections that enable them to come out safely; to be accepted and respected for who they are, live authentically and meet other LGBTQ+ people at work. This can be especially powerful when someone lacks these protections in other parts of their life. Some people are out at work and go back in the closet at the end of the day.

Once a person does come out at work, some of the benefits can be objectively measured. An important perk is increased levels of job satisfaction, which rises with every year the LGBTQ+ person has been out at work.[20] The impact also shows up in salary data – a US study found that LGBTQ+ people who were still in the closet at work or home a year after graduation earned 18 per cent less than their out LGBTQ+ peers and were 14 per cent more likely to have mental health problems.[19] Unfortunately, women currently get less opportunity to benefit – many studies find that women, especially bisexual women, are less likely to be out than men, largely due to concerns they may have about compounding the gender discrimination they already face.

It's hard to leave the closet behind

While it's great that coming out brings so many potential benefits, it is not the case that once a person comes out at work, we can put the suppression of our authentic self behind us. Some people, accustomed to hiding this information about themselves, find it difficult to move on. Tammy Smith explained: 'You create a lot of barriers in your own mind, behavioural habits that come with hiding. It wasn't like someone waved a magic wand and I felt free and out. I had to learn how to be out because my default was always to hide. Even after the law changed, I put energy into not being out because it was a habit. When your success comes from hiding, not hiding anymore feels really uncomfortable. I was making new muscles; I was sore for a while.'

Even after coming out, many LGBTQ+ people continue to encounter settings that make us feel compelled to modify our appearance, voice or behaviour to emulate a cisgender, heterosexual person and avert a perceived disadvantage or risk — the workplace equivalent of a same-gender couple dropping hands when noticing unfriendly looks while walking along a road. A Stonewall study found many people do this at the encouragement of work colleagues who think that continuing to disguise that they are LGBTQ+ will benefit their career. Lots of people, even those who are usually out and proud at work, find ourselves 'code switching', essentially playing down parts of ourselves that might be recognizable as LGBTQ+ and playing up a more 'straight-acting' persona, sometimes even on the advice of our managers who think they're being helpful, not realizing that praising an LGBTQ+ person for appearing more 'straight' is pretty homophobic, biphobic or transphobic.

Sometimes code switching can span a whole job. Director for Health and Care Workforce, James Devine, said of a past role: 'I felt I had to conform. I'd give an impression that I'm a straight white male, on purpose.' This is particularly felt in certain industries. Gautam Raghavan, Assistant to the President for Presidential Personnel at the White House at the time of our discussion, said: 'I probably felt some of that pressure at the Department of Defense as that was the culture in the place — very masculine, very straight, sometimes very white, and very formal.' Omar Daair had a similar experience when he moved to work for NATO, in a culture that he experienced as dominated by heterosexual men. Despite having been out at work for years, it had an impact: 'All the team leaders were male, all talking about football all the time… it's actually when I forced myself to get into football. I picked a team just so I could join in talking about it. When I think back to where I felt the need to fake it, I don't know why I thought I had to do it. I felt I had to do something to look more butch.'

Things can get even more complex out in the world. Keshav Suri, Executive Director at The Lalit Suri Hospitality Group, said there can be a question for some people of: 'Should I come out at all? Do I have businesses in very conservative countries where the rules and the laws don't support openly queer people – what happens to their profits, their revenues, their teams that may not accept them?'

Business trips are a significant part of many people's careers and can be helpful as we climb the corporate ladder, but numerous leaders told me that for them, travelling for work can sometimes mean climbing back into the closet, which can create stress, anxiety, practical gymnastics and inauthenticity. Some decisions are about safety. I had mixed feelings about going to Dubai for a recent conference – I knew you can theoretically go to jail for homosexual activity under civil law and face the death penalty under Sharia law in the United Arab Emirates. I could find no recent instances of these penalties being imposed and know plenty of LGBTQ+ people live in Dubai. Nevertheless, I felt unwelcome, unsafe and also conflicted about spending money there. That year I was put on the international Outstanding list of top LGBTQ+ executives, which was lovely, but the launch happened to coincide with me being on that trip, which put a bit of a dampener on the recognition – I felt genuinely afraid in case it made me less safe while I was in Dubai. A heterosexual colleague reflected afterwards that when she'd cheerily envied me the trip because I would get to enjoy a little winter sun, none of these implications had occurred to her.

It's not the first time I've felt worried overseas. I remember being asked about my 'husband' at a work event in Bangladesh, where it was not legal to be gay. Worried for my personal safety, and for the success of the project and my role in it, I described a male version of my wife and felt sick with inauthenticity. My wife Rosalind Campion, reflecting back on her time in a leadership role at the UK government's Department for International Trade, said: 'I went to a few places where if someone asked about my partner, I'd say I didn't have one as it was illegal in that country and I didn't want to cause challenges.' Ralph Breuer, a partner at McKinsey & Company who is based in Germany, said: 'Recently I travelled to a country in Southeast Asia. Only once landed, I looked up the local LGBTQ+ rules. When I realized how strict the rules are, I did not talk with anybody about being a member of the LGBTQ+ community.' And think tank convener John Lotherington said: 'I would simply be back in the closet. I de-sexed myself, didn't appear to be on the sexual scene at all. I just switch off. I avoid any form of eye contact. I'm this non-sexual, remote figure.' It's common practice for LGBTQ+ people to have to take responsibility for checking local laws and deciding whether to intrinsically modify or disguise our authentic self on a work trip – nobody I asked had received significant support from their employers on this.

Matt Burney, reflecting on his time as Director of the British Council in Japan, said: 'Japan is in some ways very open, but in male-dominated mainstream society it was always awkward because when I went to receptions people would say: "is your wife here with you, what does your wife do?" I remember thinking: this is awkward. You don't want to embarrass your interlocutors. I do feel at times that I compromised my own integrity – instead of saying "no, but my husband is", I'd just say "no". Sometimes you just can't be bothered – this is a stranger, I don't want to get into it… There's a difference between ill-intentioned homophobia and homophobia that is a product of education, socialization, culture. That was a harder thing to deal with – you had to develop the forum, the space to deal with it. Sometimes it was more trouble than it's worth. But it did make me feel shit: I've been too lazy, it's been impinging on my integrity.' Several leaders spoke about how not actively coming out in these scenarios left them feeling ashamed – but also frustrated that they had to always be thinking about whether to address it. Omar Daair said: 'Part of me would think: "am I being a bit weak?" The other part of me just couldn't be bothered.'

A sense that these modifications are needed extends beyond laws to culture, creating anxiety that being authentically LGBTQ+ could be problematic. As Senior Policy Adviser Darryl Clough said, 'When you go on an international visit, it feels like you've got to put on a front: you're representing the government. It would be a thought in my head not to be my whole self – be silent when there's a comment like "do you have a girlfriend?"' Dame Inga Beale described even more actively disguising that she is bisexual: 'I went through a phase when if I was on a business trip somewhere in Asia, if I went to the Middle East, my husband has two boys from his first marriage, they're not my sons at all but I'd sometimes use them to come off as more heterosexual, more normal. You play games all the time. I think: "I'll come across as more of a normal person at these meetings…" I worried that they would not want to have a conversation with me that could lead to business, I might not get a job in future because of it. You'd think: "Oh, I can't let that person think negatively of me". In a sector you get to be known, you can't risk making enemies.'

Alim Dhanji described a recent experience when he was attending the Advanced Management Programme at Harvard Business School in the US: 'Some of the people I met were senior government officials and business leaders from countries I know it's illegal to be gay. They said, "oh, you're so fortunate your wife is at home looking after the children" and I thought: "here I am encountering the same thing I did when I was 19." So, the next day we were doing a case study on Apple, we were talking about Tim Cook, I was able to give my point of view and I was open about my sexual orientation. There were some people in that classroom who were not going to associate with me after that.'

But it's not just about suppressing or disguising our authentic self. We all live in a society that tells us it would be better to be cisgender and heterosexual. Anyone who has had to disclose a deviation from that society-endorsed norm has a shared experience of fearing that when some people find out who we really are, they will think less of us – and many of us have experience of that happening. It is why we self-censor and self-limit ourselves and hesitate to put ourselves forward for fear the world may find us less deserving. It is also a reason some of us are particularly loud and vocal about being LGBTQ+ – we are trying to have pride instead of shame.

The impact of rising seniority on coming out

As LGBTQ+ people move into senior leadership positions, some who are not yet out double down on the disguise as the stakes feel even higher and the impact could extend beyond the personal to affect the organization. But one of the very few out LGBTQ+ Fortune 500 CEOs, Jim Fitterling, came out at chief operating officer level and reflected: 'I have no indication it's ever had any effect on our business other than positive.' He is now Chairman and CEO of Dow.

Many find that the stress, inauthenticity and just sheer effort of hiding can become untenable. Dame Jackie Daniel reflected: 'Certainly by the time I got to chief exec level, from the minute I've got into these positions I've always felt it's really important to be open. These jobs are really hard – it's made even harder if you're pretending to be someone else.' And Dame Inga Beale shared an example of the awkward guilt caused by hiding that she was bisexual: 'I was running a Swiss company. I turned it around and it was sold, a hostile takeover. I was taken out by one of my team and they said: "Oh Inga, I don't know how you managed to cope with that traumatic time all on your own, not having anyone to go home and cry to." I realized: not only have I been indirectly lying to those people, they now feel sorry for me because they think I'm on my own when I had a loving happy relationship. That night I decided at the next job interview I had, I would come out. It was for the Zurich Insurance company with the Group CEO. I came out and he didn't bat an eyelid. He just said he hoped to meet her one day.' She proceeded to get the job.

Others, while able to navigate the disadvantages of not being out at work, feel an altruistic obligation to do it anyway when they reach a senior level, regardless of the personal challenges coming out might bring because they remember how few role models they had as young people and how much difference it would have made. Dame Inga Beale reflected: 'I guess that's part of why I stayed in the closet so long. If there had been a really open and out gay leader, I think I would have felt very differently. But when I looked up, I didn't see anyone from the LGBT community and therefore I think that kept me in the closet.' Looking around, even today there are still comparatively slim pickings in many fields.

Many leaders describe deciding to be visibly out as an LGBTQ+ person specifically to show that it's possible and that it's okay, and even see it as a responsibility as they rise in seniority. Pips Bunce said: 'When I decided to come out, I'd lost several of my close and dear friends to suicide, hanging themselves, jumping in front of trains – they didn't think they'd be accepted for who they are. It'd come to a point when I wanted to be part of the solution and I thought: "if I can't be my true authentic self and best version of myself in a firm, I don't want to be part of any such firm, or their ethics." I had an incredibly supportive manager, and my firm was working on fostering a sense of equality and inclusion and the importance of authenticity in the workplace.' At the time of writing, Jim Harra was the most senior out LGBTQ+ person in the British Civil Service. He reflected that: 'Part of my job as a senior leader is to be visible and to demonstrate to people: there is someone in a senior position who is gay. You're able to get to a senior position as an openly gay person. Here's a gay permanent secretary and nobody's batting an eyelid.'

It is a responsibility willingly embraced by many LGBTQ+ leaders. Simon Pollard commented: 'For years I was almost proud of the fact that I "passed". That my sexuality was ambiguous, or that I was presumed straight. I convinced myself that my sexuality was only a tiny, almost insignificant part of who I was. But now I realize that is so fundamental to who I am as a person – it's a massive part of me and I wear it as a badge of pride. Especially in the wake of recent events [affecting LGBTQ+ people's rights and safety], I want my queerness to shine out. I didn't have any queer role models at all growing up, so now as a queer leader in the arts – especially one who works extensively with young people – I feel I have a duty to be that role model I never had and to normalize and celebrate my queerness.' Becks Buckingham said of her decision to come out: 'I had conversations with younger staff coming through who felt this wasn't a safe space. All the old stereotypes were being rolled out and I thought: "For God's sake, you're 40, you're now a role model, you can't hide anymore."'

Subverting stereotypes has always been a motivator for Allegra McEvedy. She said: 'I can't tell you how many people said I was the first lesbian they'd met. I felt I had a responsibility to be an accessible gay person – at that time there were stereotypical views about what lesbians looked like; I wanted people to understand anyone could be gay. If you can, it's a bit of a duty to show we are a percentage of the population, we always have been, we always will be, it's natural.' Rosalind Campion said of her decision to come out: 'I remember when I was at my first workplace I didn't know any gay people – how easy it is to live your life without interacting with other gay people. The choice to remain in the closet makes it easy for the rest of the population to think that's not a thing that exists. And if you know you have a gay colleague, you're a bit more respectful, a bit less homophobic. Me being out makes it easier for others to be out.'

Pedro Pina, now Head of YouTube in Europe, the Middle East and Africa, reflected: 'I'm a very visible and vocal gay executive. And the reason why I do that is I always think of the Pedros who are now 22, 23, 24 in the organization who need to see it's possible to have a career and have a family. I get a lot of feedback from the gay community thanking me for representing them. I think this is the minimum I can do. People have come out of the closet at Google with my help and I mentor a group of LGBT Googlers.' And Alim Dhanji said: 'I feel an obligation – the more senior I got, the more accountability and obligation I had; I became the role model others are looking to for signals and role models and mentorship.' The impact is clear.

Jim Fitterling shared that: 'On National Coming Out Day [in 2014] I came out on a panel broadcast to 53,000 employees. We made it a really positive and uplifting experience. Still today I'll get notes from people who were there that day or remember that day. I had parents reach out to me who said: "my son or daughter came out to us this year and we were so nervous. We were worried about their ability to get a job, all the negative things we thought would happen. For you to do this gives us hope that they can aspire to whatever level they want to be in life".' As Rick Suarez, President of AstraZeneca Spain, said: 'I believe it is our responsibility as we mature to demonstrate to others they can achieve anything – if they don't give up. The more they see us in positions of leadership, the more we inspire others to have that personal drive to get there. Do the cost benefit. What do you have to lose?'

Many leaders shared that from their observations, the most prominent out LGBTQ+ senior people often tend to be gay men – partly because men in general still tend to have various gender-based advantages in the ascent to the most senior roles. When I was young, encountering anyone who was any part of the LGBTQ+ rainbow was important enough, but people want more than that today. Lesbian, bisexual, trans, non-binary, queer people all told me that they felt a special obligation to provide that visible senior representation for people like themselves, to dispel myths and show that others like them can make it to senior roles. Becks Buckingham said: 'I didn't out myself as bisexual for a really long time and that's partly because when I was in a relationship with a man I didn't have to, and when I was in a relationship with a woman either I would pass (as straight), or people would assume I was a lesbian. When I made the senior Civil Service, I felt I had to be better and out myself as a card-carrying member of the bisexual ilk. Part of that was that people say: "oh, I wouldn't date a bi woman", or "oh, you must be greedy" – I felt a bit of shame.' And Pips Bunce said: 'I saw trans people but no one who was part of the spectrum of identities that were non-binary or gender fluid, so it was a case of helping Credit Suisse on that journey. We produced podcasts, videos, guidebooks, educating our allies about the different trans identities. As scary as that was, I was blown away by the sheer outpouring of compassion, love and support. People were sharing with me how proud they were that people could be their authentic self. It took a long time for that fear to go away.'

At the highest levels of seniority, in prominent and publicly visible roles, coming out means more than telling colleagues and managers. Jim Harra was very conscious of this: 'The challenge for me was not just that I was going to reveal my sexuality at work, but I was going to be visible as a senior gay person – I was taking on that visibility as well as coming out.' This can be intimidating.

An approach that is sometimes taken to increase visibility of senior role models from minority groups is via features and 'lists' such as the Outstanding list I previously mentioned. Dame Inga Beale was on one of their early lists. She remembers: 'I did worry about the repercussions of being "Outstanding". When I was at Lloyd's, I was asked to put myself forward. I was the first woman CEO at Lloyd's and was already getting criticism. I didn't want people to focus on my sexuality as well as my gender so I actually said no. Then I realized what a homophobic environment it was, it was really taboo to talk about it unless you were being derogatory about it, it was so terrible that it made me want to be more outspoken. I thought about the lack of role models for me and I thought: "I've got to use my position of influence and power to try to make a difference.'"

Dame Inga Beale's concern is one that resonates with many leaders – at the intersectionality of being an LGBTQ+ person who is also a senior woman, or black, or of a minority ethnicity, or disabled, some leaders feel that their visible difference already causes them so much grief in a leadership context that so often is dominated by straight white men that adding an additional difference could be the last straw. Judith Gough said: 'One of the reasons why people are not out or decide not to take on prominent roles is because of the intrusive nature of the press – it can be pretty horrible and vile. It has taken extraordinary resilience at times to withstand what's been printed about me in the media. For a lot of people in public roles, you don't want that. That does have an impact. People don't want to be on the end of that kind of abuse. If you're a woman in public life the level of abuse on social media can be extraordinary. Add being gay into the mix and it's vile. I've developed the hide of a rhinoceros. If I can't be authentic, what chance is there for younger people?'

And she didn't just have herself to think about – a senior leader being out can lead to loved ones being outed and pursued as collateral damage: 'For my partner, it's really stressful to suddenly find yourself in the paper. Maybe you weren't advertising it to your employer, then you're suddenly in the paper.' That's why Nesta Lloyd-Jones, Assistant Director at the Welsh NHS Confederation, finally took the plunge: 'I didn't tell anybody because of my unconscious bias – my director was very involved in the Church and I [wrongly] assumed she wouldn't be supportive; actually she was the complete opposite. For six months I kept it quiet, I was living with "a friend". The only reason I came out was the woman I was with was standing to be a politician. The election was happening, she had this big profile. My gran would be like "Ooh, your friend's in the paper". Everyone saw us together, so I saw it was time to tell people.'

Being outed

Of course, it is not always a personal decision. Given the sensitivities and complexities many people experience around being LGBTQ+ and figuring out how and when to tell other people, it can be extremely traumatic and harmful to be forcibly 'outed', either to colleagues or to the public, whether via malicious intent or thoughtlessness, media or social media reporting it as a bit of gossip, or even a manager inadvertently mentioning it to other staff without checking if that's okay. Nancy Schlichting shared how this happened to her: 'When I was chief operating officer at a hospital in Columbus, Ohio, a letter was sent to my board congratulating them on hiring a lesbian to run the hospital. I thought it was the end of my career. The letter was anonymous – it was sent to the CEO, to my boss. Why? Sometimes people are jealous of your success and they want to see if you could survive if people knew who you were. My board chair stood up for me, told the board members they're going to get this letter and that he supported me. What happened was I was supposed to be promoted to the head of that health system and this one person on my board who said I had no business being COO of the hospital, let alone the system, stood up and said: "If she's selected, you won't get another dime from me." So I left. I got a job at another hospital within three weeks in Philadelphia but I lost my partner after a series of moves.'

Judith Gough also experienced 'That powerlessness when people talk about your personal life in public'. The first time was when 'A Sunday newspaper bounced me into the public domain, which was pretty traumatic at the time, but in some ways liberating and reassuring because the reaction was just: "so what?" I remember the first meeting I had after the story was published was with the Ministry of Defence and I dreaded it but all they said was "lovely photo" and "my uncle was gay" – it made me think I had my own prejudices about how people would react. When I went to be Ambassador to

Georgia, a tabloid newspaper did a nasty article on me about how shocked the Queen was when I took my partner to the ceremony. I can assure you nobody at Buckingham Palace was shocked. I remember being furious because it was deeply intrusive, it was snide. When I was appointed as Ambassador to Ukraine I thought this was going to happen again, so I decided to do it my way – I did an interview with BuzzFeed. I'd told the story in my own terms, I set the narrative. It gave permission for people to talk about it.'

Matt Burney had a similar experience of using the media on his own terms after interlocutors in Japan kept asking about his wife: 'I did an interview with the Nikkei newspaper on EDI (equality, diversity and inclusion) and I remember getting into it, and it was the headline of the piece – "Remember not to ask what Matt's wife does".' They both experienced that benefit of coming out in a public and prominent way: word soon spreads. Matt said: 'A number of people read that article and it did the trick. A lot of our contacts read the Nikkei. They started asking me what my partner did.' And Judith reflected: 'What was extraordinary was expecting to get lots of backlash and finding I was getting messages from countries all around the world saying: "thank you – I needed to hear someone like you was gay". I hadn't anticipated there was a need for that. It was very liberating.' It doesn't always have to be the media. Omar Daair described that after awkwardly avoiding personal conversations with other Arab ambassadors at his current post as British High Commissioner to Rwanda, he eventually just announced it: 'During my end-of-year speech at the Queen's birthday party, I said I was here with my husband – I did all the ambassadors in one fell swoop.'

Whether it's word of mouth, or an array of biographical details including interviews, blogs and media stories just a quick internet search away, coming out in a very public way eventually means it ceases to be gossip or conjecture or something to be disclosed, and just becomes fact. Jim Harra said: 'Shortly after I came out, I was very much on the record, so I haven't had to come out again because it's out there.' Senior diversity and inclusion consultant Leng Montgomery shared: 'Someone said: "Just out of interest, why do you tell people?" I said: "So I own the narrative." It stops me being a spectacle. People say: "Oooh, did you know Leng is trans?" and they're just like "Yeah, he told me".'

For those who decide to come out in a more low-key way, there are different approaches. Senior leaders shared what worked for them. Many found it helpful to be able to refer to having a date or partner, using names and pronouns that make it clear that they are of the same gender. That's been the approach used by Simon Pollard: 'When you have a partner you're given an easy way to come out at work – you just mention your partner and you mention their gender and that's you out… being partnered gives you a shorthand to coming out.' And indeed, people can use other clues rather than having to make a pronouncement. Gautam Raghavan said: 'I was very intentional about putting up photos of me and my husband and my daughter in my office – you can't miss it. I also have on the wall a poster of the first Pride event at the Pentagon – there's things like that you can do when you're in a more senior role.'

What helps us come out?

LGBTQ+ leaders identified certain factors that helped them make the move: new situation reset, seniority privilege, political protection, international employer privilege, assumption advantage and maturity privilege. Let's explore these.

A particularly advantageous moment is new situation reset – part of what's hard about coming out is having to ask people to rearrange pre-existing assumptions about someone's sexual orientation or gender, assumptions that the person in question might even have encouraged. Ralph Breuer noted: 'If you're in a new environment you have a unique opportunity to be yourself – before you build stories. If you miss this moment that chance might be gone. I've talked to senior execs who missed this point of outing 20 years ago and now they have the feeling they cannot because they told their employees something different for 20 years.' Gautam Raghavan recognized this, saying: 'One of the challenges from early on is when is the right time to do it – I didn't want to wait so long that people felt I was hiding something from them, also I didn't want to come in on the first day and say "Hi, I'm Gautam, I'm gay…"' In many cases, moving role, even temporarily, provides a great opportunity to come out because it's often easier to present yourself as LGBTQ+ to people who are meeting you for the first time, before any competing narrative or assumption has the chance to develop and need correcting. There can sometimes be mechanisms available during a transition that help. Rosalind Campion said: 'When I was about to start a new job overseas, my boss was sending around an introductory email to the team and I asked him to mention that I was coming to the country with my wife. It meant that when I turned up, everyone already knew. Now every time I go into a new job, I always include it in my introductory email.'

Personally, I came out in my fourth year of medical school in Glasgow, Scotland. I'd intended to take advantage of new situation reset and come out on my very first day, but I lost my nerve, people made their assumptions and that opportunity was lost. I spent years feeling terrible and unable to even date in case someone found out. But eventually I summoned my friends to dinner and made them promise not to let me leave until I had told them something important. Of course, they all thought I was going to reveal something terrible like I was dying. It wasn't the smoothest coming out attempt. But it worked. And helpfully, we all ended up working in the same Glasgow hospitals for our first jobs, meaning my sexual orientation was already such common knowledge that I didn't have to come out. Learning from past regrets, and now braver, these days I try to mention my wife almost immediately when I start in a new job.

But new situation reset does not always have to mean new job or geography. Jim Fitterling shared: 'For a large part of my career I kept my personal life and my work life fairly separate. I had a diagnosis of stage 4 cancer some years ago. As I was dealing with that and coming back to work, through the cancer diagnosis, surgery, chemo, I had a lot of time to reflect on things. One thing I thought about was: "what are stressful things in my life I can eliminate or control?" I realized one of these things was keeping my private life and my work life separate. We have an employee resource group that's been in place for more than 20 years, so I reached out to people I knew there and said: "I want to do this".'

Another important factor is seniority privilege. Many people worry that coming out could have negative effects on their progression up the career ladder and decide to keep it quiet until they get a bit further. Several leaders have worried that coming out early might mean they essentially had to 'start again' with their career. Leng Montgomery said: 'I'm always curious when I see senior leaders who are visible LGBTQ+ people in the workplace – at what salary point were they at when they felt safe to come out?' Marjorie Chorlins said: 'For quite a lot of my career I hid the fact that I was gay'; she remembered worrying what her early employers might think: 'Someone who was pretty conservative, Republican… how's he going to feel about me being a lesbian, advancing in the organization?' But once some people have reached a certain level of seniority, in some ways this risk feels less of a concern. As Becks Buckingham put it, 'I just decided to be honest with people. I thought: "I'm senior enough now, what could possibly happen?"'

Many leaders concur. Jim Harra said: 'I think I did have that concern at the back of my mind that it would hold me back… It's not until I was more senior that I felt I'd proved myself and coming out properly wouldn't damage my career.' And Associate Director at Accenture, Sarah Weaver, said: 'I realized in my job I had job security because I had a 25-year career leading up to that point; whereas someone way back at the start of their career had that whole question of "What happens if… How will this affect my career?" I felt like I owed it to the trans women who came before me to help make the world better for trans people who come next.'

Tammy Smith took a similar approach, but her timeline was shaped by the law: 'In the US military it was forbidden to be in the ranks if you identified as gay or lesbian; that did not change until 2011 and I joined in 1986. For the first 25 years I couldn't come out, I could have lost my retirement had I been discovered and someone initiated an investigation. At the 25-year mark, that law was overturned and you no longer had a fear of being kicked out. I was already a colonel, a fairly high-ranking individual, I reckoned I could finish my career without this weight over me all the time. In 2012 I got notified I'd been selected for promotion as general.' She went on to note: 'I have not experienced homophobia directed at me personally – it's that halo of being the General. Who's going to be mean to a general?'

An interesting type of privilege is political protection. Gautam Raghavan said: 'When I was at the Department of Defense for the first two years I felt a bit of an obligation to be openly and visibly gay – it's such a conservative environment and at the time gay service members couldn't be out. I had the privilege of being a political appointee. I knew I had protection that those in the military did not.'

For people working in countries where being LGBTQ+ is either a legal or cultural concern, international employer privilege can be powerful. Karen Teo came to this realization in an international company in Singapore: 'I continued to hide who I was until I couldn't take it anymore and I told a senior colleague, and he was so cool about it. He told me one of the most important messages I've had in terms of developing my career. He said: "As an Asian woman working in American companies and being a lesbian, you should embrace that more, rather than hiding".' A subsection of international employer privilege is of course diplomatic privilege as diplomats are not subject to the laws of the host country; the inclusive policies and cultures, and even some protections governments may use for their own staff, can also benefit locally-engaged staff.

There is also assumption advantage. Most workplaces have a default assumption that staff are cisgender and heterosexual. When people find themselves working in a role that focuses on LGBTQ+ issues, that default assumption can switch – and it's the cisgender, heterosexual person who might feel obliged to come out. For example, Gautam Raghavan described his work for the Obama administration: 'My first two years were working at the Department of Defense – in 2010 I worked on the effort to prepare for the repeal of Don't Ask, Don't Tell. Because of that I worked closely with community groups and activists – that role led into my next job at the White House as liaison to the LGBTQ+ community. My job was not only to represent what was important to the community, but to be a representative of the President to the community.' Assumptions can also happen in roles that may not explicitly focus on LGBTQ+ issues but are stereotypically assumed to attract us, such as men working in musicals, or in hair and beauty.

And of course, there's also maturity privilege. Marjorie Chorlins reflected: 'As I've become more mature, I'm much more comfortable talking about who I am – it's not this thing I have to hide.' Sivan Kaniel agreed: 'I feel there is a certain amount of comfort and confidence that comes with age and seniority.'

Plenty of senior leaders who are LGBTQ+ have still not come out. Most leaders I interviewed told me they have many such people in their networks who feel that despite their success, or perhaps because of their professional position, they feel it would not be possible or desirable to come out. Dame Jackie Daniel said: 'There's a lot of dames. We recently had a dinner and I was astounded to find there were more lesbian dames than I knew about – a lot of them felt they couldn't be visible. These are people who've done some amazing things in their life.' Becks Buckingham said: 'People are nervous that they're putting their head above the parapet. I know there are staff who are out to me but not out – when I ask why, they say: "I don't want to be too different, I want to be looked at on my merits alone, I don't want to be The Gay One or The Trans One". You don't want to be seen as difficult.' Judith Gough reflected that concerns about colleagues' responses extend further than whether they will be accepted: 'It brings into question their integrity if it was suddenly found they were gay.'

Alim Dhanji said: 'I know quite a few in very senior positions in very large companies who are not out. I've always wanted to do a PhD to really understand – you've made it, you're a CEO of a publicly listed company, the platform you have could affect thousands and thousands of people but there's something stopping you.' He speculated: 'You get to that level then you want board directorships – that's your late-stage career plan and opportunity to make an impact at the highest level of an organization. Maybe there's a concern that you will limit yourself at that point in your career.' Tammy Smith agreed that retirement was an important barrier. She said that when the law changed allowing LGBTQ+ people to come out in the US military, 'Many people expressed: "No, they're going to take this back. I'm not going to risk my retirement".' That wasn't an unfounded concern. She noted that: 'Trans people were banned [in the US military], then for two years they could serve, then they were banned again. There's still trepidation: "even if I can, should I?"'

Intersectionality also plays a role: when people feel already disadvantaged by other characteristics, they may hesitate to add an extra one if they don't have to. Gautam Raghavan reflected: 'Earlier in my career it required more thinking and intentionality. I can't hide being a person of colour when I'm with a bunch of gay folks. But people might not know I am gay just from my appearance.' Dinesh Bhugra is a psychiatrist; he has been President of the Royal College of Psychiatrists, the World Psychiatric Association and the British Medical Association. He said: 'My hypothesis is we all have multiple micro-identities. Sexuality you can hide, but you may not be able to hide being a migrant, being Indian, being obviously not white. In some ways that has been a more dramatic factor in my career. My experiences of racism have been much more evident and close to the bone.' Peter Gordon, the New Zealand chef often described as 'the godfather of fusion cooking', said: 'I had this Māori heritage which was usually fine, but I had a little bit of racism; that stuff would have had more of an impact on me than being gay.' But ultimately, those micro-identities become a package deal. Loren Fykes reflected: 'I think because I can't hide the fact I'm African-American, hiding the fact that I'm gay didn't make sense for me. It feels like I'd be cutting off a part of who I am, living a lie, living a duality.'

While it's a great frustration to many LGBTQ+ people that some senior leaders with significant privilege still feel unable to come out and help reduce inequalities for the next generations, we generally recognize that it is complicated, it is hard, it is personal and nobody should be rushed. Pips Bunce reflected: 'I can see where they're coming from – people have different reasons about why they feel they can or can't be out. The more people that can and do, that inspires me. Whatever level they're at, they're helping so many people behind them. People should, where they feel able or comfortable to do so, aspire to being open and out. I would always encourage people to do that if they can and be proud of who they are.' And Jim Fitterling advised: 'It's a personal choice. You want everybody to feel comfortable making that decision but, like in my case, sometimes you need help and it's not an easy thing to reach out and get that help. The act of coming out is one of the most positive things we can do for our community.'

One heartening message was that having come out, most people found it was not the problem they feared it would be. Keshav Suri reflected on the impact on the Lalit Suri Hospitality Group in India of finding out their executive director is gay: 'It's been accepted well. Especially people you'd think would be strait-laced fully accept it. A lot of fears and thoughts I had were mainly in my head – I honestly thought a lot of the barriers I put on myself. I had to simply say: "Okay,

I'm queer, I'm gay. This is my sexuality – can we just park that aside and move forward?"'

Overall, coming out at work can be hard. Telling people about being LGBTQ+ often harks back to previous experiences of anxiety, fear and rejection and even today comes with perceived and actual career risk due to other people's homophobia, biphobia and transphobia. But despite the fear and the risks, none of the LGBTQ+ leaders I interviewed said they regretted coming out at work. They found the risks were outweighed by the benefits of being able to work in an honest and authentic way, and being able to provide visible LGBTQ+ role models for colleagues and contribute to progress towards inclusion. Because coming out at work is just the start of a journey.

5

Being LGBTQ+ at work

'It requires you to have the resilience, the self-worth and self-esteem to say: "look, anything's possible", knowing you'll get a lot of "no" along the way' – Rick Suarez, President of AstraZeneca Spain

Coming out or transitioning at work can be a major hurdle, but it is not the end of the story. Studies have found gay and lesbian people around the world have up to 15 per cent lower levels of job satisfaction than their heterosexual colleagues.[15] There are many constraints that affect the extent to which LGBTQ+ people can be our best selves at work and prevent us from being in the most conducive position to reach the next rung on the career ladder. That said, there are also advantages and opportunities. This chapter will explore both.

Diversity as a performance advantage in the workplace

Beyond the advantages identified in Chapter 3, leaders recognized aspects of being LGBTQ+ that they consider have helped them to thrive in the workplace. One is a 'diversity of thought' advantage. CEO of Brooks Brothers Ken Ohashi said: 'If I wasn't gay, potentially my world would be a little more myopic. I think being gay opens you to greater possibilities, it broadens you, it makes you more curious about the wider world.

That gives you one leg up to think about things from a different perspective. I'm not sure where I would be if I didn't have that.' Mitch Mitchinson made a similar observation: 'I think I'm a better human being because I'm queer – I feel it has given me an opportunity to mix in environments with people who think about the world differently, who challenge the status quo. It's a deeply freeing space to be.'

LGBTQ+ people may also have a 'diversity of action' advantage. Liberated from the constraints of what is expected, there is more space to raise new ideas, do things differently and innovate. Peter Molyneux has found: 'I do think you can get away with saying things that someone else couldn't.' British Ambassador to Sweden, Judith Gough, observed: 'Because you're already different, it gives you permission to do it your way, and I think that's a superpower in some ways. There's no pressure on me to conform – because I can't in their eyes.' Part of that is a degree of freedom from expectations of gender. Major General (retired) Tammy Smith said: 'Because I was a lesbian I didn't buy into all of the reflexive male/female role type activities. I didn't have to live any stereotypes.' Dame Inga Beale considered: 'I actually know quite a few lesbians who are quite successful at work because I guess their behaviour is a little bit different, not being seen as sex objects. I was more like a guy and therefore I was more accepted by the guys.' Mitch Mitchinson described the experience of being non-binary: 'I basically got rid of the shackles of expectation – when you present or modify your body so as not to look so much like one gender, there are no expectations. It's a different kind of freedom.'

Another benefit of having personal experience of being different can help increase LGBTQ+ people's empathy for other people's personal challenges, especially those that might affect their work. Judith Gough noticed: 'I think it gives you a better understanding of what it's like to feel like an outsider, to feel different. It helps with empathy – if you've been in your workplace and felt terrified because of who you are, I think it gives you a different perspective. It gives you much broader insight into what people can go through. Does it make you better? I hope so.' Alim Dhanji, who was President of Adidas Canada, described: 'The level of empathy, relatability, you can understand adversity better, you can understand when somebody's feeling excluded. I focus on building psychological safety in a team – that's the foundation for inclusion, innovation, risk-taking. I'm more alert as a leader, as a result of being gay.' And Chairman and CEO of Dow, Jim Fitterling, said: 'It made people realize I deal with the same things as everyone else. It makes you more approachable. It made it easier for me to understand employees who had different challenges. I think it just made me better, more empathetic and more in touch with the human condition.'

LGBTQ+ people are often practised in sharing in a very authentic way, even when it feels risky, which can have benefits. Ralph Breuer, a Partner at McKinsey, said: 'I've experienced it – making yourself vulnerable helps create an environment when others can share. I intentionally share what went well, but also what didn't go so well in my career. It's making it much easier for younger colleagues to be human and open up. Sharing also opened up a lot of opportunities for much deeper conversations – for example, with clients.' Chief Executive and First Permanent Secretary of HM Revenue and Customs in the British government, Jim Harra, noted that: 'It does cause me to think that there are different people who are motivated in different ways and have different lives outside of work – that comes more naturally to me than some of my managers in the past who start with an assumption and have to be disabused of that.' And Ken Ohashi reflected: 'I think I'm really empathetic when people are struggling in their personal lives. I just believe whatever's happening in your personal life bleeds over into your work. I take a personal understanding in what the push and pull are for staff outside the office, I'm keyed into personal hardships like anxiety, not feeling a certain way, I'm very sensitive to that. I give people a lot of affirmation and try to create a safe space for everyone. I think that has everything to do with me being gay.'

There is also significant benefit in having an elevated sense of resilience, personal insight and emotional intelligence as you progress as a leader. Diplomat Matt Burney said: 'The fear of being swept to one side because you're not accepted actually leads to a greater level of resilience, self-discipline and self-responsibility.' And Associate Director at Accenture, Sarah Weaver, reflected: 'As a transgender person I think I'm a lot more in touch with who I am because of the process I've had to go through to get here – I imagine that's the same for all people questioning their sexuality. If you're going through that journey of understanding who you are, it's not that simple, it's about how you present to the world, who you are, and then who you're attracted to and how you relate to them, how I perceive intimate relationships with other people. Maybe cis-het people don't always ask these questions.' Assistant to the President for Presidential Personnel at the White House, Gautam Raghavan, mused: 'It has given me more licence to flex my management style – to be either more directive or softer. That doesn't have to do with being gay but the freedom of how I express myself emotionally, being gay makes me comfortable in a range of emotional spaces.'

Networking as an LGBTQ+ person

Another area where LGBTQ+ leaders describe both challenges and advantages is networking, a key function widely recognized as critical to many people's professional success. BVG CEO at the time of interview, Eva Kreienkamp, said: 'I do feel shut out of particular networks because I'm not quite conformative.' It is in fact very common for LGBTQ+ people to be excluded from standard networking opportunities. In the US a fifth of LGBTQ+ people have avoided a work event like a lunch, happy hour or holiday party because they felt unwelcome or awkward due to their sexual orientation or gender identity.[32] Tammy Smith reflected that when it came to networking opportunities in her roles: 'It was difficult to determine if I felt excluded because I was a woman or because I was a lesbian.' But some networking opportunities set up to counter that 'old boys' club' culture also fail to include LGBTQ+ people. Diplomat Becks Buckingham said: 'There's still a real boys' club around playing golf, whisky nights, it still very much happens.' John Lotherington, thinktank convener, observed: 'I think a particular code of straight male-style masculinity has dominated. It's the lads in lots of corporations that play rugby, go drinking, have a homosocial experience that LGBTQ+ people are not going to be involved in. There's something about straight men, the club you belong to, the power plays... You can form bonds, where favours may be done.'

Networking events that involve inviting partners can be a particular minefield – as I remember well from my time as a diplomat's wife. Many leaders, like Dame Inga Beale, describe: 'If people know you're in a same-sex relationship sometimes you don't get invited to corporate events – somehow you'd find out you weren't invited because it was a couples thing and they didn't want to invite you and your partner.' As a bisexual person, Dame Inga got to see the difference in action: 'With my current husband, we got invited to all sorts of things and I realized: gosh, all these things were happening when I was with my female partner for 12 years and I wasn't invited.'

Of course, given the challenges of coming out and being out at work explored in the previous chapter, it will be no surprise to learn that plenty of LGBTQ+ people encounter barriers to networking because success relies on informal, authentic conversation and personal sharing that some people feel less able to do. Some worry that by responding authentically their interlocutor could respond with homophobia, biphobia or transphobia, potentially putting at risk their safety or the business relationship. Others worry about failing to find commonalities with which to relate, with many examples of men stereotypically talking about sports, or everyone talking about spouses and children. Senior Policy Adviser Darryl Clough reflected: 'Because I'm gay, because I'm not into football, there's something separating me in general chit-chat.' But it's not insurmountable. Ralph Breuer said: 'With clients, some of the connection points are not there, but for example I have a dog and sometimes I intentionally bring this into the conversation to build a bridge, in contrast to other parts of my life where there may be less commonality.' Of course, when we happen to encounter other LGBTQ+ people, commonality is often there and can be powerful. Pedro Pina described this benefit: 'I may not be able to network certain networks that may be interesting, but at the same time you basically find gay people everywhere and there's something meaningful that connects you to them. There's an extra connection that's established that helps, at least at first.'

That connection can indeed be helpful – for example, Rosalind Campion reflected on how her hosting a reception at the Ambassador's Residence in Washington DC to celebrate equal marriage coming into law in England, when she was a diplomat, led to many previously hard-to-reach LGBTQ+ interlocutors coming along, enabling her and her colleagues to forge new connections. And David Quarrey, currently British Ambassador to NATO, reflected of his time as Ambassador to Israel: 'People were genuinely very interested and once you've opened a conversation, you can take it into all sorts of different areas, whatever communication objectives we had. In a country where the UK has a lot of historical baggage, it told a different story.' There are other opportunities too. Peter Molyneux noted: 'I think occasionally if you're a gay man you get treated like a court jester so you can say things that others can't. You have this funny role – it's not always very comfortable, but you can sometimes get further with an issue.'

There are also specific spaces for LGBTQ+ people to network, including through professional networking groups and chambers of commerce. Loren Fykes set up the Japan chapter of the LGBTQ+ business networking association, Fruits in Suits, after attending their events in Sydney. He said: 'It was a place where you could talk about your work rather than trying to hook up. When I went to my first mixer, I was very impressed by all these queer business owners, talking about stuff that was important. When I got to Japan, none of this was happening, nobody was going to raise their hand and say they were gay and owned a business… I'd seen many people being scared to come out of the closet, scared to be themselves at work. The fear of visibility and bringing attention to oneself, rocking the boat. I thought – "this is ridiculous". So, I started with the mixer and a chamber of commerce grew organically out of that.'

Of course, these descriptions of networking with peers and with external interlocutors are very focused on the LGBTQ+ part of people's identities. But no person has an identity composed of just one part. Different aspects of our identities interplay with our sexual orientation or gender identity, creating our own personal 'hierarchy of diversities', which can have a significant impact on networking. The LGBTQ+ leaders I spoke to described their identity and interactions being shaped by factors including: being a man, being a woman; being an immigrant, being of a particular socioeconomic class or caste, growing up poor; having gone to Oxford, Cambridge or an Ivy League college; being from a certain part of the country or the world, having a certain accent; being of a majority or minority ethnicity or religion; being of a different political persuasion than others in an organization; having a disability, health condition or other physical difference, even being shorter than average.

This mosaic of commonalities, differences and intersectionality can be distilled to just a handful of elements that make up a person's identity in the workplace. We talk a lot about bringing our whole self to work. But some LGBTQ+ leaders said they tend to focus on the most visible or obvious part of their diversity. This means the LGBTQ+ element of a person's identity, often less visible, can sometimes be diminished, including in equality, diversity and inclusion conversations. Leng Montgomery reflected: 'We make snap judgements based on looking at someone – people might think: "oh, here's this white middle-class man". I am actually trans, mixed race, I was brought up on benefits, but I look a way that makes people jump to assumptions.' And Darryl Clough shared: 'You have to pick your identity in certain situations. When Pride is the same weekend as Notting Hill Carnival – you've sometimes got to choose: "am I relating to my gay or race characteristics today?" Black Pride is quite nice for bringing everything together.' Some leaders observed that having 'too many' types of diversity can compromise opportunities. Loren Fykes reflected: 'It's been challenging to be black and gay. Affinity bias drives people's behaviour so much. I feel white men tend to help other white men. And this can also occur among white gay men. When I started my start-up, I spoke to a hundred different VCs [venture capitalists]. Not one white VC gave me money, [or even] entertained that it might be a good idea. The people who ended up giving me money were a Japanese person who had lived overseas, and another African-American man.' Although diplomat Omar Daair wryly noted that in the hierarchy of diversities, it sometimes feels like being gay neutralizes other types of prejudice: 'I remember thinking when I was doing security interviews that being gay slightly helped if he was worried I was some secret Islamic fundamentalist – I wasn't that kind of risk.'

Trans people describe particular challenges in networking that come at the intersection of the gender they were raised in and their current gender. Sarah Weaver said of the years before she transitioned: 'I alternated between being a bloke and being a complete introvert. I was performing masculinity – I was trying to perform in a role I was told society expected of me, but I was really bad at it… because I'm not a man… Since I came out, in calls with women I suddenly feel so much more comfortable than I did before in a group of men. I see completely different forms of socialization, of interaction.'

Leng Montgomery reflected on a different challenge: 'If you're first socialized in a female identity, you're taught to give space to others, sit down and shut up – then you become a man and you're told "you've got all that male privilege – be aware of that, and give space to other people". There's a shyness to the trans men that I know. I don't know how to put myself in a space – you need to make yourself smaller.'

Another problem is that LGBTQ+ people can get less access to support associated with our other diverse characteristics – in particular, many described feeling unwelcome as an LGBTQ+ person in spaces that focus on shared identities based on gender or race. This can disadvantage us in the workplace. I have attended several networking groups designed for professional women where it was all going well until I disclosed I was a lesbian and didn't have children. At that moment it always felt as though the other women closed ranks. I realized their unofficial commonality was bonding over shared experiences of men and children. I felt rejected, almost resented for being there. Rosalind Campion had similar experiences: 'I feel like I am more disadvantaged by being a woman than by being gay – but by being gay, I'm excluded from lots of the supportive women things. I think there is an alliance between cis straight women that I'm not a part of.' Rosanna Andrews, a programme lead at NHS Employers and an asexual woman, said: 'I didn't see a lot of strong female figures around me at work; if I did, I just couldn't relate to them. They tended to be covered in clouds of perfume... they could always tell I was never going to be one of them.' For trans people, this issue has an extra layer, as research tells us transgender employees are at particular risk of being excluded from gender-specific networks.[35] Digital content officer Rosemary Tickle reflected: 'At a previous job we had a trans-inclusive women's group; someone had a problem with that and tried to push for a more exclusionary way of providing these services. It was one of these things when it makes you second-guess how supportive people are going to be when you come out; it keeps you in the closet a little bit longer.'

Even within LGBTQ+ settings, people can feel excluded. Pedro Pina reflected: 'The LGBTQ+ community still has a long way to go in its own inclusiveness. There's so much fracture and friction even within our community. We demand others to accept us but we still have a long journey to be made to accept ourselves. You can see the tension around trans rights, between gay people and lesbians, it's heartbreaking. We're still in a very early, unsophisticated stage of our evolution. We've done a lot – we came out of the dark, we're visible, we're getting places, we're starting to be accepted, but there's still a way to go.'

Practical opportunities and challenges in the workplace

Flexibility can open up extra opportunities at work – being able to work late, change plans unexpectedly, take on risky contracts, go on last-minute business trips and seize good opportunities that require relocation can be advantageous, and all can be more challenging if you have caring responsibilities. LGBTQ+ people have historically been able to leverage that flexibility advantage, being less likely to have family commitments; anecdotally, some companies have recruited with this in mind. Jim Harra felt his career benefitted from this: 'I've been able to move around the country when it suited my career – I haven't had to make the compromises and choices that others had.' Although he also noted that he may have been disproportionately moved around for this reason and therefore disadvantaged in his personal life. It's important to remember that everyone's out-of-work priorities are diverse, valid and worthy of respect.

Hospital CEO Dame Jackie Daniel described that in the more than 20 years she has been with her wife, she has been able to access a level of flexibility that might not have been available if she had been married to a man with children: 'She really supports me to do what I do. When we were both working as chief execs we tended to live apart during the week – a practical thing to get the jobs we wanted in different locations. We've cut each other a lot of slack in pursuit of our professional personal ambition and found a way to make that work in terms of our life together. I think if I had a husband, it could have been different. I feel really blessed that I didn't have to have that difficult conversation about who's going to stay home and who's going to have the career.'

Part of that flexibility for some LGBTQ+ women is avoiding the disruption to career and salary associated with maternity leave because we are less likely to have children – in the 2019 US Census, just 15 per cent of same-gender female couples had at least one child under 18 in their household (only 6.6 per cent of same-gender male couples), compared to 38 per cent of mixed-gender couples, and LGBTQ+ people are more likely to have just one child.[36] However, as society progresses, more and more LGBTQ+ people have spouses and children, and these previous flexibility benefits are being overshadowed by different challenges like ensuring inclusive parental policies, securing visas for same-gender partners and feeling restricted in which countries or states feel safe and offer the opportunity to live life openly with our families, which we will explore in Chapter 7.

There are some specific practical challenges that get in the way of LGBTQ+ people being able to perform to our full potential at work. Some of these challenges may seem superficial but they are important in terms of simply being able to feel comfortable. LGBTQ+ leaders gave examples of gendered dress codes, uniforms and workplace clothing policies requiring them to dress in a way that has felt incongruous to their identity – for example, having to wear high heels or skirts. In the US, one in every five LGBTQ+ people have been told to dress in a more feminine or masculine way in the workplace, as opposed to one in 24 people who are not LGBTQ+.[32] Rosalind Campion said: 'My clothes and hair have changed over the years – I think they have gone from being more "straight" to more "gay". I now don't really think about it, but when I was younger I tried to look like everyone else.' Surveys tell us about a third of non-binary people, a fifth of trans people and one in 10 cis lesbian, gay and bisexual people feel obliged to wear work attire that doesn't represent their gender expression. Making these modifications, despite them causing discomfort or humiliation, can get in the way of someone trying to be their best, authentic self at work.

Some practical challenges go beyond comfort to become a health risk. Due to various political discourse, policies and inadequacy of workplace facilities, some colleagues may find themselves subjected to intrusive, inappropriate questions to determine which bathroom they are allowed to use, or told to frame being trans or non-binary as a 'disability' to use facilities designed for disabled people. Many trans people end up lacking access to any bathroom where they feel safe to pee with dignity during the working day. Instead, they can be subject to humiliation, discomfort, dehydration and potential urinary tract infections and other medical problems when they feel unable to use a toilet at work. As a trans man, Leng Montgomery reflected: 'I wonder how many trans people are going to start getting more urology-based illnesses. I get kidney stones, I've been having ongoing issues for six years. A lot of the time I don't want to go near public toilets – I feel scared. If I menstruated that would be an added stress. A lot of trans women won't drink anything, they just won't use the toilet out and about because of all the violence that's happening, lies in the media, that "pervert in a toilet" narrative going on.'

There are also particular considerations associated with people transitioning gender. For example, people who bind their chests can experience back and chest pain, overheating, shortness of breath, dermatological issues, scarring and rib fractures.[37] Gender-affirming hormone therapy and surgery can have mental and physical side effects, but also practical implications, as Rosemary Tickle remembered: 'I was spending a lot of time and money on transition (between 7–10 per cent of my salary each month), so that meant, say I wanted to go for an interview in London that would be tricky, if I wanted to do a course in my spare time that would be difficult to finance; in terms of time, I'd have appointments and check-ups that I'd need to fit in. I had to chase up blood tests. I didn't have time to look at vacancies.'

Bullying, harassment and discrimination at work

LGBTQ+ people encounter homophobia, biphobia and transphobia from colleagues, managers, contractors and clients, which can affect our performance at work and therefore our career opportunities.[38] In America, more than half of LGBTQ+ people who are out to at least some colleagues experience discrimination or harassment – and so do 18 per cent of people who are in the closet.[16] Across Europe, 11 per cent of LGBTQ+ people described feeling discriminated against when seeking work due to their sexual orientation or gender, and 21 per cent felt discriminated against when at work; this went up to 36 per cent for trans people for whom it's getting worse rather than better.[39]

Whether it was thanks to support, luck, or not coming out until they were already quite senior, many leaders I spoke to largely managed to avoid or navigate the bullying, harassment and discrimination that can hold LGBTQ+ people back from achieving senior positions. This behaviour is often motivated by historical and cultural narratives, including pornography and other sexualized depictions of LGBTQ+ people in the media, and by religious beliefs – many LGBTQ+ staff describe colleagues telling them they are going to hell, quoting Bible passages at them in the workplace and praying for them to become heterosexual or cisgender. Many trans women experience additional discrimination motivated by currents of societal prejudice and beliefs that trans women should not have the same recognition, rights and access as cisgender or biological women.

Microaggressions

One of the most common experiences that affects LGBTQ+ people at work is something cisgender, heterosexual people might not even notice, or might inadvertently be doing all the time:

comments, actions and behaviours about sexual orientation or gender identity that make LGBTQ+ people feel uncomfortable, invisible, belittled, disrespected or demeaned at work. This can happen regardless of whether the perpetrator has malicious intent or is entirely well meaning and would be surprised and horrified to realize the negative impact on some colleagues. Previous President of Adidas Canada, Alim Dhanji, said: 'The term I've learned is "microaggressions" – the discomfort comes from people's biases and prejudices that make them feel they can make a certain comment.' Overt bullying and harassment can be obvious, but microaggressions can be harder to identify and address, regardless of whether they are intentional or inadvertent.

Sometimes microaggressions can be well-meant, social clumsiness, or intended as a positive attempt to be inclusive. But just like intentional belittlement, they can cause stress, embarrassment, awkwardness and a sense of not belonging or being respected. Leaders gave examples they have experienced: a colleague talking to them about a TV show featuring gay characters may be an attempt to be inclusive but when it comes out of the blue it can feel like stereotyping – after all, nobody assumes heterosexual colleagues enjoy every TV show that features a straight person. Or upon learning a colleague is gay, saying 'oh, my friend Bob is gay too – do you know him?', presuming all LGBTQ+ people know each other, or worse, 'you two would make a great couple!' on no other basis than having the same sexual orientation. Darryl Clough said: 'There's definitely been a few microaggressions. Stereotypes and assumptions about what gay people do at weekends, how easy it must be without kids, a lot of assumptions that they haven't considered.'

Often microaggressions come in the form of jokes. Alim Dhanji gave an example: 'They open the door and say: "ladies first". When that's unaddressed and accumulates it becomes a toxic environment. Over the years I've become more comfortable addressing that discomfort with people, doing it in a way that's not making it a major conflict but using it as a teachable moment. By them understanding what the impact was, it maybe changes their behaviour next time. For younger people in the organization it is a much bigger challenge because they don't have the courage to address it in that way – you either withdraw and you leave, or you go back to when I was younger and adapt – you may double down on the joke and that will bother you.' Chef Allegra McEvedy said: 'Be aware that what is sometimes called joshing or joking is hurtful and can be homophobia. The types of things that have been said to me, with a smile on their face – that's not okay.'

A particular subset of microaggressions leaders find frustrating is making an assumption that everyone is cisgender and heterosexual by default – and acting accordingly. Matt Burney reflected: 'People just don't really think. They see the world in their own image and haven't necessarily been given an opportunity to think about the diversity that's inherent within the world.' This shows up in admin, in policies, and of course in everyday conversation. Almost everyone I interviewed wearily described the same experience: colleagues repeatedly asking about an opposite-gender partner. Dan Farrell, Company Director at Sparks Film Schools, described it as 'getting wifed', by which he meant people at external networking events asking: 'Is your wife here tonight?', or 'What does your wife do?' without stopping to think that he might have a husband. Or indeed a partner or partners to whom he is not married. This is not usually done with any malice. But 'getting wifed' puts LGBTQ+ people in the uncomfortable position of having to either lie or come out.

Jim Harra said: 'There's obviously a general culture that you do get invited to things with your wife and you have to point out – "I have a husband, is that alright?"' Dame Jackie Daniel said: 'These assumptions are still happening. When you're in a queue to go to a meal, it's "What does your husband do?" It drives me mad. It's easier now when someone asks about my husband to say: "I'm going to stop you right there. I've been with my wife for 27 years. It's really problematic when you do that – you might want to have a reflect".' Of course, when you are more junior, or shy, or not universally out, or feel vulnerable or worried about the repercussions, or just don't have the time or energy, that can be harder to do. Or sometimes you may just be speechless: Rosalind Campion remembered when she worked in Tokyo and referred to her wife (me) in Japanese, interlocutors would kindly tell her that she had got the vocabulary wrong and she actually meant 'husband'. These assumptions are pervasive, especially if children are in the picture. Alim Dhanji reflected: 'When I had kids it made me straight again, apparently – whenever I talk about kids the assumption was I was heterosexual and I had a wife at home.' That said, avoiding the topic altogether because a person might be LGBTQ+ can also be harmful. Matt Burney said: 'Not asking about family is an indication you're being othered, because of what's not said.'

Another microaggression leaders describe is the use of pronouns. Often, people decide at a glance whether to refer to someone as 'he' or 'she', based on clues from their name or appearance, which may not be accurate. Assuming someone's gender inaccurately can make colleagues feel disrespected, disparaged and unseen, that they do not belong, or that they are potentially unsafe at work. Intentionally using the wrong pronouns to make a point that someone does not personally approve of their colleague wanting to exist as their authentic self in the workplace can amount to bullying and it is pervasive. In a Stonewall survey in the UK, almost one in six trans respondents (15 per cent) reported they were not addressed with their correct name and pronouns at work. Ken Ohashi said: 'I can't tell you how many conversations I've had about people not wanting to use the proper pronouns for people.'

Pronoun diversity might feel new to some people, but they are an intrinsic part of everyone's identity. If you are a cisgender woman, imagine how you would feel if your colleagues insisted on calling you 'he', even after you asked them not to. If you're a cisgender man, would repeatedly being called 'she' make you feel respected at work? For anyone whose current pronouns are different from the ones used at birth, they have been on a journey to understand themselves, often a hard journey that has included facing prejudice. Making the effort to learn and use correct pronouns can tell colleagues that they are valid, respected and accepted. When people do not use these pronouns, it can have the opposite effect. Linked to this is the disrespect caused by using a trans person's pre-transition name, also known as a 'deadname', especially when it is used on purpose with the intention of causing distress. Leng Montgomery said: 'I've had some people be really stupid. One person was insistent on knowing what my deadname was, and then kept referring to it in the third person. One person was asking for photos of how I used to look, like I keep them for show and tell.'

Another part of assuming everyone is cisgender and heterosexual is colleagues feeling comfortable describing LGBTQ+ people in a derogatory way or framing being LGBTQ+ as a negative thing or a punchline. The LGBTQ+ staff group members at my organization describe these as 'yikes moments' when they pause and wonder: 'Yikes, did my colleague really just say that?' Peter Molyneux gave an example of a previous chairman he worked with who 'said he loved Westerns... but obviously not *Brokeback Mountain*.' Rosemary Tickle remembered: 'When I wasn't out to anyone, there was a point when everyone was talking about Caitlyn Jenner [a prominent American athlete who came out publicly as a trans woman in 2015]. Someone in my work team had very pointed opinions and felt she could air these to what she thought was a room of cis people, just deadnaming, saying she was weird. Obviously, I wasn't in danger as I was still closeted but if I'd wanted to come out the next week, I wouldn't have been able to, because I'd known she'd think these things about me. These things really put you down.' Rick Suarez says of these comments: 'I've corrected them in the moment and clarified: "what did you mean by that?" if I feel it is something against who I am and those I represent.' There are also 'oh... moments'. Rosanna Andrews described: 'I still find if I mention I go to the LGBTQ+ staff network, everyone does this subtle "backwards pull". It's just like: "oh…" Acknowledging you're part of any marginalized community makes people squirm a bit. So many things are still not talked about.'

Microaggressions can come from unexpected places, including during conversations about equality, diversity and inclusion. In the 'hierarchy of diversity' that we discussed earlier, several leaders reflected that the 'primary' type of diversity to address in the workplace tends to vary by country. Being LGBTQ+ is an aspect of diversity often given less focus, investment, measurement or commitment than other diverse characteristics like race, the inclusion of women and, in certain places, religion in the competition for public and institutional focus. Peter Molyneux reflected on his work representing LGBTQ+ issues in the wider inclusion space: 'It has given me lots of examples of feeling othered and this is quite triggering as it happened so much during the HIV period. I think it's quite hard to talk about but when you're talking about other protected characteristics you have to "remind" people that some black people, women and disabled people are LGBTQ+ too.' This can show up in staff networks, or employee resource groups. Director for Health and Care Workforce, James Devine, reflected: 'In some organizations it seems that perversely, BAME networks [an acronym commonly used at the time of writing in some places to mean: black, Asian and minority ethnic] have reduced network time for other networks. After the George Floyd murder, the presence of BAME networks has rocketed and most boards now appear more interested – it has elevated the BAME network, which is positive in addressing discrimination. I think that's also pushed the other networks much further down the priority lists. LGBTQ+ and disability networks have a potentially important role but there's no headspace.' Peter Molyneux also spoke of microaggressions coming from other LGBTQ+ people: 'In the past I was talked to by other gay men about being "too out" – you were on the receiving end of other people's internalized homophobia, and of course you had some of your own. I think that's quite tiring.'

Beyond microaggressions

When microaggressions progress to bullying and harassment, whether from staff, peers or managers, a sense of not belonging turns into a workplace that is not safe for LGBTQ+ people and impacts our ability to perform well, get promoted and succeed. It is telling that very few of the LGBTQ+ leaders interviewed for this book describe having experienced significant bullying and harassment at work. We can speculate on a correlation because these experiences do hold people back. The scale of the problem can be hard to quantify because many LGBTQ+ people who are bullied, harassed or assaulted at work never report it, fearing a negative impact on their career and work relationships, but also because they feel embarrassed, or are not comfortable talking about their sexuality or gender identity with their manager or Human Resources. Many also say they don't report it because they don't believe employers will take appropriate action against the perpetrator. And others don't act because it can be subtle. For example, Peter Gordon has owned or consulted to restaurants in London, Auckland, New York, Istanbul and Wellington. He said: 'There have certainly been times, even as a restaurant owner, when I've been in a position of having to discipline someone. Sometimes you're having this discussion and you can sense they're thinking: "you're just a fag, why should I take you seriously?"'

The 2021 survey by the Williams Institute at UCLA School of Law in the United States found that more than a third of the 1,000 LGBTQ+ workers they surveyed had experienced harassment in the workplace because of their sexual orientation or gender identity.[16] This included verbal harassment from supervisors, co-workers and customers; physical harassment, including being physically assaulted; and sexual harassment, all of which were even more likely for trans people and for LGBTQ+ people from black and minority ethnicities.

A survey by Stonewall working with YouGov[33] asked 5,000 LGBTQ+ people in England, Scotland and Wales about their experience of physical harassment associated with their sexual orientation or gender identity. In the past year, 3 per cent of white LGBTQ+ staff had been physically attacked by customers or colleagues; this increased to 10 per cent of LGBTQ+ staff of black and minority ethnicities, and 12 per cent of trans staff. An example: Allegra McEvedy described a co-worker coming at her and her gay colleague with a knife.

Sexual harassment

LGBTQ+ people experience significantly more sexual harassment at work than many people imagine. The Williams Institute survey found about a quarter of LGBTQ+ employees in the US had experienced sexual harassment in the workplace because of their sexual orientation or gender identity, especially bisexual people and trans people;[16] a Trades Union Congress survey in the UK found it was seven out of ten. One in 20 LGBT workers reported being sexually harassed on a work visit – for example, to see a client or a patient – but the majority of incidents happen in the physical workplace; a smaller amount at work-related social events, conferences and other work gatherings.[40]

About half of LGBTQ+ people's sexual harassment experiences come in the form of sexual comments stemming from colleagues assuming that if an LGBTQ+ person is out at work, that is an invitation to talk sex lives and genitalia. Offensively stereotypical sexual assumptions are often disguised as 'banter' – for example, implying a gay man is promiscuous or a bisexual person fickle or likely to enjoy threesomes. James Devine shared that just a couple of weeks before we spoke, he encountered a woman he knew at a conference. She commented that he looked well: 'We joked and talked about me looking fit and healthy. She said, "Maybe I'll get a chance to touch a six-pack later!" I felt this was really inappropriate. Did she say that because I'm gay and she thought it was okay? I got the impression she wouldn't have said it otherwise.'

And it is very common for people to ask LGBTQ+ colleagues personal, intrusive questions that they would never dream of asking their heterosexual, cisgender colleagues: sexual preferences, the mechanics of sexual practices, body parts, medical procedures, demanding to know the precise method used to conceive their children. Trans and non-binary people are particularly likely to be asked about their breasts and genitals and personal medical and surgical details with questions from colleagues who have no need for this personal information. The assumption that LGBTQ+ people should be perfectly happy sharing private information with anyone who asks – and indeed that colleagues are somehow owed this information – can feel humiliating, dehumanizing and horribly inappropriate in the workplace.

Moving beyond verbal sexual harassment, one in every six LGBT workers receives unwanted emails with sexual content from colleagues and almost as many get this via their social media accounts.[40] Of the quarter of LGBT men and third of LGBT women who had received unwanted verbal sexual advances or threats at work in the Williams Institute survey, many of them had been about rape and 'turning them straight'. The British Trades Union Congress survey also found that more than a third of LGBT women and a fifth of all bisexual people had experienced unwanted touching, unwanted kissing attempts, or unwanted touching of their legs, breasts, buttocks or genitals; one in eight LGBT women and one in 14 men had been seriously sexually assaulted or raped at work. In most cases the perpetrator was a co-worker; in a fifth of cases, it was a client, customer or contractor, and in 12 per cent of cases it was a manager. In the survey, some respondents spoke of these assaults being deemed amusing by colleagues and supervisors.

The role of intersectionality is hugely important here. Lesbian, bisexual and trans women of colour are much more likely to experience unwanted touching and three times as likely to experience serious sexual assault or rape than LGBTQ+ white women (this pattern wasn't seen in men). And disabled LGBTQ+

people experience far higher levels of sexual harassment than the wider LGBTQ+ population.

Discrimination

Beyond bullying, harassment and assault, discrimination affects many LGBTQ+ people's careers. In the European Union and the UK, 21 per cent of LGBTQ+ people felt discriminated against when at work; 36 per cent of trans people. Nearly a third of LGBTQ+ workers described experiencing unfair treatment in the past five years on the basis of their sexual orientation or gender identity.[39] Part of this is supervisors and managers judging LGBTQ+ people more negatively than they would cisgender, heterosexual people, which affects opportunities. In a US survey that has been repeated a number of times between 2008 and 2018, a consistent one in 10 workers have heard their supervisor make negative comments about LGBTQ+ people.[32] Many leaders said of previous roles: 'if I'd come out, I don't think I'd necessarily have been as welcome', especially when their supervisors were religious, conservative or simply perceived as older or traditional in outlook. Prejudice can be overt but may also be subtle, especially when there are policies and cultures that seek to prevent it. John Lotherington described the uncertainty: 'Whenever you're in a minority that at least in the past was threatened, you have antennae, you're aware of it, you're looking over your shoulder. There was one person superior to me who I thought was keeping a distance; possibly because of reasons of religion they disapproved of my sexuality. Like with any boss, they might make a decision influenced by that – one was wary.'

Many of the leaders I spoke to felt negatively judged by their seniors because of characteristics or behaviours deemed to be associated with being LGBTQ+. Several leaders described instances where their boss advised them to eliminate certain characteristics or behaviours to appear more cisgender and heterosexual – for example, criticizing women's voices being deep, or men's voices judged to be effeminate, or being told that they should act 'normal' and complimenting LGBTQ+ staff when they 'don't act gay'. Becks Buckingham said: 'I find that what happens is I get labelled as loud, bossy, a bit "much" – I get told to tone it down. A bit much of what? You're not saying that to the man who just interrupted me!' Darryl Clough described: 'People will say, "Oh, are you going to say something sassy?" I feel if I was a straight man being direct, it would just be direct; because it's me, I'm being attributed a characteristic.'

Darryl Clough also shared: 'There's been times when I've delivered a presentation, I felt quite confident, but some of the feedback was like "quite soft and not very confident".' Later, and not necessarily linking it to that feedback, Darryl revealed he had internalized its impact: 'When I'm presenting, I'm very conscious of voice – maybe my intonation is a bit soft, I feel people can tell I'm gay when I'm speaking. I sometimes feel the need to change the way I speak to be a bit more straight.' The feedback had knocked his confidence and made him feel that disguising his sexual orientation was a legitimate professional development objective. Ken Ohashi remembered: 'A few times in my career a boss or someone more senior than me has said: "You don't act very gay". Or: "Why can't more gay people be like you?" In that I don't come off as what they perceive a stereotype to be.' Alim Dhanji had the same experience: 'I've had people say "I didn't know you were gay – why can't more gay people be like you?" They think it's a compliment. It isn't.'

Some people described that senior leaders' homophobia, biphobia or transphobia became implicit in decisions that affected their opportunities and promotion. For example, James Devine recalled a time when 'in a previous role there was a particular senior leader who had called me an attractive young man initially, found out I was gay, then changed her style toward me – she became overly critical. I felt excluded from opportunities, often unjustifiably. I felt a result of her finding out that I was gay was certainly treating me unfairly and differently than she treated others. Previously if there was an opportunity to represent colleagues within the area on an issue, I'd be seen as someone who was a confident speaker, well informed, a good person to engage with external parties. I felt that when she found out I was gay, I never got the chance again. And I felt I was "called out" unfairly for things that others were not.'

6

How being LGBTQ+ affects hiring and firing

'I didn't always look like someone people wanted in their organization. I hadn't colluded with someone's idea of normative' – Peter Molyneux, Chair of Sussex Partnership NHS Foundation Trust, England

Looking around, the casual observer might ask: where are all the LGBTQ+ people we'd expect to see in senior management positions? Even with the various factors holding us back that we explored in previous chapters, we might have expected to see more. A significant explanation is discrimination within hiring, firing and promotion processes. Both self-limitation and limitation by employers reduce options and make for a harder climb up the corporate ladder, leading to disproportionately few LGBTQ+ people at the upper echelons of the workplace.

Dame Inga Beale, former CEO of Lloyd's of London, describes it well: 'There's a ceiling that is put upon you by others – their biases, their views, beliefs. There's also a ceiling you can put upon yourself – they can hold you back.' Alim Dhanji agreed: 'There is definitely still a rainbow ceiling there. If you don't fit, if you don't conform – I see it now.' And Mitch Mitchinson said: 'I think that we've got to start thinking about those insidious barriers and blockers – being more aware and talking about it more. People say "yeah, but we've protected their rights..." That's circular – we need to look at what exactly is it that's genuinely stopping people.'

So let's look.

A huge survey of almost 140,000 LGBTQ+ people in the European Union in 2020 found that 11 per cent felt discriminated against when seeking work due to their sexual orientation or gender.[39] That's because research tells us that regardless of laws and policies around the world, being LGBTQ+ is often a devalued characteristic associated with negative discrimination in hiring, firing, setting wages and promoting.[41] More than one in four LGBTQ+ employees in the US and in the UK say they are aware of having been fired or not hired at some point in their lives at least partly because of their sexual orientation or gender identity. This proportion rises to nearly half of transgender people and LGBTQ+ people who are also black or of minority ethnicities.[16] This is not a historical issue. In the year of that survey, 8.9 per cent of employed LGBT people in the US believed that they were fired or not hired because of their sexual orientation or gender identity, including 11.3 per cent of LGBT employees who were black or of a minority ethnicity, and 6.5 per cent of white LGBT employees. The percentage was five times as high for those who were out as LGBT to at least some colleagues (10.9 per cent) compared to those who were not (2.2 per cent). Things get worse the more senior people become. Omar Daair recalls working in the British government's Department for International Development when the current senior champion for their LGBT group was leaving and asked him to take over: 'She said: "You're the only choice because you're the only one."' I was shocked that I could be the only out LGBTQ+ person in the whole of the Department's senior Civil Service. I looked around – gender diversity was very good, ethnicity was getting there... then to see LGBTQ+ had one person? It was kind of shocking.'

The impact of history

There's one really tragic answer for why gay and bisexual men are missing from senior leadership positions: that cohort was decimated when they were younger. John Lotherington shared a haunting story from the beginning of his career as a history teacher in England, during the period when the law made it impossible for teachers to be openly gay at school. He said: 'I got the idea when I was 23 that I could live a straight life at school and a gay life on Fridays and Saturdays in central London. So, I hiked my way down to Heaven [a gay nightclub], heart thumping – I was finally going to talk to people like me! I went into the nightclub and I started making eyes at a man. Then I looked at the dance floor and saw one of my sixth form students. I left. I went back into the closet for the next 10 years. I look back at that kid on the dance floor in 1981. He may have saved my life. That boy died about seven years later of AIDS.'

Many of the men who were born in the 1950s to 1970s, who would have been the right age to be CEOs, presidents and other senior leaders round about now, died prematurely of AIDS as young men, before they had the opportunity to fulfil their potential. They might have filled more Fortune 500 CEO posts today; they might have been role models and mentors for thousands of young LGBTQ+ people and achieved brilliant things. But by 1995, one in 15 gay men in the US had been killed by AIDS[42] and most other gay and bisexual men were deeply affected by it, many starting their careers while simultaneously fearing their own death, nursing and mourning loved ones, experiencing self-esteem assaults stemming from the huge isolation, prejudice and discrimination, and believing that the authorities did not value their lives as much as heterosexual people's lives. Some became activists in response to a slow response by politicians, which affected their job options. Meanwhile, most heterosexual men who are now CEOs, presidents and in other senior positions were largely unaffected by that period, able instead to focus on honing their work experience and racing up the career ladder. For example, 40.7 per cent of men who had sex with men in San Francisco were infected with HIV compared to 1.5 per cent of heterosexual men.

But the impact of HIV is only the start. For a significant part of the 20th century, LGBTQ+ people in many countries were formally discriminated against in employment with laws and policies explicitly preventing certain employers from hiring them. For example, as mentioned in the introduction, the US, from the mid-20th century until the 1970s, ran a campaign of discrimination known as the 'Lavender Scare'. LGBTQ+ people were banned from working in federal and local government employment, as teachers and in the military. Assistant to the President for Presidential Personnel at the White House, Gautam Raghavan, said: 'During the Lavender Scare of the '50s, people were actively sought out and fired for being gay. Then for a period of time it was hard to get security clearance, because being gay was seen to be a security risk as you could have been blackmailed for it.' The impact lives on. The Executive Order that originally banned gay and lesbian people from government service in the US wasn't fully repealed until 2017 and it's only recently that all LGBTQ+ people have been allowed to serve openly in the military. In many countries it is still currently legal to discriminate on the basis of sexual orientation or gender identity. Some countries offer partial protections, so for example government employees cannot discriminate but the private sector can. In many places, LGBTQ+ rights today are not a guarantee for tomorrow. It's hard for all of this not to still colour some people's assessment of candidates. Some discrimination policies may have been lifted, but older hiring managers can well remember systemic homophobia and transphobia being officially the right thing to do. This reinforces other prejudices stemming from personal or religious beliefs, for example.

The history lives on in the minds of candidates too. Judith Gough said: 'I kind of knew I wanted to join the diplomatic service but as a youngster coming to terms with my sexuality, the idea of joining an organization that was very traditional, that had banned people like me from joining it until the 1990s was a tall order. If I wasn't gay, I would possibly have dared to go into the Foreign Office earlier.' Another barrier is imposing limits due to personal prejudices and practical worries about safety and cultural acceptance in certain jobs (which may or may not turn out to be valid). But this is changing. Gautam Raghavan, looking at today's White House personnel, said: 'Culturally it's shifted so much – some of my younger colleagues, I feel like I have to teach them a little history. It would never cross their minds they couldn't get a job because of being LGBTQ+.'

Getting to interview

But it's not just about history. A good place to start in understanding the impact of being LGBTQ+ on a person's career is how it affects hiring today. Up to half of all LGBTQ+ people report experiencing discrimination in their first decade in the labour market after graduating.[19] And many describe self-limiting in what they apply for. Let's consider why.

First is the wide range of factors discussed in Chapter 3 that can create low self-esteem, interfere with our education and aspiration potential, and affect LGBTQ+ people in how we climb the career ladder.

Then, there's the impact of gender psychology. Most people grow up with gender stereotypes that deem men and women intrinsically suitable for different jobs and not suitable for others. This prejudice starts in childhood, with a general feeling that girls have more appropriate traits for artistic or caring-type roles like beauticians or nurses, while boys have the right traits for technical and leadership-type roles, like scientists, engineers or CEOs,[43] and society is uncomfortable with people bucking the trend. According to role congruity theory,[44] if people contravene this 'wisdom' and opt for a role stereotypically associated with a different gender, it can feel so incongruous with employers' expectations and ingrained beliefs about the roles of men and women that they subconsciously assume that person will be less competent at it. In 1983, Madeline Heilman,[45] now a Professor of

Psychology at New York University, developed a concept called the 'lack of fit model' to explain why women find it harder to succeed in fields typically seen as 'male'. She described that as well as other-directed bias, in other words discrimination from others, gender stereotypes cause self-directed bias, which leads to people limiting themselves. These two factors combine to shape people's beliefs about whether a particular person is suitable for a job, the extent to which they're doing well at it and even what they should be paid for it. This particularly disadvantages men who choose to work in stereotypically 'female roles' who, by failing to demonstrate typically 'masculine traits', and indeed being considered to have 'feminine' traits, can be considered less worthy of respect and reward.[46] What's more, if employers and other staff have to concede that someone does actually seem good at the job despite having contravened gender stereotypes, they are often deemed unlikeable.[47]

So, what does this all mean for the far-less researched LGBTQ+ community? Are LGBTQ+ people subject to the effects of 'lack of fit' or role incongruity? Are specific roles considered to be 'gay'? And what is the impact of this? There is evidence that some gay men are less likely to be invited to interview than heterosexual men for stereotypically 'male roles'[41] but may be more successful in applying for stereotypically 'female roles' than heterosexual men thanks to hiring manager biases.[48] And researchers have found that lesbians who demonstrate stereotypically masculine traits may be deemed of greater leadership potential – as long as they simultaneously demonstrate so-called 'feminine' traits.[22]

Even in countries like the US, the UK, Canada and Australia and many European countries where it is currently illegal to discriminate against LGBTQ+ people in the workplace, it still happens. A survey run by Stonewall[33] found that 18 per cent of LGBTQ+ people looking for work felt they were discriminated against because of their sexual orientation or gender identity while trying to get a job in the UK over the past year and more than a third of those looking for work specifically worried about being discriminated against or harassed in their new role.

Pedro Pina said: 'You never know when you're not invited. I don't know how many longlists of search companies I've been removed from because I'm gay – I will never know. I've had some suspicions.'

This is not paranoia. Dame Jackie Daniel remembered: 'There was certainly one job I applied to. I was a senior nurse looking for my first director of nursing job. I felt discrimination and bias during the process. I was told when I didn't get through to shortlisting it was attributable to the fact I was a lesbian. I didn't challenge it at the time.'

Alexandre Flage from the Université de Lorraine brought together the results from 18 high-quality studies in 2020 to look at the evidence for discrimination against gay and lesbian people in hiring decisions.[49] He found that at the initial stage of hiring, with applications providing the same information, openly gay or lesbian job candidates had 36 per cent lower odds of receiving a positive response compared to the general population. This level of discrimination is similar to that experienced by people from ethnic minorities. He also found evidence of higher levels of discrimination in Europe than in North America, that applications for more junior roles were subject to higher levels of discrimination and that gay men faced more discrimination than lesbians, except for jobs that are considered particularly 'feminine'. The biggest disparity was in low-skilled jobs, where straight men had double the chance of being hired than gay men, despite providing the same information on application. This book's focus is on the impact of being LGBTQ+ at the upper echelons of people's careers, but a whole other book could – and should – be written on LGBTQ+ discrimination at the bottom of the pyramid.

In the UK, research found that equally qualified gay men and lesbians are 5.1 per cent less likely to be invited to interview for the same job as heterosexual applicants.[41] When recruiters spot indications that candidates might be gay or lesbian through CV/résumé details like belonging to LGBTQ+ clubs at university, whether subconsciously or not, they tend to rate these candidates lower in competence, social skills and 'hireability'.[41] This is particularly unhelpful because many people get relevant leadership experience from student and staff networks. CEO Eva Kreienkamp confirmed that this has happened to her: 'I have had application processes where I didn't get a job because I was out and they didn't understand why I'd put that into my CV.'

When an application states that the candidate has been involved in activism around LGBTQ+ rights, that can compound the bias. LGBTQ+ people, disproportionately subject to discrimination and reduced rights, are often involved in some kind of activism, which can be off-putting to future employers. Peter Molyneux shared: 'There are examples of how I closed down choices for myself because I accentuated the activism – it became easier to be in the voluntary sector than in other sectors. Because it's easier to accommodate activism in a voluntary sector setting.' Pips Bunce, who works in investment banking, also saw this as an issue: 'I know how risk-averse some firms are and some firms still conflate activism with politics. Activism, as defined in the dictionary, also covers working to drive positive societal change, be that climate, our environment, human rights, etc. Standing up for human rights, most people would see that as an incredibly positive thing. When you step into more politically aligned things, in vetting they may feel less positive – they always try to keep a step away from politics. A lot of firms would be more welcoming to me because of the work I'm doing and the values I hold dear and know that having someone like me in their firm speaks volumes about their firm, their values, their ethics and their franchise; you may get some that look less favourably on it and for whom such causes are not a concern.'

References can also prove a minefield, particularly in terms of previous managers being homophobic, biphobic or transphobic in their response, either overtly or in how they assess or describe the candidate. And trans and non-binary people in particular may have had different names and gender expression in past jobs; requests for references may expose their gender history, out them in ways that might be distressing or unsafe, and cause other practical issues. Sarah Weaver said: 'I'd have to give them my deadname so they could ask previous employers: "did this guy work there?"'

Another challenge is employers struggling to imagine people in roles with an LGBTQ+ focus taking on other roles. Gautam Raghavan reflected: 'If you're gay or any identity you can get pigeonholed – people will say "oh, that's the person who does that issue". At the White House my whole job was to be LGBT+ Liaison and transitioning out of that I found to be difficult.'

But discrimination does not just come from the outside. LGBTQ+ people self-censor and hold ourselves back from opportunities in many ways. Matt Burney, now His Majesty's Consul General in Shanghai, reflected: 'I think I've not taken the opportunity to apply for things as some sort of internalized homophobia told me I'm not good enough to do these things. In the early days I probably didn't push myself forward.' We will explore this further in the promotion section.

Another form of self-censoring is in deciding which jobs to apply for, including level and sector. Sarah Weaver described the complex interplay of gender influences as a trans woman: 'I try and unpack my own experiences of masculinity – men will aim higher than women will. We have internal guidance: when you're this far in your career you should be applying for this level. But men were applying for the top level; women were applying for the bottom level and still not sure they were going to get it. It's social conditioning. The reason I struggle with this is as a trans woman who was closeted, I struggled to say "I want the top level".'

She also reflected that before she was out as a trans woman, her efforts to perform a masculinity that felt unnatural to her contributed to her being introverted and anxious, which made a career in IT appealing: 'I was like: "hey I'm good with computers" – if I'm working with computers I didn't have to work with people.' Others gravitated to industries with a reputation for being inclusive. Dan Farrell, who works in film, said: 'I think lots of people go to the arts sector because everyone knows it's full of really inspirational gay people. The sector is fundamentally about expressing yourself and that goes hand in hand with being gay. There are loads of really good role models.' Loren Fykes, who has worked in television in business development and as a general manager from Nickelodeon and Fox Kids to Time Warner Turner, including the Cartoon Network and CNN, based in Japan, Australia, Singapore and Hong Kong, reflected: 'My experience in TV is that it's an industry that is friendlier towards queer people – I was out at work and didn't come across any bad treatment based on my sexuality.'

Now at Google, Pedro Pina said: 'I probably self-selected out of certain industries as I didn't think they'd be welcoming... banks and consulting firms are safe organizations, a lot of the consumer-facing brands are safe too, because they understand the market and the value of the "pink dollar"; I know very senior people in the oil and gas industry who are still not out.' Alim Dhanji had some of these concerns when being recruited into Adidas: 'I was confronted: will I go into an environment full of jocks? Will I be embraced? But right from the start they didn't shy away from it – there was a genuine authentic curiosity. What I found is sport can actually be inclusive – there are places where there's toxic masculinity, but I didn't find that to be the case at Adidas. I was promoted within six months, and two years later I was President of the Canadian organization.'

People also self-select out of jobs because of the impact that the role might have on their partners, spouses or children. Judith Gough said: 'I've tried not to self-censor but had I not been gay, I would probably have looked at jobs in the Middle East and Africa.' Indeed, Becks Buckingham, the British government's Head of Mission in Caracas, said: 'Every out LGBTQ+ Head of Mission acknowledged they had not applied to roles because of either their LGBTQ+ status or the impact on their partner or family. We're losing people because they self-select.'

At the interview

Having applied and made it through the selection process to interview, many panels are put off when candidates don't display stereotypical masculine or feminine looks or behaviour, leading them to surmise that the candidate may not be a good 'fit'. Managers hiring in their own image, either consciously or subconsciously, is a pervasive challenge for companies seeking to diversify their workforce. There are numerous descriptions of LGBTQ+ people being rejected at interview for tenuous reasons that boil down to either 'you don't look right' or 'you won't fit in as one of the lads or girls', or for vague reasons. As I described in the Introduction, while I know in theory this happens to other people, I was chilled to learn that fairly recently it happened to me when a key interview panel member reportedly argued against my selection because I mentioned being gay. What felt galling was that this one visible episode could be the tip of an iceberg. I have gone to many interviews where I didn't get the job and I have no idea if being a lesbian played a role. As Rosalind Campion reflected: 'You don't know what you don't know. I applied for nine jobs and came second in all of them – who knows why.' Sometimes, you do have a hunch. Sarah Weaver said: 'I did five job interviews last year and in every one of them they told me I wouldn't be a cultural fit. I suspect I was just ticking a box in the interview process – "make sure we have a trans lesbian woman on the panel". This was in some very large public companies who have statements about inclusion policy. Now I have to ask recruiters straight up: "am I just the diversity candidate?" I come across as an angry trans woman – I *am* an angry trans woman. It does make it hard to build a career.'

Several people who applied for jobs that involved relocation, especially overseas, described a feeling that they had not been successful at interview because the panel had brought the complication of taking a same-sex or non-binary partner or spouse into consideration. One leader described: 'I applied for an overseas role that would have been difficult to be accompanied, but not impossible. The person who got it was qualified so I think that's okay... but I knew there was questioning about how that would be handled for me.'

Sometimes people experience homophobia, biphobia or transphobia during discussions with a potential employer, including in the interview itself. Even if the person is offered the job, this can still mean they miss out on the opportunity. Matt Burney reminisced: 'Before I joined the British Council I interviewed with a pharmaceutical company in Japan and the CEO used a derogatory term to ask me directly the equivalent of "are you a fag?" [in Japanese]. At 26 I can't believe I had the wherewithal to say it was none of his business. I was actually offered the job, but I turned it down and I told HR why – I said: "clearly the culture in your company is not the kind of company I want to work for".'

Sarah Weaver described her girlfriend's first job interview: 'One of the questions they asked was: "how will you deal with transphobia from our customers?" That's illegal in Australia to ask that in an interview. It's the organization's job to deal with transphobia from customers.' Senior diversity and inclusion consultant Leng Montgomery described his experience of interviewing as a trans man: 'It took me nearly three years to get a full-time job after transition. I realized it was very different from being a lesbian. In one interview they were very surprised to hear I had a trans identity; one person was so shocked they poured an entire jug of water over the table; one asked which bathroom I would use. There was a correlation about whether I told someone I was trans and how the interview went.' And Pedro Pina remembered: 'I was approached to work at a company and they said: "we don't have a problem you're gay... but at the Christmas party, you're not going to come with your boyfriend, are you?"'

Going for promotion

Once LGBTQ+ people do get a job, it is often harder for us to get ahead than our cisgender, heterosexual peers. In the

UK's Stonewall survey in 2018,[33] one in 10 LGBT employees felt they didn't get a promotion they were up for at work in the past year specifically because they are LGBT. This rises to 16 per cent of LGBT and disabled workers, 19 per cent of LGBT and BAME workers, and 24 per cent of trans people, compared to 7 per cent of lesbian, gay and bisexual people who aren't trans. The reasons that prevent us being promoted can largely be split into three groups: holding ourselves back, being held back by managers and employers, and not working in conditions that are most conducive to developing, thriving and being ready for promotion.

Holding ourselves back from promotion

One restriction we impose on ourselves can be summarized as: 'better the devil you know'. Surveys tell us a full quarter of LGBTQ+ workers elect to stay in their job when they could be seeking promotion because the environment is accepting of LGBTQ+ people and they fear this might not be the case if they move.[32] As a trans woman, Sarah Weaver said: 'Moving between jobs is terrifying – even if you feel you're not getting progression you're safer where you are than applying for a new job.' Matt Burney remembered: 'I stayed with the British Council for so long because it's an organization that has a really strong ethos on equality, diversity and inclusion. There are times I've wondered if it's held me back career-wise because it's been so comfortable.' Organizations do benefit from this competitive advantage in recruitment and retention. Karen Teo, who works in Singapore, reflected on diversity and inclusion approaches of employers: 'Meta has spoilt me so much it's hard for me to want to go to a local company that does not embrace diversity, equity and inclusive practices.'

Another restriction we may impose can be a mindful one. As we explored in previous chapters, many LGBTQ+ people, lacking the privilege to just go with the flow, have invested more time and effort than others may have done just thinking hard about who we are and what we want our life to be like.

Part of that consideration is often quality of life. Consultant Ralph Breuer said: 'It's important not to generalize LGBTQ+ people. Some have leadership ambitions, others don't. We talk about what's important for us in life, what balance do we want in our life, how much do we want to achieve? For myself, do I want to be exposed in the media all the time like some CEOs?' Sarah Weaver had similar thoughts: 'Going back to when I started my career, I was all for advancement – I think part of that was performing masculinity: "that's what men do – they get promoted!" Now I spend more time thinking about what I want out of life – I'm not so driven by the white cis-het male version of what life ought to be.' These self-aware considerations may play into decisions about whether, where and when to pursue promotion.

But of course, LGBTQ+ people who are actively seeking promotion can also hold ourselves back in ways less conducive to our wellbeing. Our own homophobia, biphobia or transphobia often creates a type of imposter syndrome that tells us we shouldn't apply for a senior role. Matt Burney described it as: 'that internalized homophobia that you take on board, subconsciously, the fact that somehow you're not quite good enough.'

Theatre director Simon Pollard said: 'I think as gay people we carry a lot of emotional, psychological, mental baggage with us, a fear of rocking the boat, a fear of upsetting people. We've had to hide ourselves for so long, I think sometimes we go through life in an apologetic way. We're always apologizing for ourselves, censoring ourselves to keep other people happy – our family, our school, our workplace. I'd think "oh, I probably shouldn't say that", and "I should feel lucky to have been accepted in the first place – I shouldn't push". It's internalized shame that's keeping us quiet, holding us back. A straight counterpart may be more used to bashing through without obstacles. In our lives we pick our battles.' Matt Burney believes that all this comes through in promotion discussions: 'If you're putting yourself on a platform that gives you visibility and high profile and there's this undercurrent of fear about your very identity, it puts people off.'

Being held back by people making promotion decisions
As LGBTQ+ people ascend in seniority, questions about suitability become an increasingly toxic narrative that gets in the way of going for promotion – and being recognized as ready for it. Part of this is a sense that as an LGBTQ+ person, we need to perform better than other people to get the same level of respect or access the same opportunities. Dame Jackie Daniel explained how it affected her: 'I felt like I always had to go a bit further to prove I could do the job. It can be really disabling when you're feeling that amount of prejudice – the way it erodes confidence, self-belief and ability to create your own opportunities. To reach these levels of being a CEO, you've got to have these levels of self-confidence.'

It's not just a personal feeling of whether you are good enough; there is a widely experienced sense that many employers feel that LGBTQ+ people do indeed somehow need to do extra to compensate, prove ourselves and be validated. Retired President and CEO of the Henry Ford Health System, Nancy Schlichting, reflected: 'I do think people who are diverse have to be perfect – I don't think you can get away with being an average CEO if you're gay, I think you have to be exceptional. The bar is high.' Leng Montgomery agreed, saying: 'I feel there is no space to mess up, ever.'

Digital content officer Rosemary Tickle described how she sees people thinking about trans women's careers: 'If she's just quite good but not the best, it feels like she wouldn't have permission to succeed. She's treated like she's invading; she's taking up space other people should be in instead.' Chef Peter Gordon remembered: 'The New Zealand Society had created this New Zealander of the Year award. I'd been invited to come along as one of the nominees. We looked a bit queer and you could see other people who didn't know anything about us being a bit judgey. Then I won the award and those people who'd been dismissive wanted to say hello.' Intersectionality only exacerbates the problem. As an African-American gay man, Loren Fykes reflected that in his experience: 'People from marginalized identities who are queer have to work five times, 10 times as hard to advance their careers versus cis gay white men, often.' Eva Kreienkamp said: 'Understand that you're always under scrutiny in one way or another, even if you don't see it. People sense that there's something different about you. Always be clear the backlash is just around the corner.'

Other people's homophobia, biphobia and transphobia is obviously a huge factor too. As LGBTQ+ people climb the career ladder, concealment, bullying, harassment and discrimination can all affect our ability to perform at our best, which can affect our work attendance and performance as well as make it harder for us to access the networking and professional development opportunities that are so important in promotion.[38] For those who make it to senior roles, it becomes more complex. Allegra McEvedy reflected: 'There's enough of us that it's seen to be acceptable – but not enough that it *is* accepted'; as Judith Gough put it: 'At senior levels, the revolution is still coming.' Many people cited religious or conservative colleagues and managers as a barrier to promotion. Dame Inga Beale remembers: 'I worked at one company when I was with a woman – I only found out a couple of years later the CEO, a very religious man and driven also by the views of his family, he couldn't get his head around my partner being a woman – he didn't want to give me promotion, he didn't want me in the company at all. I didn't get the promotion. I didn't know why at the time. I found out years later. Probably if I'd got that promotion, I'd have had a different career.'

An interesting question is whether some LGBTQ+ people find it easier to climb the career ladder than others. Several leaders reflected a sense that the more 'straight-acting' an LGBTQ+ person is, the better their likelihood of getting promotion. Becks Buckingham reflected: 'It would be impossible for there not to be a rainbow ceiling. When I see some of the senior gay men, they might as well be straight – they have conformed hugely, because they've felt they had to. They've been told to tone down what could be seen as campness because it makes people feel uncomfortable.' Nancy Schlichting agreed: 'I think for men it's harder than women. If they appear gay, if they have effeminate features, people get nervous because of the public nature of these roles.' However, on reflection, she added: 'It's probably true of women too, if they're butch. It's all about image for the company.'

There are theories that at junior levels, women who have stereotypically 'masculine' traits like confident leadership may experience an advantage in hiring and promotion because hiring managers tend to discriminate for these traits. This effect ebbs with seniority. Judith Gough is one of the leaders who has noticed this: 'You don't see so many gay women in senior positions. It's partly that idea of women being likeable in order to get on and part of that is being "fanciable" [deemed sexually attractive by heterosexual men]. That's not necessarily a game that gay women are willing to play. I'm hitting up against some real subconscious bias and – on occasion – prejudice at senior levels around what a woman is supposed to be like in the workplace. If you don't fit a certain mould as a woman, it is harder.'

Mitch Mitchinson has had similar experiences: 'What if I'd looked more the part, been more feminine? I've always looked queer and I think that is very difficult. I do think there's something about society wanting women to look a certain way, to look feminine. When I was in my late twenties and still relatively junior I was butcher, I was heavier, and I used to feel if men didn't want to sleep with you or be mothered by you, they didn't know what to do with you. I had top surgery – people don't know what to do about that. Although I don't think I've ever worked in an organization that's been small-minded enough to think: "oh no, we don't want gay people around", there was definitely an atmosphere of "oh, I don't know what to do with you". You're not allowed to think like that anymore, but I think people still do… It leads to people not wanting to engage as much.'

Programme Manager Rosanna Andrews has experienced this at different levels: 'So much of life is playing the game, and knowing you have the tools to play the game. In a workplace, if you don't play the part of a woman, you know you're just going to be talked about – it impacts your ability to work well and be a strong voice. If you don't feel confident or able to be yourself in front of people, that takes away any opportunity you see within yourself. Then when there's opportunities for speaking at events, or training, or participating in forward planning for the organization, you do just feel very disempowered.' This is important. Mitch Mitchinson observed: 'In a private company, particularly at the junior ranks, promotion and development is simply not just about skill, it's also about favour. Naturally we gravitate, engage with, understand better, want to develop those that we can relate to and where you are one of the few people who sit outside of the "norm", who is there to nurture that talent?'

Another issue identified by several leaders I spoke to is anxiety that employers would be less likely to hire or promote them if there was already a LGBTQ+ person on their senior leadership team or board, as this could be seen as creating an 'excess' of LGBTQ+ people (and indeed some have been criticized for favouritism or bias for hiring another LGBTQ+ person).

Many LGBTQ+ leaders observed that employers often lose their nerve when appointing to the most senior roles, even those that consider themselves inclusive and embracing of diversity. Eva Kreienkamp reflected: 'The necessity to conform in a business context is still very, very high, I think. It's okay if it's middle management – but do we really want to have someone at the top who is so different from the rest? It has to be a special company to say: "I don't care".' Senior civil servant Jim Harra noted: 'Most organizations have a culture and people advance if that culture fits with them. If you're gay, if you're black, if you're a woman, often you've got to push against that. That's a bit stressful for the individual – and sometimes the culture pushes back.' Several leaders described rather bitterly that their employers had been keen to publicly showcase them as an

LGBTQ+ staff member when it was helpful to demonstrate diversity in their organization and receive good PR – but that same public profile sometimes worked against them when it came to considering them for more senior appointments. Judith Gough said: 'I genuinely think I'm about to hit that rainbow ceiling. I think it's about to have a chilling effect on my career – when you get to a senior level, a lot of the very senior jobs are super-fought over. Someone with a public profile like me, it really limits my choices.' LGBTQ+ people are further limited by geography. Alim Dhanji remembered: 'I went through a period, from when I left "start-up land" to Adidas when there were a number of exciting opportunities in countries, CEO-level roles, where the company would be taking too much of a risk.'

Being held back by a non-inclusive environment

Several leaders described approaches and targets put in place to increase workplace representation for women, diversity in race and ethnicity, and to some extent disability, albeit at less senior levels, but pointed out that from what they have seen, there tends to be less focus on LGBTQ+ people. Simon Pollard said: 'For anyone who is othered, it's going to be potentially harder for the people in power to see their younger selves reflected back at them', which is why Dame Jackie Daniel advised: 'We do need to be thinking about *all* the minority groups.' And this should apply across all levels of seniority.

Executive roles can be challenging enough, but an important next step in senior leaders' careers is to secure positions on boards. In Chapter 4, we saw that fear of discrimination in board appointments was a concern holding many senior LGBTQ+ people back from coming out of the closet or transitioning. Pips Bunce has observed: 'There are still far too many companies who are not truly or representatively LGBTQ+ inclusive – there's a big difference between celebrating diversity and tolerating it. It's going to be a blocker to a firm's progress – if a firm wants to hire people into the boardroom who only all look the same, feel the same, think the same and with the same lived experience, this will provide no diversity of thought, reduced innovation and less opportunity... there's not enough firms who are as inclusive as they should be when you look at the hard and fast facts on boardroom diversity.' Consultant Ralph Breuer reflected: 'I see a bit of a pattern. The way in which board positions are filled sometimes follows a "mini me" bias – the next generation is chosen to have similar qualities as the current generation.' Psychiatrist Dinesh Bhugra said: 'It is possible that the "otherism" stops people from appointing people who are not like us. Very few leaders are willing to be challenged, to say they want people on their boards who will ask them difficult questions.' Sure enough, several leaders described that commonly search firms tasked with building a diverse shortlist come back to employers claiming that they were somehow unable to find appropriate diverse candidates; one leader reflected: 'Most of it comes with hindsight – I see it actually wasn't right that they didn't ask me to be on the board when I was so senior. I'm fairly sure if I was a white heterosexual man that would not have happened.'

Alim Dhanji said: 'Now I'm exploring non-executive board directorships, the perceptions are that if you're of a minority group, you've got an agenda – there's more focused questions around how you feel about political issues like the Recognition of Marriage Act in the US – I don't think that would come up normally in a director interview. They're asking: do they want to invite that agenda into the boardroom? My optimistic view is maybe they're trying to understand my views on inclusion, but if you're in that position, knowing the hurdles you've had in life, maybe you will choose to protect yourself.'

Dame Inga Beale said: 'I have had some discrimination. It could be happening even now – people might be saying "she has great experience but she's a bit out there about the LGBTQ+ topic so we don't want her on our board".' However, there is also a sense that change is in the air. Pedro Pina said: 'When you see the boardrooms changing as they are, the reason why I'm not disquieted is I see the progress and I understand it takes time. I'm part of the diversity council at Google and at first I was impatient and wanted to see change almost immediately. But now I look back and I see all the progress made and it's incredible what we've done.' British Ambassador to NATO, David Quarrey, has similarly noticed: 'The environment is infinitely more positive than it was a few years ago.'

As people work their way up in seniority, one very practical issue often gets in the way of promotion: international restrictions. Being internationally mobile can be very important for career progression. In some ways, LGBTQ+ people who are less likely than the general population to have family ties restricting their mobility should be advantaged here. However, not only is that difference equalizing with the passing years, any benefit is outweighed by the extra challenges LGBTQ+ people face that can leave us having to hide, be unsafe, or simply be unable to take certain steps up the career ladder.

As an example, successive British governments banned LGBTQ+ staff from serving as diplomats all the way up until 1991. As part of an apology by Foreign, Commonwealth and Development Office Permanent Secretary Sir Philip Barton 30 years later, he said: 'The ban was in place because there was a perception that LGBT people were more susceptible than their straight counterparts to blackmail and, therefore, that they posed a security risk. That meant LGBT+ individuals were not able to join the Diplomatic Service or serve their country overseas. It also meant that LGBT+ people who worked for the Diplomatic Service could lose their jobs if they were open and honest about who they were and who they loved, even though that would have removed the blackmail risk... Because of this misguided view, people's careers were ended, cut short, or stopped before they could even begin.' This apology was both powerful and deeply important to people. However, working overseas remains a challenging area for LGBTQ+ inclusion.

When my wife got the opportunity to become a senior diplomat, we gazed together at the array of potential postings she could apply for – and then cross-referenced them against a spreadsheet that had been informally created by the UK's Foreign and Commonwealth Office's LGBTQ+ staff group. This spreadsheet noted for each country whether it was legal to be LGBTQ+, whether, if not legal, you were likely to be prosecuted or subject to vigilante justice. Whether your spouse would be recognized as your spouse. Whether they'd be able to get the visa or work permit or diplomatic immunity that would be automatically granted to other spouses. These are considerations that generally do not exist for mixed-sex couples, and in our case, my wife felt unable to consider several jobs that would otherwise have been great for her career.

She was not alone. David Quarrey reflected: 'I've self-censored what I might apply for. I haven't pitched for stuff where I've thought that was going to be a big problem. The reality is it's still quite challenging in a lot of places that are interesting for foreign policy people to want to go.'

Becks Buckingham said: 'I know someone who would say they've been deliberately sidelined. They'd say their cohort when they joined have done better than them, progressed quicker. They think it's because they're gay – there are postings they wouldn't be able to take, they're seen as a bit difficult.' This can be particularly true when there are partners, spouses and families to consider and has affected Becks personally: 'It can make it harder to get a job – if you want to be accompanied you may not get recognition and thus diplomatic immunity for your same-sex spouse. My wife uses they/them pronouns. When the Head of Mission to an East African country job came up, I felt I had all the right experience, but I still didn't apply – I couldn't put my wife through it and there was a real risk that the country would refuse to accept me as Head of Mission – or if they did, I would be attacked by all sides and it would be impossible to be anything other than the "gay" ambassador.'

Even some jobs designated as particularly conducive for LGBTQ+ families have their issues. When my wife now looks back on her previous role, she acknowledges: 'Being in Tokyo was the first time I found myself back in the closet – at times it felt really unacceptable being gay.'

A good example of someone facing an international rainbow ceiling at the time we spoke is Omar Daair, who has built his career as an Africa specialist. He is currently British High Commissioner to Rwanda and Non-resident Ambassador to Burundi, but as he approaches his next promotion, he is realizing that many of the ambassador jobs coming up in Africa are in countries where he and his partner could not live openly as a gay couple. He said: 'I'm feeling [the rainbow ceiling] more than ever now. I was kind of a bit of a hopeless optimist when I was younger – I wouldn't let being gay hold me back. I kept on this Africa path, thinking it would all be fine. I've suddenly realized as Head of Mission you're so much more exposed, on show, and your partner is more on show. I just can't do a whole load of these jobs. Now if I look backwards, I wish I'd chosen a different path – I've created myself as an Africa specialist and I can't go to work in so many of the countries. A lot of people have felt what I hadn't felt before but I'm now feeling – my options have narrowed.'

He reflected that he may need to expand to other geographies if he wants to both be promoted and be safe and able to live openly. But it's not that simple – he is not confident about getting senior jobs in regions in which he has less experience, especially with fierce competition for these roles. 'How do I make myself a Europe person? I do think that's a bit tough. I've been talking to people about how to make me a credible candidate. Because of my past career choices, I've not given myself the best shot of hitting these jobs.'

Omar Daair said: 'There are people who just leave. For same-sex partners to follow, it's an added problem, you just maybe pull out and the numbers shrink.' Rosalind Campion is one of the people who left. She remembered: 'As a diplomat there were lots of jobs that weren't open to me because it was really important to me that my wife was able to thrive and that we could live openly.' And Becks Buckingham said: 'I have a gay male colleague who said he couldn't see any postings where he could take his husband – the response of HR was: "Aren't you being picky, trying to bring your husband?"'

Losing jobs

John Lotherington told me: 'I finally came out to my mother and her immediate question was: "Will you lose your job?"' In the UK, 4 per cent of white LGBTQ+ workers, 11 per cent of trans workers and 12 per cent of BME LGBTQ+ workers reported that they lost a job within the last year specifically due to being LGBTQ+.[33] And in the US, one-third (34.2 per cent) of LGBT employees said that they left a job because of how they were treated by their employer based on their sexual orientation or gender identity.[16] When I asked senior LGBTQ+ leaders around the world whether they had ever lost a job or opportunity on that basis, many had not – congruous with this cohort of people who made it to senior roles. But I was shocked by the deluge of stories.

Some chose to leave jobs because the work environment felt homophobic or transphobic. John Lotherington said of his former role as a teacher in line for promotion: 'I needed to leave to come out of the closet. Undoubtedly there was a need to change course. I couldn't conceive of it being possible to be out and the headteacher of a boys' school in the 1980s. In the years of Section 28, I was too cowardly to make a stand. It was fight or flight.' Thinking back, he would have warned his younger self: 'Don't be so stupid as to go into teaching, where you're going to be trapped.'

But John is only one of numerous LGBTQ+ leaders I interviewed who made that decision to leave despite having invested sometimes years in the role. Another said: 'I tell the story that I left because I didn't like the sector, but it was also based on having outed myself and having lots of mildly sleazy men laughing and I didn't want to be there. If that hadn't happened, it's relatively likely I would have progressed in that sector and my wife would be living in a palace with my multi-million-pound salary.' And 'In one of my appraisals my new boss made a homophobic comment about how it wasn't normal to be gay. It made me sad. It's probably one of the reasons I left that job so early, which has probably ruled out a career in that sector. If I had still had my previous boss, I'd have been much less likely to leave as I felt more welcome and accepted.'

Others were not given the option to decide and spoke emotionally of having been fired or managed out of senior leadership roles or otherwise obliged to leave at least in part because of being LGBTQ+. In Chapter 4, we saw how Nancy Schlichting, on the cusp of a promotion, felt she had to leave her senior role at a hospital when she was maliciously outed to the hospital board. Several spoke about having seen mergers, acquisitions and even new appointments create a culture shift away from inclusion. One leader gave a very current example of doing well in a leadership role until a change of management brought different values than their predecessors: 'The people who hired me wanted me to bring the company into the 21st century; these people aren't there anymore. My supervisory board now want to get rid of me… It can happen at any age, at any time – you don't know when it's going to happen. It's about being not part of the gang.'

Several leaders gave the example of having their performance judged more harshly than their cisgender, heterosexual peers, saying: 'The experience of leaving was linked to one person being unjustifiably critical. I have no doubt that I'd probably still be doing my senior leadership role if I was a straight white male. I've seen other people's performance being significantly worse and still be in post.' And 'I got fired. I'd done something that was a misdemeanor but I'm pretty sure he was homophobic and had decided that enough was enough.' The effect is not evenly spread among LGBTQ+ people. Trans people are three times as likely as lesbian, gay and bisexual people to lose their job.[50]

Yet another example is losing opportunities through the impact of #metoo. One leader gave an example of having met a potential collaborator: 'After one of our meetings he propositioned me, said it felt like a bit of a date when I thought it was a meeting. I said: "Oh, good job it's not as we both have boyfriends!" I very much batted it off. However, that opportunity never materialized. I was really gutted. I thought this was someone I could collaborate with, but now I thought: "Oh, did he only want sex? Did I wound his ego by batting him off?" He then got a job at a high-profile company and as many times as I applied for an opportunity there, I got refused and I can't help wondering if it's part of that.'

It is clear that being LGBTQ+ can lead to significant barriers in getting jobs, keeping them and being considered for promotion. Then again, sometimes it can act in people's favour. Dame Jackie Daniel said: 'People see diversity as a real strength, a real plus.' Many employers are actively seeking diverse candidates and being LGBTQ+ can in that context act in candidates' favour. For example, one male leader said that: 'During the selection process I was told by the agency that when I did my presentation, to drop in that I had a husband, to make it obvious and move them away from the stereotype of assuming I was another straight white male.'

7

The impact of life outside the workplace

'We need to talk about our staff's lives, not only about their work. When you talk about work-life balance, it feels like one thing weighs more than others. I believe it comes together. If one of your children is sick and you go to work, you can't really be yourself at work as you're worried about your child. Creating an environment where you understand that life unfolds as a mix is healthier' – Pedro Pina, Vice President and Head of YouTube in Europe, the Middle East and Africa

What happens outside of work exerts a huge impact on people's ability to thrive and reach their full potential in the workplace. We saw this in Chapter 3, so now let us consider what happens when LGBTQ+ adults leave the workplace at the end of the day and interact with partners, family, friends, strangers in the street and on the internet, politicians and the media, and how all this affects people's work.

Public homophobia, biphobia and transphobia

LGBTQ+ people are more likely than the wider workforce to experience prejudice and discrimination at work. But with its anti-prejudice, anti-discrimination and anti-bullying culture, policies and protections, the workplace can also feel like a harbour in a storm – and there are often harsh repercussions for people who harass a colleague. As a result, some people feel safer to be out in the workplace than they do in other parts of their life; as noted in Chapter 4, some even go back in the closet at the end of the working day.

A large European survey of LGBTQ+ people in 2019[39] found more than half of adolescents and 41 per cent of LGBTQ+ adults had experienced offensive or threatening situations and felt discriminated against within the past year in settings including the street, public transport, in shops, cafés, restaurants, bars, nightclubs, schools, universities and healthcare settings. That proportion rises to nearly seven in 10 trans people and intersex people. One in every 10 LGBTQ+ people were physically or sexually attacked in the last five years and a full quarter said that fear of a homophobic, biphobic or transphobic reaction from the police would put them off reporting it – in fact, only 14 per cent said they reported their last attack. Fewer than half of the people surveyed felt that violence against LGBTQ+ people has decreased in recent years; 43 per cent think it has increased. They seem to be right. Despite the under-reporting we just considered, annual data from the UK's Home Office tell us that from 2021 to 2022, sexual orientation hate crimes increased by 41 per cent and transgender identity hate crimes increased by 56 per cent, the biggest rise in a decade.[51] Leng Montgomery reflected: 'I still leave my house and it's not acceptable. I'm being treated as a sub-human, being humiliated. There's no protection. I have to walk into situations where I have to be pragmatic and wonder: what level of trauma is it going to be?'

And that is before considering the deluge of homophobic, biphobic and transphobic abuse that at least one in 10 LGBTQ+ people and a quarter of trans and non-binary people experience on the internet, particularly via social media.[52] Rick Suarez, the President of AstraZeneca Spain, reflected: 'The bullying is easier today – it's anonymous and it's so much more consistent because of what social media can do. That's an angle I didn't face – on a nightly basis getting comments and messages that someone's against me.' James Devine shared: 'When I was a chief executive I had a stalker, and part of his reason for stalking me was that I was gay. He'd follow my social media and referred to things me or my partner were doing, follow me to the shops, found out where I lived. When we met unexpectedly face-to-face, he made derogatory comments about me being gay. When you have an experience like that it almost puts you back years – what you say can be twisted and be used against you in a very unpleasant way. The experience still impacts me today and I am more cautious about what I say about me or my family on social media.'

Many people use homophobia, biphobia and transphobia as an activism tool and propagate this ideology online, including personally threatening and attacking LGBTQ+ individuals and allies. In fact, some trans people were afraid to talk to me in case I was another transphobic person posing as a writer to gain information to use against them, or fearing that being featured in this book could direct further transphobia towards them. Associate Director at Accenture, Sarah Weaver, said: 'Outside of the workplace, I've been assaulted, I've been called slurs, received targeted harassment on the internet, I've had some abusive commentary on LinkedIn, I've received transphobic and biphobic abuse from people I used to know.'

Often politicians, celebrities, activists and the media create and encourage homophobic, biphobic and transphobic rhetoric and threats. In a 2021 blog, the Council of Europe's Commissioner of Human Rights, Dunja Mijatović, juxtaposed the good progress across Europe in LGBTQ+ rights such as protecting people from discrimination and hate, or recognition of same-sex relationships, with a tide of discriminatory legislation, often designed to win over so-called traditional or conservative voters through popularizing mechanisms like suppressing LGBTQ+ people's rights to marry and adopt children, stopping trans people using public bathrooms, or prohibiting books for young people that mention the existence of LGBTQ+ people. Such activities endorse homophobia, biphobia and transphobia as culturally legitimate and even desirable, leaving LGBTQ+

people navigating a culture of shame and fear. I found it startling talking to some trans people to hear of how many online death threats they receive as a matter of course. LGBTQ+ people are routinely, publicly blamed by some parties for earthquakes, floods, the financial crisis. This propagation of hate about LGBTQ+ people regularly inspires real-life violence, such as attacks during Pride parades or shootings at gay nightclubs, and violence towards individuals around the world.[53] If I hold hands with my wife in the street in cosmopolitan London, it's not unusual for someone to shout something hateful at us.

As well as experiencing repeat assaults on our dignity and safety, LGBTQ+ people do not know whether or when our hard-won rights are about to be snatched from us for political expediency, leaving us in a constant state of low-grade insecurity. In many countries, politicians have recently made good on their campaign promises of blocking or rescinding LGBTQ+ people's rights. Just as Dunja Mijatović described many new laws in progress across Europe designed to reduce LGBTQ+ people's rights, the American Civil Liberties Union (ACLU) is tracking hundreds of anti-LGBTQ+ Bills across the US, including many affecting freedom of speech, rights in educational settings and access to healthcare as well as allowing more workplace discrimination. This feels like an active risk all over the world and it takes its toll. Sivan Kaniel said: 'I have a pride flag in my apartment, I am the CEO of one of the around 22 LGBTQ+ organizations in Israel… There was a lot of tension in the days after the new, very right-wing government was elected. I came home, there was a delivery guy on a scooter, he said, "Hey, do you know Sivan?" I said, "Yeah, that's me" and he turned to get something, and I realized I was scared. I had this really random moment when I thought: "I have a family, do we need to be less visible?" He was just delivering a package.'

At the time of writing, organized discrimination has been particularly targeted at trans and non-binary people with significant scapegoating of trans people for political gain in public discourse.[54] Leng Montgomery said: 'I've never regretted my transition, but I sometimes wish I wasn't trans because of how people have been given a lot of power to ruin my life… All the media bias is poisoning people's minds left, right and centre. It's this constant drip-feed of negativity about a set of people. People don't realize how much they reflect what they've just heard or read.' And Pips Bunce, who works in investment banking, shared: 'I certainly face more challenges outside the workplace – in society over the last two or three years the levels of intolerance, bias or prejudice have gone up, a rise in the people who think it's their place to put you down. This is driven by the legacy press, parts of the media, some of the narrative being pushed from the government. This is further evidenced by the UK until 2015 consistently achieving number one place in the Rainbow Map and Index, which ranks European countries on the support for LGBTQI+ people, hate crime, policies, etc. The UK has been plummeting in this table, slipping to position 9 in 2020 and in 2022 dropping to 14th place.' In 2023 the UK had dropped still further to 17th place.

The UK is not alone. Sarah Weaver reflected on the personal impact: 'It's a minority of people with very loud voices, but some of them are in positions of power. In Australia we've recently had a federal election. One of the candidates had been shown to be transphobic. The then Prime Minister stood by her, said she's an amazing person asking valid questions. I was like: "What's going on in our country?" We've got this politician saying we don't deserve to have the same rights as other people enjoy; we've got the PM essentially saying she's on to something. There's nothing like having your existence debated. That creates stress and fear and anxiety that you can't just walk away from, put that aside and say I'm just going to do my job and not be affected. It absolutely affects you – in your relationships, where you'll decide to go out, in your work life… it affects you everywhere.'

More widely, as a think tank convener, John Lotherington reflected: 'There's a terrific variety of what people have to face – in those countries where they still have homophobic laws, their careers are always on the line. Every day they're lucky to keep their jobs; if the political weather changes, they might lose their job or go to jail.' It's not an exaggeration to say that our current rights to live life as our authentic self are fragile, tenuous and as LGBTQ+ people learn more about what has come before, it becomes all too clear these rights could be easily lost. People are afraid.

Health

Given the impact of prejudice and discrimination that LGBTQ+ people encounter, it is not surprising to learn that we are at higher risk of developing mental health problems. Research tells us that about half of LGBTQ+ people have experienced depression in the past year, including two-thirds of trans people. Almost a third of lesbian, gay and bisexual people and nearly half of trans people think about suicide in any year. In the year of the survey, one in every eight LGBTQ+ young people between the ages of 18 and 24 attempted suicide. Anxiety affects 71 per cent of trans people, 65 per cent of queer women and 51 per cent of queer men. Rates of eating disorders and addiction including alcohol and drugs are also disproportionately high.[55] Alcohol, drug use and smoking are all generally higher in LGBTQ+ populations, which stems from a complex mix of a response to stress, anxiety and the impact of discrimination and a legacy of drinking establishments being historically one of the only safe places to meet, and continuing to be one of the most common places to meet. There's evidence that LGBTQ+ people are at higher risk of domestic abuse. And men who have sex with men continue to be at higher risk of becoming infected with HIV than many other demographics; of note, treatment is now very effective.[56] Plus, some people are subject to so-called conversion 'therapy', a diverse range of practices often disguised as medical or religious procedures that are based on the false promise of turning an LGBTQ+ person cisgender or heterosexual; this 'therapy' lacks a basis in science and has been condemned by the United Nations alongside most respected experts and organizations as being akin to torture; it is banned in many jurisdictions. As well as failing to deliver its intended result, conversion 'therapy' can cause significant physical and psychological damage. It's believed to affect about one in every 20 LGBTQ+ people.

Many health inequalities stem from LGBTQ+ people having a harder time accessing healthcare. Gender care waiting lists can be far longer than for other health needs and are often hard to access; in the UK, 63 per cent of trans and non-binary people reported that this wait had a negative effect on their work life.[37] And LGBTQ+ people who want children can require additional and more complex care. But more widely, many LGBTQ+ people avoid or postpone accessing the healthcare they need due to fears of prejudice and discrimination. These fears are not unfounded. Leng Montgomery described his name change not being correctly processed on his health records for two years, leading to him struggling to get his medication and at one point, surgery. He also described an experience of going for a gynaecological examination: 'I've had receptionists laugh in my face, saying "There must be some terrible mistake". Having paramedics or doctors saying "Oh, you're trans – I thought you were a normal guy". Having an internal examination by a person who asked *while inside me* "Why have you done this to yourself?". She was brushing over the fact that I had kidney stones, a fibroid, a cyst on my ovary – I was hearing about her political views.' In the UK a quarter of all LGBTQ+ people have witnessed discriminatory or negative remarks against LGBTQ+ people by healthcare staff and one in eight have personally experienced discrimination when accessing healthcare – this puts a lot of LGBTQ+ people off from going to the doctor when they need to – including for some cancer screenings, and even during pregnancy.

Pregnancy

Of the many things that make life more complex for LGBTQ+ people, having children is high up the list. It is also an incredibly important part of many people's lives. US surveys tell us that around a third of straight people and bisexual women and a fifth of lesbians live with children in their homes; gay and bisexual men are less likely to have children. Many LGBTQ+ leaders told me that they had regrets about not having had children, but it had not felt it was a possibility when they were the right age. Diplomat Matt Burney reflected: 'I do feel a bit of regret sometimes. I think growing up when I did, you kind of put the idea of kids to one side. I told myself I don't like kids. I wonder if it was a defence mechanism. Had the options been available in the way they are now we might have acted differently. It's a bit late in the day now.'

Increasingly, this narrative is changing and plenty of LGBTQ+ people have children. For instance, Alim Dhanji shared: 'I always wanted to have a family. When you're part of the LGBTQ+ community society has no expectations of that – you have a blank canvas. I always felt parenthood was something I really, really wanted to do but it hadn't been on the cards until I met my husband and it was just an immediate thing. Three years after meeting him we had our first child, and now we have a second one.' However, for LGBTQ+ people who have children, there can be particular considerations.

LGBTQ+ people are more likely to need fertility, surrogacy and adoption services and can experience sexism, homophobia, biphobia, transphobia and significant discrimination during that journey – for example, from health professionals, foster agencies, adoption agencies and in custody cases. We can also experience far more practical logistics. Lesbians and bisexual women who want to get pregnant are 12 times as likely to need access to fertility treatments, including funding them and having time away from work to accommodate them, compared to heterosexual women. Men in a same-gender couple are particularly subject to additional cost and complex logistics, as well as workplace policies that do not always recognize their needs. And trans people may have to navigate considerations about how to preserve their fertility during transition and manage disruption in their hormone therapy during pregnancy as well as manage exacerbations of dysphoria. Overall, LGBTQ+ people are more likely to have to navigate multiple people being involved in the conception and pregnancy. And they are more likely to need access to good, inclusive parental policies around adoption, both at the time and over the course of their working life as parents. Often workplace health insurance and other policies are designed for cisgender, heterosexual couples and do not take these extra complexities into consideration. As well as the financial and other practical implications, it can feel pretty distressing and unfair for LGBTQ+ people to see our employers looking after our colleagues' families but not our own.

Many LGBTQ+ people feel paranoid that due to societal prejudices and expectations, they may not be afforded the same accommodation as their peers if they want children. Theatre director Simon Pollard reflected: 'At some point we might adopt. I have a real fear about doing that while in a job. I think that as a straight couple there's an expectation that at some point you might have children – if you do, it's going to be an inconvenience for a company, but they're used to it, they'll deal with it. I think as a gay person knowing I want to adopt, if you land that on an employer, I'm worried about the stigma attached to that – like "you could have planned to do that at a different time, why don't you wait until after this job is over?" That is something I'm worried about moving forward. I think there's never going to be a right time for me to adopt as I'll always feel I'm letting someone down, that I'll be thought of negatively, like I deliberately plotted to get a well-paid job then ask to go on parental leave. Even if on paper we should all be treated fairly, so much of my work is about reputation and making connections. If I have to go on leave in the middle of a job, people are going to be pissed off. Maybe a reason we've delayed and delayed is I don't want to upset anyone. If I was straight, I don't think I'd feel the same because there's this expectation that straight people have kids – that straight people deserve kids, it's part of their life plan. There are so many gay people who live a fabulous life without kids. I can't think of many gays within the industry who have adopted. Whereas if I think of all the straight people in the industry, the majority do have families.'

Having made the move towards starting a family, pregnant LGBTQ+ people often don't feel able to access the healthcare they need, like pre-natal care, access to abortions and post-partum care due to fears and actual experiences of prejudice and discrimination from fellow parents and from healthcare teams providing services that are almost universally designed with cisgender, heterosexual people in mind. This can be anything from awkward to humiliating. As a result, LGBTQ+ parents underuse the health services designed to achieve a healthy pregnancy, experience more prejudice and anxiety, and have worse outcomes. The rate of pregnancy success is nine times lower for lesbian parents and two times lower for bisexual parents than for those who are heterosexual; there is less data available for trans parents, but the outcomes are generally considered likely to be worse.[57] LGBTQ+ people are more likely to encounter complications during pregnancy including miscarriage, still birth and pre-term birth and depression, and if the pregnancy does not work out, distress may be particularly sharp because of the extra barriers to pregnancy that we may face, as well as the challenges of accessing support services that may not know how to meet the specific needs of LGBTQ+ people.[58]

Transgender men and non-binary people are particularly likely to experience psychological distress during pregnancy, both because of discrimination in maternity services designed to meet the needs of women only, and also due to complex feelings of gender dysphoria exacerbated by pregnancy, which can mean regressing to distress caused by a feeling of mismatch between biological sex and gender identity. All of these barriers are likely to make pregnancy more complicated and difficult for LGBTQ+ people and contribute to worse outcomes.

Children

Then there are bureaucratic complexities and biases once LGBTQ+ people have had children. James Devine said: 'My husband and I recently had a baby via a surrogate. A simple task such as registering him with our GP [family doctor] was difficult because the practice said they usually register the baby to the mother's record – even when I said that would be impossible, they said they would only temporarily register him until we got the parental order, despite one of us being his biological father. It took a complaint to the practice manager to resolve. And registering his birth, the official had to go and ask, as she "doesn't deal with many of these", referring to us being gay.' And Sivan Kaniel shared: 'We needed to go to court as my son was born in the Netherlands so there was bureaucracy to prove he was an Israeli citizen. In Israel we struggled so much to get that recognition. There are legal implications. If we were heterosexual, I know we'd need to prove nothing.' Then her second child was born in Israel and she and her wife faced a new set of challenges, this time in registering both women as parents: 'Usually if there's a husband, he goes into a booth, signs something and gets a certificate. I mean, he could be anyone! LGBTQ+ people have a very long procedure – it takes a few months, a few thousand shekels – we had a good few months where I was officially the only parent. That was really painful.'

The decision about whether to consider taking an overseas job takes on new gravity when LGBTQ+ people have to factor in children's risk of being bullied or worse for having LGBTQ+ parents, or lies that might be needed to keep them safe. Ken Ohashi said: 'I have two children – we were having a conversation about Qatar. Being gay is illegal in Qatar. My boys made a joke: "Could the whole family go?" I said we just couldn't go. I'm never going to put us in a situation where we're going to have to lie about our family. I wouldn't put us in that position.'

Judith Gough had a similar concern: 'I was perfectly happy to go to Ukraine and Georgia when my children were young but I was very clear I didn't want them growing up having to defend me from the prejudice.'

There are extra concerns about the risk and intrusion to which children of a visibly LGBTQ+ leader in a prominent role may be subjected. Judith reflected: 'I keep my children well and truly out of the public domain. I did an interview with a British newspaper and they asked: "How did you conceive your son?" I thought: "Would you ask a straight person?" I found that really intrusive.'

The links between family life and professional attainment

When it comes to career progression, ambitious professionals can deeply benefit from background support in the form of a long-term partner. People who have secure, stable relationships tend to have better income, health and wellbeing, and support to thrive at work – although this benefit generally favours the career of one half of the couple; in heterosexual couples it is usually the man. But how does this affect LGBTQ+ people? There are two key questions: are LGBTQ+ people as likely as cisgender, heterosexual people to benefit from stable, live-in relationships? And for those who do, does it confer career benefits in the same way or do something different?

Just 42 per cent of American gay men and 30 per cent of bisexual men live with a partner or spouse compared to a resounding 64 per cent of heterosexual men. Lesbians and heterosexual women tend to live with their partner or spouse at fairly similar rates (53 per cent versus 59 per cent); only 40 per cent of bisexual women tend to be living with a partner. Asexual people have the same rates of intimate relationships as other LGBTQ+ people. This data tells us that overall LGBTQ+ people, especially gay men and bisexual people, are less likely to access the particular career benefits that come from living with a partner.

Marriage confers additional advantages on top of cohabitation in the form of stability, support and social recognition; however, around the world, depending on the jurisdiction, marriage is either not available or only recently available for LGBTQ+ people. Even where it is available, some couples may choose to avoid it for personal reasons – for example, because of patriarchal connotations. In 2019, the US Census found that just 58 per cent of same-sex couple households were married compared to 88 per cent of opposite-sex couple households.[59] Transgender people are in general less likely to be married than cisgender people; American surveys have found somewhere between 33 per cent and 41 per cent were married; a further 3–15 per cent were not married but did have a partner.[13]

People who are part of a live-in same-gender couple are more likely to be working, more likely to own our home and less likely to be poor.[12] But the benefits seem to be distributed more equitably than for our cisgender, heterosexual peers. Think of that adage 'Behind every great man is a great woman' (sometimes adapted to say 'Behind every strong man is a strong woman'). It became popular in the 1940s and was first printed in 1946 as a newspaper quote from Meryll Frost, an American football quarterback, talking about how his wife had enabled his sports career success – the implication was that she had done this by supporting him psychologically and all-importantly, practically. This resonated at a time where many husbands did the paid work while their wives, who did the bulk of the underappreciated behind-the-scenes housework and caring work that freed men to invest unrestricted time and effort in their career, needed a self-esteem boost. What's disturbing is that the message still resonates today.

The balance in gender roles has obviously changed in the intervening decades as more women have entered the workplace and progressed into the top jobs. But of course, there is still a glass ceiling, partly because it remains very common for one member of a couple to receive disproportionately more behind-the-scenes support that gives them extra time, space, flexibility and energy to invest in their career. More often than not, in heterosexual relationships, the career beneficiary is the man. Most studies looking at how mixed-gender couples distribute work (paid work, housework and caring work) come to the same conclusion: men do more paid work than women. The amount of paid work women do is affected by maternity leave of course, but the effect goes far beyond that. Regardless of how much paid work they do, in mixed-gender couples, women on average are responsible for far more hours of housework and caring.

LGBTQ+ people are not immune from this housework gender gap, but it plays out differently. Traditionally the gap starts with teenage girls being expected to spend more time on cooking and household chores than boys. This sets up a dynamic that persists into adulthood and plays out in the households of mixed-gender partners where women just keep on doing more housework than men. Once children enter the picture, this housework gap widens even further, especially when the couple is married, and even if both parties are working full time. There are umpteen studies that show this to be true everywhere in the world. In mixed-gender couples where both work and have children, women are three times more likely than men to spend an hour on housework every day;[60] in Britain, 85 per cent of all sole carers for children and 65 per cent of carers for older adults are women who are, unsurprisingly, three times as likely as men to have their careers held back due to caring responsibilities.[61] This includes formal decisions like taking extended time off work, working part time to allow for childcare, or not applying for a new job or promotion; and also informal decisions like spending less extracurricular time networking to be with family and choosing not to pursue certain opportunities or aspire to particular career tracks because they would involve more hours at work, relocation or something else that would interfere with current or future family ambitions.[60]

It's intriguing to consider that the more married mothers in opposite-gender relationships earn, the greater the proportion of housework and caring they take on.[62] Why? Gender theorists suggest that it's thanks to the socialization of male and female roles – being the caregiver is such an ingrained part of the traditional stereotype of being a woman that many mothers subconsciously feel the need to over-compensate for their career ambitions within the relationship dynamic by taking on extra housework and caring work. This means these women are left with little time for rest, leisure, exercise and social activities, and therefore are less likely to be able to come into work feeling refreshed and ready to perform at their best. Unfortunate, since the discrimination women face in the workplace often calls upon exceptional performance to progress in our careers. It also means less time and capacity to take on more demanding jobs that may come with longer hours, or engage in networking events, overnight work trips or other extracurricular activity linked to furthering our careers.

Meanwhile, men may be subconsciously pulled in the other direction – by acting as breadwinner, they are fulfilling a stereotype from 1950s TV shows; by doing more housework and caring, society implies they are inadequately fulfilling the masculine stereotype.[61] It's a recipe for guilt, stress and burnout for women and part of the inspiration for Anne Marie Slaughter's landmark essay in *The Atlantic* in 2012, 'Why Women Still Can't Have it All'.[63] Meanwhile, men in general are better set up for career success by default. Stereotypes from the ideal 1950s home continue to benefit men's careers deep into the 21st century. Behind every great man there is still a great woman – but the reverse is so much less common that it still accounts for a significant amount of gender disparities in the workplace.

So what does this mean for same-gender couples? In my home, I have a framed print by the artist Amy Gardner called 'Behind Every Strong Woman…' The print shows Lynda Carter who played Wonder Woman in the 1970s TV series being carried by her stunt double Jeannie Epper, both dressed as Wonder Women. I bought that print because it makes me think of my wife and me. Other people helping you succeed is a lovely part of life. But what resonates with that print is that in our same-gender marriage it feels like we support each other to succeed at work in a very equitable way. My wife said: 'We work well as a team – we try to spur and support each other and see each other as our cheerleader.' That's the equalizing career opportunity of being LGBTQ+. I say opportunity, because not everyone takes it.

LGBTQ+ people usually grow up surrounded by cisgender, heterosexual stereotypes about the roles of men and women, just like everyone else. But as we explored in Chapter 3, realizing that we are different unmoors us from that path of societal expectations. When people demand of same-gender couples, as they so often do: 'Which of you is the man?' they sometimes mean the mechanics of your sex life, but more often than not, they mean: "Who washes the dishes? Who takes out the garbage? Who is the primary breadwinner?" That's an offensive question, and it rarely has an answer.

For all its challenges, being LGBTQ+ tends to free us to think beyond stereotypes and traditions and make active decisions about how we want our household to work. There is no default when both parts of a couple are the same gender, or if one or both have transitioned away from the gender they were assigned at birth. That's why research tells us that from Australia to the United Kingdom to France and the US, same-gender couples tend to divide their housework, paid work and caring responsibilities much more evenly than mixed-gender couples,[64] tending to split chores according to ability and availability (especially lesbians[65]). The result can lead to approaches that are better suited to the individuals involved, to modern life, and to individual and shared ambitions, including career ambitions.

People who have ascended to senior leadership positions have often benefitted from this approach. Marjorie Chorlins at the US Chamber of Commerce reflected of her relationship: 'We've always been there to help each other and split the responsibilities; we both make a good faith effort to do what we can to keep the trains running.' Gautam Raghavan, who works at the White House, said: 'There's a working assumption that we take turns. We've been together 17 years and we've had times when one of us has had the most consuming job, for a period every two or three years we would switch. We don't have any view that one of us is the primary breadwinner.' James Devine said: 'We play to each other's strengths – both our careers are very important to us, and we're very respectful of each other's careers and the time commitment. My husband is doing a master's degree so that distribution of household chores might be a bit skewed because of that. We've always communicated about what's important to us.'

When they become parents, one member of the household often pivots to doing more paid work and the other to more housework and caring responsibilities. Again, this tends to be a more conscious choice based on an analysis of preference, logistics and circumstances rather than being steered by a heteronormative assumption about who will do what. But there is still often a principle of task sharing. Ken Ohashi shared: 'We don't have a gendered relationship – the default parent. People ask us all the time: "Who's the mommy, who's the daddy?" For us, we really volley back and forth. My husband has also been CEO of a company. There's been times when I've leaned forward in my career and he's leaned back; then he leans forward and I lean back. I think it's also about personality – I'm a tasker so I like cooking meals, buying the boys' clothes, planning activities and helping them with schoolwork.' Even with differences emerging in task sharing once a child is in the picture, in Sweden researchers found that lesbians were much more likely than heterosexual couples to close their income gap after having children while inequalities in mixed-sex couples' salaries persisted.[66]

We haven't quite achieved a utopia of gender equality free from stereotypes though. Regardless of whether they have children, same-sex male couples do more paid work on average than same-sex female couples.[67] There is lots of speculation about reasons for this – a key suggestion is that being the breadwinner is so entrenched a part of male gender stereotypes that it is particularly hard to break free. However, gay men in partnerships in particular seem to earn less than their single peers – it's speculated that having a partner leads to them being more visibly LGBTQ+ at work, causing discrimination that in turn leads to reduced salary opportunity; they may also be more likely to take time out for children.[12]

Of course, we have mostly looked at couples in this section. As we explored in Chapter 4, many LGBTQ+ people often find it easier to come out when they are in a monogamous couple, because it is such a culturally accepted and recognizable relationship model around the world. But there is no rule that shared households have to be arranged in couples. Just as LGBTQ+ people are more likely to be single than our cisgender, heterosexual peers, we are also more likely to be creative in our approaches to romantic and sexual partners and to cohabitation. With no traditional script, all of this is far more up for discussion and negotiation. Having already deviated from societal expectations and binaries, and potentially spent extra time thinking about sexual and relationship diversity, this may empower some people to think beyond the constraints of the default two-person monogamous model to consider what works best for them. For example, more LGBTQ+ than cisgender, heterosexual people choose consensual non-monogamy such as open relationships and polyamorous relationships with multiple partners.[68]

Interestingly, some people reflect that coming out of the closet as being in a polyamorous relationship can be harder than telling colleagues you are LGBTQ+. Just as the world is set up for a default of cisgender, heterosexual people, so too it is set up for couples. Romantic love directed at more than one person incurs social stigma and having multiple sexual partners incurs moral judgement. Even though one in nine people have engaged in polyamory at some point, many people feel so unfamiliar with non-monogamous and polyamorous relationships that they struggle to relate to them as equally legitimate and deserving of dignity, leading to an extra layer of prejudice and discrimination. Not much research has been done on how well polyamorous people thrive in the workplace. These types of relationships are often hidden, and unlike the protections given to LGBTQ+ people in many workplaces, are rarely recognized or supported in workplace culture or policy, usually with no provision for health insurance or other benefits for the household. In those Monday morning chats, polyamorous people may find themselves editing one or more loved ones out of their stories; bringing one partner to a colleague's wedding while the other stays home, pretending not to exist. People can become marginalized as a result of being polyamorous, lacking both societal endorsement and legal protections for their relationships, including with their children. This should be remembered in the development of policies and communications.

Overall, being LGBTQ+ can empower people to move away from gender stereotypes and share responsibilities more flexibly and equitably. This may go some way to counterbalance some of the other inequalities we face. So perhaps LGBTQ+ people who want both children and a career have a little more potential to achieve Anne Marie Slaughter's aspiration of 'having it all' – despite the additional complexities.

The role of the extended family

One factor that might get in the way of that aspiration is support from extended family. To bring in another adage, when it comes to raising children, it 'takes a village'. This means accessing support from outside the home, frequently from extended family members. Often this support is more available for cisgender, heterosexual people.

LGBTQ+ people are at particular risk of having been rejected or otherwise estranged from some or all members of our families due to homophobic, biphobic or transphobic attitudes. We are also quite likely to be geographically remote from them due to moving away, particularly from rural to urban settings in pursuit of more LGBTQ+ peers, amenities and infrastructure, acceptance and greater anonymity (although several leaders noted they have good lives in the countryside). People who have moved to cities may have better career options but are less likely to have roots and long-standing and dependable local support systems.[13] Sivan Kaniel has worked in Ireland, the Netherlands and Israel. She reflected: 'I want to work and live in a place where I feel 100 per cent comfortable and supported, that my relationship with my wife will be acknowledged, my family will be acknowledged. We constantly think about what sort of life we want to give our family.'

For these reasons, LGBTQ+ people are overall less likely to have convenient local access to reliable support from our extended family. For similar reasons, we may be less likely to have maintained as many school friends into adulthood. That said, we may be more likely to have support from other quarters. The author Armistead Maupin coined the term 'logical family' to mean the set of people who provide love and support for LGBTQ+ people when our biological family does not fulfil that role. The term, alongside the concept 'chosen family' has deeply resonated with many LGBTQ+ people and is a good reminder that traditional parameters of the nuclear and extended family may be less relevant to us and assumptions about the relative importance of certain people in our lives should be avoided.

Insecurity and bureaucracy

Sometimes there is just a lot more bureaucracy for LGBTQ+ people. Matt Burney shared: 'My husband has had to rescind his Chinese nationality when we got British citizenship but we needed that so we could include him in my will; we couldn't jointly own property. None of that would have been an issue if he'd not been a same-sex partner.' Keshav Suri reflected: 'I think right now a lot are quite worried about what happens next – it's a basic thing not being a criminal but what happens about marriage equality, about shared bank accounts… after Covid a lot of people are worried about a will: What happens if I fall ill? If I don't get along with my mother and father; I want my partner at the hospital.'

Work is just one part of our day. We all bring our experiences from other parts of life into work with us – our worries, our fears, our frustrations, our wins. LGBTQ+ people may be bringing additional experiences of prejudice, discrimination, assault, inequalities, marginalization, fear, anger, rejection and disconnection into the workplace. The possibility that we are walking out the office door to death threats, or to prejudice when we try to access healthcare, needs to be understood. So too does the fact that being LGBTQ+ is not a recipe for sorrow. For many of us, our climb up the career ladder is boosted by love, mutual support, opportunity, creativity and an empowering sense of having consciously coloured our home life outside the lines, creating something beautiful.

8

How employers can help break the rainbow ceiling

'You need to come to work every day and be who you are – and we need to be okay with that. I want you to be comfortable at work, I don't want you to feel you have to hide anything' – Jim Fitterling, Chairman and CEO of Dow

It is in every employer's interest to have a diverse workforce. The research has consistently found companies that recruit and nurture diverse talent perform better. They have access to wider talent pools and by creating environments where everyone can perform as their best self, are better able to retain staff and benefit from greater productivity plus a wider range of perspectives that make them more creative, innovative and resilient.[38] All of this helps them to be more competitive, to access new markets and to improve financial outcomes. Clearly, it's tricky to assess the size of the impact when organizations get this right, but many have tried. For example, a report by Research and Markets published in 2022[69] found that companies with diverse staff can achieve 2.5 times more cash flow per employee and they estimated inclusive teams to be 35 per cent more productive. A report by the organization Board Ready,[70] using the S&P 500 index of 500 leading publicly traded companies in the US, found that organizations with diverse boards achieved more revenue growth and had more resilience during the Covid-19 pandemic. There are three key steps to realizing this so-called 'diversity dividend': 1. recruit and retain a workforce and board full of diverse characteristics; 2. make sure these people are all able to thrive and develop within the workplace to reach their full potential; and 3. empower, value and meaningfully include people in all their diversity in creativity, analysis and decision-making.

Sivan Kaniel, CEO of LGBTech, remembered: 'When I started working for Airbnb, they had a very diverse workforce. They had just opened a headquarters in Dublin, so people were coming from all over the world. It was such a defining moment in my career. This was the first time I had ever been surrounded by such a diverse group of people. It helped me to acknowledge we're all special, each of us brought something completely different to the game, we started working together really well. That helped me to feel more empowered but at the same time understand the importance of inclusion.'

Umpteen books and reports have been written on the topic of how to improve diversity and inclusion at work – despite the patchy implementation, this is hardly new information, so let's not repeat it here. Instead, let's go straight to some of the world's most senior LGBTQ+ leaders and ask them simply: what helped them succeed? As LGBTQ+ people, what did their employers and managers do that made them want to join the organization or company, and once there, feel able to be the best version of themselves? What meant they kept progressing to the next rung of the career ladder to reach their potential? What policies really mattered to them? And how can managers and workforce leaders make changes now that will recruit and retain more LGBTQ+ people and support them to thrive and succeed?

Bring LGBTQ+ into the diversity fold

Many organizations have strong plans for recruitment and retention of a diverse workforce, but across the world, leaders have observed that being LGBTQ+ does not always seem to be given parity of esteem with other minority characteristics. In the 'hierarchy of diversity' they see employers often putting LGBTQ+ people low (or nowhere) on their inclusion priority list. This is often because employers, while systematically measuring, monitoring and reporting on certain aspects of diversity like gender and race (often required by law), may not know even how many LGBTQ+ people work in their organizations, much less the challenges we may experience along our career paths. Or they may assume the discrimination we encounter is somehow 'not as bad' or less worthy of prioritization. Often employers will decide to focus efforts on one particular minority group and hope this will help all of us; sometimes they might, but often the root causes of inequalities are very different and need tailored approaches. So LGBTQ+ leaders encourage employers to start by asking good questions: monitoring demographics, understanding the experiences LGBTQ+ staff are having and bringing diversity and inclusion of LGBTQ+ people more explicitly into the organization's plans if they aren't there, or strengthening them if they aren't sufficient.

Some employers assume that their organization is a lot more inclusive of LGBTQ+ people than it really is. Sivan Kaniel, whose role focuses on improving inclusion for LGBTQ+ people in the workforce, has observed this on many occasions. She said: 'Often I find there's a very big gap between how employers feel and how employees feel. It doesn't matter what company, the employer's initial response will be: "We're great, we're liberal, no worries, there's no issue". It's very shallow.' In fact, sometimes the employer is so confident that they're great that they encourage their LGBTQ+ staff to promote their inclusive practices on the public stage. In theory, a good idea – showing visible inclusion and success of current LGBTQ+ staff members can help encourage more diverse people to apply for a job there. But less good if that positive assumption is wrong. Sivan described LGBTQ+ people seeking her advice, saying: 'My company wants to organize a media interview with me, talking about how it's great being gay... but it's not great being gay in the company.' Developing a deeper understanding of how the organization's culture and policies affect LGBTQ+ people avoids making false assumptions and helps employers understand the true situation and make more strategic decisions to achieve diversity and inclusion ambitions.

Diversify yourself

Most managers and other senior leaders are not LGBTQ+ people themselves, but that does not mean they cannot develop insight and empathy into the specific challenges that can affect our work. Reading this book is a great start. Alongside that, many LGBTQ+ leaders recommend managers consider how to diversify their inputs. Mitch Mitchinson said: 'If managers can't conceive of the impact of differences, they're probably not immediately able to provide the best support. Do you have a basis for yourself to be able to actually understand what some of those differences are, or how they could affect someone? Because if not, any other advice is meaningless.' Public transit CEO Eva Kreienkamp suggested: 'Have as diverse a senior management as possible. Challenge yourself and be clear on who you hang out with privately – if they're all like you, it doesn't matter what you do at work.' And British Ambassador to NATO David Quarrey said: 'Talk to people, try to understand even what might seem obvious. If you've got a sibling who's gay or relatives who are LGBTQ+, get them talking about how it is for them, what they find straightforward, what they're concerned about.'

Several LGBTQ+ leaders recommended both standard and reverse mentoring, which simultaneously gives junior LGBTQ+ people a professional development opportunity, and managers, CEOs and board members insight into diverse experiences. Dame Inga Beale, former CEO of Lloyd's of London, advised: 'I would try to remain as curious as you can – it's by asking the questions rather than giving advice you get a better understanding of what might be limiting them. The only way you can find out and give better advice is to pursue questioning rather than jump into advice too soon.' Simon Pollard said: 'I've been mentoring a young non-binary person and it's led me to question how I would do things differently.' And Senior Policy Adviser Darryl Clough reflected on experiences of reverse mentoring: 'I feel like my role isn't to educate a senior leader, it's maybe to spark interest, get them to question where it's working and not working, and how to get the best from your staff by creating that safe working environment.'

Show, don't tell, that your organization is inclusive

Karen Teo, who was Vice President of Sales at Meta when we talked, said: 'When I look at companies, I look at the culture, I look at their diversity and inclusion work. I don't just look at what they say – I ask about what they do.' She is not alone. Prospective LGBTQ+ staff may be particularly interested in a company's equality, diversity and inclusion activities when considering whether to apply for a role. Several LGBTQ+ leaders noted wryly that when they were young, they felt grateful for anything they got. Not being actively bullied, harassed, outed or overtly punished for being LGBTQ+? What a great employer! But diplomat Omar Daair reflected: 'We had narrower expectations, a lower bar for success. Just being able to be open was a bonus… I think some of the younger people are pushing for stuff that wasn't even in my mind when I was younger.'

As a chairman, Peter Molyneux has observed: 'The millennial generations are more interested in the equality, diversity and inclusion practices of their employers and we stand to lose if we don't keep up.' Today, LGBTQ+ people are far more likely to expect clear and enthusiastic inclusion, which impacts decisions about where to work. Annie Bliss, Policy Adviser at the NHS Confederation in the UK, said: 'It's important for my organization to be in line with my values, not having to think about coming out and if that would be accepted.' Alim Dhanji noted: 'I deliberately choose companies where there is not tolerance. I hate the word tolerance – dandruff is something you might tolerate. I want to be celebrated for who I am. I choose organizations that very overtly welcome LGBTQ+ people.' And Pedro Pina said: 'I don't want to belong to an industry that I know would not accept someone like me, I'm just not interested.' They are looking for inclusive actions, not just 'virtue signalling'.

One famous example of virtue signalling has become known as 'pink washing' or 'rainbow washing'. Often organizations will take the opportunity of 'Pride month', generally observed in June or July, to demonstrate their support for LGBTQ+ inclusion. This can benefit the organization in lots of ways: for example, it can make LGBTQ+ staff feel recognized, it can show prospective staff and clients who support equality that this organization shares their values and it can directly generate income. In a country where being LGBTQ+ is not widely accepted, just putting up a flag can in itself be a bold act of allyship. Senior diplomat Becks Buckingham noted: 'You might think it's lip service, but it means so much more, particularly in countries where it's illegal, to see that Progress Pride flag flying at your embassy post. If you have country-based staff who are in the closet, that small gesture makes a difference.' Sivan Kaniel reassures employers in these situations that: 'it can start with really small things: a small Pride flag in the HR room, or around the office; bringing content to the office – a conversation, or a workshop.' And Ralph Breuer said: 'The major element is to talk about the topic – bring it into the room. For example, by celebrating a day of pink, by mentioning LGBTQ+ inclusion in a speech.'

But in countries where LGBTQ+ inclusion is culturally and legally accepted, pasting a rainbow on to an organization's logo, doing a quick internal video, or selling a Pride-themed sandwich or t-shirt is often easy to do and may not really improve things for LGBTQ+ people. These approaches, if not accompanied by more meaningful support, are increasingly viewed cynically by LGBTQ+ people who see the shift from furthering inclusion to taking advantage of a marketing opportunity. Keshav

Suri, Executive Director at The Lalit Suri Hospitality Group, recommended: 'Don't try to fool your customers by using the right hashtags or doing one thing in one country and not in another. Our customers are not fools. Let's actually put our money where our mouth is. Whether you're queer or not, if you're a strong ally to our community, you're not someone who's doing it for the cash.'

There's also the risk of making diverse staff feel exploited rather than included. Senior diversity and inclusion consultant Leng Montgomery said: 'I'm a little bit fed up that companies think: "It's June: let's bring our unicorns out of the stable!", then it's October and it's: "Oh, we know five black people!"' Internally, Matt Dabrowski, Founder and Director of OutBritain LGBTQ+ Chamber of Commerce, said: 'There can be such a disconnect from executive leadership to everyone who works there. It's nice they show up on a video in Pride month, but then I'm like: besides this PR stunt, what long-term difference are you making? What are you doing for internal employees, for consumers, for suppliers?'

Ultimately, to get this right, employers need to think beyond warm words and rainbows, across the whole organization and not just where it's easiest. As chef Peter Gordon said: 'I think you've got to show you really truly mean it – there may be all this lovely stuff, but what does your company actually do?' Pips Bunce, Director and Head of Investment Banking Technology Strategic Programs, suggested: 'Recognizing and supporting this every day of the year, showing inclusion doesn't stop at the end of June when Pride month finishes. Make sure you're giving visible signage in your communications, in newsletters, across the firm. The message from the top of the house is absolutely key. If very senior people are giving a message that this is something they stand by – they fundamentally care about creating an inclusive space – it makes people feel safe to come out and it encourages people to step up as allies.' That can mean speaking up and calling out prejudice and discrimination. Annie Bliss reflected: 'It's so important to have colleagues around who are allies – it's really hard to call things out.' It can also include marking other events beyond Pride, like LGBT History Month in February, International Day Against Homophobia, Biphobia and Transphobia (IDAHoBiT) on 17 May, Coming Out Day on 11 October, or Trans Day of Remembrance on 20 November.

One practice sometimes wrongly derided as virtue signalling is having people include their pronouns on email signatures – trans and non-binary staff have described having people widely do this as making 'a massive difference' because it reminds colleagues that not everyone uses the pronouns they might assume and it allows anyone who has changed their pronouns at some point to alert their colleagues in a clear and appropriate way. More widely in terms of making assumptions, people will identify using different words, like gay, lesbian, bisexual, pansexual, trans, non-binary, queer and many more. It is more respectful to ask than to assume.

Diplomat Matt Burney recommended: 'Don't just use words to say how you are supporting equality, diversity and inclusion (EDI) for LGBTQ+ and other people – really look at how you can embed EDI into your policies, your processes, your programmes, so it doesn't become about showcasing, virtue signalling or profile-raising. Don't confuse corporate social responsibility with EDI – they are very different things. This is about fundamental human rights and equality which needs to be seen as part of the day-to-day running of any organization or company.'

Jim Fitterling gave an example of what happens at Dow: 'In Latin America we actually have a transgender intern programme. We've had people transition out in the manufacturing workplace, not just the office. It's been very positive. Every time you have a positive experience it builds the inclusive culture.' Keshav Suri shared examples of what they do to improve LGBTQ+ inclusion in his business: 'We're the first hospitality chain in India to start hiring trans people, to train them. We also have scholarships we have been giving LGBTQ+ young people to pursue Food Production and Baking Training. The point on inclusion is it's a never-ending learning spectrum. We're learning. We're getting there.' Karen Teo shared some examples of actions that have felt truly inclusive or not during her career: 'I received these emails about how they were hiring transgender engineers, how they were embracing LGBTQ+ people, and I was so inspired. But I'd look up from these emails and I'd hear all these homophobic slurs. That aspiration to be inclusive at HQ didn't translate to APAC [Asia-Pacific]... When I started in my current workplace and someone came to me and said: "Hey, your partner is taken care of as well" [in the company healthcare policy], I thought: "Huh, this is a place that walks the walk".'

President of AstraZeneca Spain, Rick Suarez, said: 'Every leader has the responsibility to find the beauty and strengths of what every person brings to the table and must allow the space for every person at that table to contribute. It is our duty to pause, include and stop always having the same conversation with only those we know. Broaden your table, invite more people and understand that diversity is the beauty of your organization.' Corporate policy gives organizations key opportunities to genuinely walk the walk and make decisions that improve the lives of LGBTQ+ staff. Let's examine some of the options that LGBTQ+ leaders think are important.

Be inclusive in recruitment

Recruitment is the first time that prospective LGBTQ+ staff get to know the organization – experiences at this point can colour a person's understanding of that employer's approach to inclusion. In Chapter 6 we saw some of the pitfalls, but Gautam Raghavan, Assistant to the President for Presidential Personnel at the White House, shared opportunities: 'There are so many options in hiring and retaining talent where there is bias. I think we are at a time and a place where we can think about the systems we use: how do we write job descriptions in a way that expands options? What networks do we go to? How do we do outreach? How do we conduct interviews? On our forms, we offer a range of gender identities and sexual orientation options – it signals to applicants: your identity is important to us.' There are other practical opportunities, such as including a line in application forms about whether referees may know the candidate by another name that should be used in reference requests; making sure there is access to toilets and changing places that are safe for all people to use regardless of their gender when they are attending an interview; and avoiding any assumptions or judgements about a person's sexual orientation or gender identity at interview.

Employers can also think more creatively about how to make their roles more inclusive for LGBTQ+ people. A particular issue for inclusion that LGBTQ+ leaders raise is how cultural or legal barriers prevent us from taking up opportunities in certain countries or states. Leaders acknowledge geopolitical constraints, but within these, many felt employers could do more to maximize inclusion. Civil servant Rosalind Campion said: 'Start acknowledging we're a minority that's not protected: we're the only group of people that can't travel safely to a large proportion of the world.'

As an ambassador who has seen his career limited by where in the world he can live safely and comfortably with his partner, Omar Daair reflected on the content of previous post reports, part of the British Foreign, Commonwealth and Development Office's job descriptions, written by senior leaders located at that post, that describe what it's like to live there: 'A lot of posts would just put in a line that it's illegal to be gay. It was a bit of a cop out – essentially, if you wanted to come out, fine, but they couldn't do anything to help your partner, you had to understand you couldn't be yourself. I want young LGBT staff not to just rule out Africa. Embassies should do more thinking about what they can do to help. We haven't done enough to improve that. You can say: "this is difficult, but these are the places it can work, and this is how we can help…" What has been the experience of gay staff who've been there? Just even telling people about that makes the posts more appealing.'

Organizations operating internationally have power (including financial and diplomatic) they can choose to leverage to improve inclusion for their staff. Becks Buckingham suggested going further to improve inclusion in host countries: 'Get with likeminded colleagues and lobby the Ministries of Foreign Affairs together to get better rights for your own staff and their families.' The efforts of the British government to do just that in Washington and Tokyo meant that I was able to get a work visa in both these countries as the same-sex partner of a diplomat. In both cases I was one of the first same-sex diplomatic spouses to benefit from these agreements; just a few years ago it wouldn't have been possible and as a result, my wife wouldn't have felt able to take these jobs, so would have lost out on opportunities.

Sometimes inclusion may need to come in the form of investment in practical changes and reasonable adjustments so that LGBTQ+ people can take up roles and participate fully and meaningfully at work. Simon Pollard gave an example from the theatre industry that is thought-provoking: 'It's brilliant that we are seeing more and more trans and non-binary performers on stage within the musical theatre industry. But it's so important that these performers are completely supported, and that appropriate adjustments are made, both on and off-stage. This may mean making small changes to a script, or changing the keys in which songs are written.' Leng Montgomery said: 'Don't think of trans people as a problem – that's an area where we might need to work a little differently, but we are always innovating anyway.' Opportunities to apply innovative thinking like this abound in all sectors.

And finally, in the hiring process, visibility matters. Prospective staff will often look to see whether there is evidence that LGBTQ+ people can be successful in that organization. Ralph Breuer described how he takes personal responsibility for making sure candidates see senior LGBTQ+ leaders at McKinsey in Germany: 'I spend my time investing into the next generation of LGBTQ+ leaders. A partner is not always available to join all of the recruitment events, but I free my calendar because it's important.'

Make diversity count in the workplace

Once in the workplace, visibility matters even more. Knowing that you are not the only LGBTQ+ person in your team, department, or even organization is important to people, and being able to see other people like you succeeding in the organization can be powerful. Most of the LGBTQ+ leaders I spoke to spent much of their career with no visible role models, which led them to feel that expressing that part of themselves would hold them back. Hospital CEO Dame Jackie Daniel reflected: 'It was less visible at senior level in the early part of my career – everyone was so busy trying not to have that label attached to them. I couldn't see other gay people.' But seeing successful people from any part of the LGBTQ+ population was empowering. Karen Teo remembered: 'I met a transgender engineering director on a work trip. I thought she was great: she started a web comic, she has a family, she has kids. The fact she was successful in the company made me desire more for myself in my career. I should be working for people and companies who let me be who I am.' And Rosalind Campion said: 'I was super-lucky when I first joined government – my director was a legendary gay man in the Civil Service, there were other senior gay people in the department, and it gave me a vibe that being gay was something a lot of civil servants were. It had a really positive impact on me, seeing these senior people being so out and confident. I remember how I felt and the shadow they cast – and now I want to do that for other people.'

There is an opportunity for employers to support the development, confidence and ambition of junior LGBTQ+ staff by making sure more senior LGBTQ+ people are in the organization and are empowered and supported, included with time and resources to do role model work if they want to. As Gautam Raghavan said: 'The more that we can lift up and showcase people who are successful and who are out is helpful – it shows people there are options available to them.' Several LGBTQ+ people reflected that the increase in virtual working associated with the Covid-19 pandemic actually improved visibility because people who worked at home or in small offices that were part of bigger organizations became more exposed to diverse colleagues in different parts of the country and the world.

Today, many LGBTQ+ leaders reflected that there is growing visibility of gay men and to some extent, gay women in the workplace, but fewer visible role models across other parts of the LGBTQ+ spectrum. For example, Becks Buckingham reflected: 'In terms of senior bisexual role models, there are so few about who are prepared to be out.' But LGBTQ+ leaders have noticed that people entering the workplace today are increasingly expecting more: they want to see not just LGBTQ+ people in general, but senior versions of people like them, recognizing the expanding identities within the LGBTQ+ umbrella – not to mention broader intersectionality. That means further widening of diversity at all levels – a solitary gay, white, cisgender, able-bodied man in a workplace no longer has the impact it once might have done when people were grateful for any representation at all of LGBTQ+ people. I have often joked about feeling like the 'token gay' – but that concept, rife throughout my career, is becoming increasingly passé.

LGBTQ+ leaders across the world also emphasize that getting diversity and inclusion right means more than just having staff with diverse characteristics existing in the workplace being 'visible', being photographed to showcase diversity on the organization's website. Annie Bliss reflected: 'You could have a workplace with loads of LGBTQ+ people who are all marginalized.' And Ambassador Judith Gough said: 'There is a false comfort in assuming diversity just means numbers – it means accepting diversity of thought and needs. A greater sense that diversity actually does mean accommodating different views and ways of working. Not just:"Oh, we have X women or X gay people in post"... We do work differently, have different needs.'

LGBTQ+ leaders agree the key to getting the most from diversity is by empowering people to bring their diverse perspectives to be heard and valued in all aspects of creative thinking, planning, problem solving and decision-making within an organization. Opportunities exist at every level of seniority. Becks Buckingham advised: 'Give LGBT staff a seat at the table in key decision-making forums. And don't assume they will be the LGBT lead.' This meaningful inclusion in the fabric of an organization needs to extend all the way to the top. The rainbow ceiling can stop people reaching the most senior roles, but Rosalind Campion advised: 'Look around your senior leadership table and think about whether any are out. If nobody is, something is wrong – either you haven't been promoting LGBTQ+ talent, or you've made it so that they're in the closet. You need to decide what you're going to do about that.' The so-called 'diversity dividend' for organizations comes from genuinely valuing diverse perspectives and that means letting staff know they are safe, welcome and encouraged to express their diversity. Jackie Daniel said: 'Try and create an environment where people feel confident in being who they want to be, not settle for who they can be.'

Provide safety as a part of inclusion

LGBTQ+ people should be able to think of their workplaces as a safe haven, where no matter what happens outside the doors of our job, once we are inside, the organization's policies sit alongside national or regional law to protect us from homophobia, biphobia and transphobia. We know from the disproportionately high number of LGBTQ+ people who experience bullying and harassment at work that this opportunity has not yet been fully leveraged. For example, Pips Bunce shared: 'I've got friends who are trans and work for a well-known company and they say there's no way they'd come out – if they did, they'd be beaten up, they'd face so much abuse. There are so many companies that don't stand by their staff, that don't make a safe space for everyone and that have much work they could do to make the workplace they provide open and accepting to all, regardless of their points of difference.'

But it can be done. As senior civil servant in the British government Jim Harra said, 'Don't underestimate the extent to which people look to you to lead.' Jim Fitterling advised: 'When you're a leader of an organization you're responsible for your people – you have to make them feel safe, treat them with respect. Imagine you've got an employee who every day feels threatened in their environment. I don't want someone to come to work and feel less safe than they did outside of work. That's not something that happens by accident – people responsible for creating the work environment need to work to make that happen. It has a huge impact on your ability to hire and retain people, it has a huge impact on your ability to operate at a high level of safety.'

Leadership is key to set the tone of what is expected – making sure that everyone in the organization knows prejudice and discrimination will not be tolerated and will have repercussions. LGBTQ+ staff need to know that if they do experience a problem, the organization will genuinely have their back. Pips Bunce shared some advice for leaders: 'Make sure that focus on LGBT inclusion is second nature, embedded in everything you do. The stronger that message comes from the top of the house, the better. Stand up and step up as an ally – it's good for your business.' Keshav Suri has invested particularly strongly in inclusion in his hotel chain. He describes: 'At the Lalit we say we have an army of allies who understand and stand strong with our LGBTQIA+ community in their journey. We get an equality pledge signed at the time of joining itself, which talks about no discrimination on race, caste, sexual orientation and gender identity. Let's say a person has a problem with that – they're more than welcome not to join us… make sure your company has created a safe environment wherever it may be in the world. If you're in countries where it's still a criminal offence [for people to be LGBTQ+], all the more reason. Please create safe spaces. Understand what you want to do and if you feel it's right for you and your company, take that leap – don't be on the sidelines.' Jim Fitterling said: 'We conduct business in countries where it's still against the law. We don't try to work around the laws but instead try to create an environment that's safe.'

So how to create a recognizably safe space? Pips Bunce suggested: 'If you're thinking of coming out, you look around and try to ascertain it's a safe space, then even after you come out, you still look around. One thing people will overlook as cliché, but isn't, is visible signposting – rainbow lanyards, or showing you're an ally in your email signature including pronouns.' Several leaders emphasized the importance of not making assumptions about who someone might be attracted to, or how they might identify. Nesta Lloyd-Jones, Assistant Director, said: 'Don't put pressure on people – if they want to talk about their partners or sexuality, they will – you've got to give them the space, the open-ended questions to do that when they're ready'. And if someone does come out, it's incredibly important not to share that information with others without permission.

Associate Director at Accenture, Sarah Weaver, shared a practical example of her organization thinking creatively about how to use their footprint to reduce staff exposure to homophobia, biphobia and transphobia beyond the workplace: 'We as a company have an agreement with every organization that is our client that basically says: if your staff harass or intimidate our staff you could be in breach of our contract. Were you to start saying nasty things, I can go to my HR department and they'll talk to your HR department.' And several leaders noted that since LGBTQ+ people feel there are barriers to reporting bullying and harassment associated with their sexual orientation or gender, having clear, safe procedures and independent advocates can help.

Enact inclusive practical changes

Employers can improve inclusion simply by making practical tweaks to systems that have been set up by default with an assumption that everyone is cisgender and heterosexual. IT and administration offer many opportunities for inclusion. For example, when a form asks about a person's gender or sexual orientation, it can be a small but impactful matter to extend the options so that more staff members get to select an option that aligns with their personal identity. Annie Bliss described feeling 'miffed' whenever she is asked to fill in a sexual orientation box that does not include 'queer' as an option, but just as frustrated if she notices there are no options relevant for her colleagues to describe their identities. Nothing makes a person feel 'othered' like having to tick the 'other' box. Though of course that's better than having only binary options. Pips Bunce highlighted the implications of non-binary people filling in forms like these: 'If you're trying to truly hire diverse talent and the first system they have to register their details on has only male or female, they have to invalidate their identity or lie to you about who they are as your systems and forms are not inclusive – this will galvanize (or not) their view on you as a firm and how inclusive you really are.' Although it's important to also stop and think about whether any changes intended to be inclusive make sense and are not offensive or ridiculous. Rosalind Campion remembered: 'In a previous department, our IT system kept flipping back to deadnaming trans people. And in another department when I inputted to the system that I was a lesbian it asked me to state the date this started and the date I expected it to end.'

Leaders also described the importance of IT systems responding promptly and reliably to staff's changes in gender. Several people expressed frustration that systems able to easily process staff's name changes associated with marriage cannot cope with name and gender changes associated with transition. Several people described having their deadname frequently reappearing in different parts of the IT system such as below their name in video conferencing calls, causing distress and confusion each time, and this taking months, or even years to resolve. Some people struggle to get a new photo identity card for their work systems. Particularly for some non-binary or gender-fluid people who may need more than one photograph. Pips Bunce remembered: 'For me it was some of the simple things – like putting changes in place so I could have a dual picture on my passcard.' Getting these things right is fundamental to creating an inclusive work environment.

Dress code is another area that inadvertently makes some people uncomfortable and can easily be made more inclusive. Employers often require that people wear certain clothes. This can have a disproportionate impact on LGBTQ+ people because the approved clothes may not feel in line with our gender expression, which can be humiliating, and affect our sense of belonging and ability to do our best work. Clothing matters. Rick Suarez remembers turning up to the first day of his first job in pharmaceutical sales in Kentucky in the US: 'I was so excited to get on my career path I went and bought a new shirt, it was salmon colour. I walk in to meet my new counterpart and she goes: "You can't wear that here! They're going to think you're... you know." And I said: "I am, and I'll be wearing this shirt." At that moment I decided to be my full self in my career whatever the cost.'

Omar Daair described developing a personal dress code as a diplomat that enabled him to express himself: 'I've always been straight acting – I've been able to pass. But I have tried to be a bit flamboyant in ties – I have a loud tie collection that's become my signature here. Some people find them too colourful, but I feel that's at least a bit of showing personality.'

Broadening clothing policy to make sure everyone has an option that feels congruous with their identity is an inclusion tool. Pips Bunce described their company's approach: 'We went through every policy to make sure where appropriate they were non-gendered. As an example, it was really important to make sure the dress code policy wasn't talking about just binary male or binary female and enforcing conformant dress expectations on either; all genders can wear trousers as can all genders wear a skirt. Such cases [where gendered dress codes apply] could exclude the gender non-conforming or gender expansive people we are trying to hire.'

Another practical issue is toilets. Anyone who feels they can't safely use a toilet during the working day clearly cannot do their best work, much less feel included in the workplace. But as we have explored, trans and non-binary people are often prevented from using bathrooms or feel unsafe doing so and can end up humiliated, uncomfortable, attacked and even unwell. Employers need to be sure all staff have safe access to toilets. Karen Teo reflected with frustration: 'Something as simple as gender-neutral bathrooms – it's not as easy as you think. There can be country policy or building management policy that says you need X percentage of male and female bathrooms. Sometimes companies for all their best intentions can't overcome these. It was surprising to me that something that should be easy is as difficult as this.' Keshav Suri recommended his approach with hotel staff in India: 'We had conversations about toilets. I told my team: "Bring your biases. Now put yourself in the shoes of a trans person. They have to sit at their desks for eight hours and hold their pee because you are not allowing them to use the toilets. Put yourselves in their shoes – what would you like to do now?" Now every hotel of mine has a toilet and locker room that is gender-neutral and people can use whatever toilet they identify with.'

Matt Dabrowski recommended taking the opportunity to be more inclusive across the wider corporate footprint – for example, taking the opportunity to diversify supply chains: 'Corporates could say: "We'll support LGBTQ+ suppliers. We're changing the dynamic." They could say: "We're working with diverse groups even in countries where they're not welcomed by government. We want as much diversity in this company as we can get".' And Jim Fitterling reflected on the role of organizations in driving external change, saying: 'We've been part of a number of amicus briefs [legal documents that a person or organization can supply to a court about a case in which they are not directly involved] to the Supreme Court on employment non-discrimination.'

Make policies inclusive by default

An intrinsic part of enabling LGBTQ+ people to thrive is creating the support structure that provides a conducive environment. Workplace policies are incredibly important in creating that inclusion. Major General (retired) Tammy Smith said: 'Everybody has the same opportunity to be an ally but at the senior level you have the opportunity to create ally policy. So, teach them how to be a personal ally, how to stay abreast of the barriers the LGBTQ+ community face. Then remind them being an ally is the start – you have to create ally policy in your organization. As you learn about the barriers, start recognizing the barriers in your policy.' Matt Burney recommended: 'Be clear about monitoring equality, make sure new policies do not unjustifiably discriminate against LGBTQ+ people, have a toolbox to make sure that's applied to all of the policies.'

Retired President and CEO Nancy Schlichting described: 'One of the most difficult moments I had was sitting in a board meeting and having the board reject a policy we were bringing forward to include sexual orientation in our anti-discrimination policy. This was before I was out. I remember presenting on why this was important and they didn't do it. I thought: "Gosh, I don't know about working in this organization – how can I work in a place that doesn't protect me?" After I was outed and they could see me, they adopted that policy. It showed when we're open and able to be who we are, life can get better.'

One of the most frequent examples raised by LGBTQ+ leaders of policy discrimination in action is not being able to access the same employment benefits for family members as everyone else. Karen Teo described the problem: 'In terms of benefits coverage for family, how do you define family? If you're straight and married, defining family is a no-brainer. If you're gay, we don't even talk about it. It's: "Sorry man, it's just you". What about your loved ones at home? I can imagine a LGBTQ+ person with a sick partner, or kids who are not theirs by name – how do they take care of them? We need to level the playing field. It all feeds into whether you can do your best work. When some people are given the bare minimum, everything else in their lives is not considered, that's not equity.'

Many leaders described having encountered barriers to accessing benefits designed with a married-with-children default in mind. Marjorie Chorlins, now at the US Chamber of Commerce, said: 'Before gay marriage was legal, there were a lot of years I didn't enjoy the same benefits as my straight peers.' And Eva Kreienkamp shared: 'In Germany, health insurance usually works for the spouse as well, and we never got the opportunity to actually use it. As long as we didn't have any marital rights, we were separate people – there were always issues around that if you have spouse benefits.' Many leaders described jobs in the past where they had no access to compassionate leave for the people who meant most to them because their relationship wasn't covered in company policy, or their partner or family could not access the benefits their cisgender, heterosexual colleagues took for granted, leaving them without healthcare for instance, or without a visa to move to a new country when required by their partner's job.

But 'fixing' benefits inclusion for LGBTQ+ people is not just a matter of extending benefits to married couples of all genders. A little more thought is required. First, same-sex marriage is not legal and recognized in all jurisdictions, so some couples cannot get married. It's also worth remembering that LGBTQ+ people are probably the only part of the adult population who may be married in one part of the world, or even one part of the country, and not have that marriage legally recognized in other places. Tammy Smith described how, even after she got married, support available to her wife as a spouse in the US military was still withheld because the marriage was legally recognized only at state level, not at a federal level. When that eventually changed, it transformed her wife's experience and thus her own: 'Tracy was recognized as my legal spouse and because of that we now qualified for military family housing, she could have healthcare benefits, if I were going to be permanently reassigned she was considered a family member so I didn't have to pay for her plane ticket or to move her personal possessions, families had access to daycare, Tracy could now shop at the commissary for groceries like any other military spouse, she could go to the post exchange. The daily trappings of everyday military life became available to us.'

It's not only about whether someone's marriage is legal – LGBTQ+ people may feel marriage is not right for them and choose to cohabit or indeed choose diverse arrangements with more than one partner, or short-term partners, or chosen family members to whom they may not be officially related but consider just as close and just as deserving of appropriate benefits.

Some benefits policies may be drafted externally; others, such as compassionate leave policy, may be internal. Either way, the key is to make sure that restrictive definitions of family in policy documents do not discriminate against LGBTQ+ people for having different arrangements. Keshav Suri explained that it is not hard for employers to offer this sort of equity once they are aware of the problem: 'If our insurance company would not cover same-sex couples, we will go with someone else – as we wanted people to find themselves in the policies.'

Karen Teo shared the impact of experiencing benefits inclusion for the first time: 'I started at Facebook as a senior manager. On the first day people were so warm and caring and nice. One of my old friends was here, she knew I'm gay, she knew I had a partner, and she said: "If you come out and tell them you have a partner at home, they will cover her medical costs." I was shocked. No other company had covered such things. I took the form, I filled it in, nobody batted an eyelid and I suddenly felt the privilege of heterosexuals, filling in forms about their spouses without even thinking about it and getting benefits for them – this was my first taste of equity as a LGBTQ+ person.'

There are other policies that do not automatically extend to LGBTQ+ people, particularly when it comes to children. This does not just create practical issues but denotes a lack of respect and commitment to inclusion, which is seen and felt by LGBTQ+ staff members. There are two potential problem areas.

The first is that LGBTQ+ people are less likely to have children than heterosexual, cisgender people and many voice frustration that work policies and cultures are often child-centric and afford less regard for other types of commitments and priorities that may be just as important to different people. For example, Nesta Lloyd-Jones reflected on HR approaches she has seen: 'In her work my partner always got Easter shifts and nights over Christmas because we don't have children. There's no clear concrete evidence. But it's that attitude: if you haven't got kids, you keep getting given the really crap shifts.' Being aware of the negative impact this may have can make things fairer for everyone.

Secondly, LGBTQ+ people who do have children may have different needs because we are far more likely to use surrogacy, undergo fertility treatment, adopt, foster and have step-children.[36] Plus, there is less likely to be a link between a staff member's gender and their particular role in the journey of having and caring for children – there should be no assumptions and policies need to be designed accordingly. But often they are not. LGBTQ+ leaders described how when they went to access a certain policy, they found it had not been written with them in mind. Nesta Lloyd-Jones said: 'When we were going through IVF, I just couldn't see where our circumstances fit in with our policies: do I go off on sick? What do I do?' Director for Health and Care Workforce, James Devine, shared: 'My husband and I had been working with a surrogate for the past two years. We both went to our respective employers and spoke about time off. His company sent him the maternity policy initially, which of course does not apply as he's not a female giving birth; then they sent him the paternity policy, which only allowed for two weeks off. He asked if there was a policy specifically for surrogacy with same-sex couples and there wasn't, so he was then given an adoption policy. Whereas my company had a surrogacy/ adoption policy for same-sex couples. The latter gave a feeling of pride that my company had policies that were genuinely inclusive.'

Sometimes workplaces need entirely new policies, or sections of policies to address needs that are specific to LGBTQ+ people. Leng Montgomery explained: 'In certain cases you need a very clear understanding so anyone in the company knows what their company stands for and what they need to do. It's having a clear line so if people say: "Oh, I don't think it's right that a trans person is in that space", you can say: "The person is female – according to our policy, they can use that space".' And Karen Teo said: 'We are pushing really hard to make sure our health benefits cover transgender folks who might need to go through transition. We're trying to make this a base standard worldwide.' Jim Fitterling noted that this is not as hard as one might think: 'When I talked about gender reassignment surgery as a benefit, one of the major reactions was: "Oh that's going to be expensive for us". But if you think about it, the number of people who would take advantage of that benefit is relatively small. It's important for that person, but for the company it's not significant in terms of cost. It isn't a monumental hurdle – just treat other people the way you want to be treated.'

There are significant advantages to transitioning while at work in terms of having a financially and emotionally stable setting in which to transition[71] but a survey of over 1,000 transgender people in the UK found that fewer than half of those transitioning while at work had felt supported by their workplace.[37] Often there is a lack of relevant workplace policy to steer them through the process and understand their rights.

Many leaders described being the first person in their organization who needed a certain policy to be adapted or created to meet their needs as an LGBTQ+ person. While they universally expressed gratitude that their employers were willing to make the relevant changes, and appreciated the opportunity to shape the policy to make sure it suited them, some of them also shared a little frustration about this extra hurdle making life unnecessarily complicated and underlining the experience of feeling 'othered'.

Digital content officer Rosemary Tickle put it well: 'It felt like something that was quite new to the HR team. They were lovely about it, and it was nice to have the ability to dictate my own needs, but it did feel unstructured. Having that extra bit of structure, some "in the past we did this", some extra rigour would make it easier.' Pips Bunce said: 'Knowing we've got these policies in place, and a lot of education to staff, is incredibly important because I feel seen and heard and valued and better understood. It helps create that sense of belonging.'

LGBTQ+ people should not always be the ones having to call for inclusive policies. At a programme manager level, Rosanna Andrews noted: 'Even though I feel open and able to be who I am now, I still wouldn't feel able to say: "Oh, I think you should have this and that diversity policy"!' But leaders did describe the benefits of meaningfully involving LGBTQ+ staff groups or employee resource groups in the development of workplace policies to make sure they meet the needs of these people. But while it's great to empower that input, they also warn against employers putting the onus on random staff members to have to request these policies and spend personal time working on them just because they happen to be LGBTQ+. They are experts by their own experience, but employers should not assume that these staff members also happen to be experts in workplace inclusion policy and fully rely on their feedback to develop high-quality inclusive policies. As well as engaging staff, it may be helpful to engage LGBTQ+ NGOs or other consultant services to help develop these policies using the latest evidence in LGBTQ+ inclusion if this expertise is not available in-house.

Support an LGBTQ+ staff network or employee resource group

One way to make sure LGBTQ+ people can meet role models, feel a sense of belonging, access professional development, raise concerns and positively influence workplace policy is by joining a staff network or employee resource group for LGBTQ+ people. It's a good way for organizations to hear what matters to their LGBTQ+ staff and can help reduce inequalities as they do for other marginalized groups. Nancy Schlichting identified this as one of her key recommendations for employers: 'Make sure you have an employee resource group for LGBTQ+ people so they know you value them. We relied on them for advice on how to recruit and retain people within their group, and how to market to that group.' These groups are widely recognized to empower staff and help break the rainbow ceiling, and several leaders reflected that once a network was established and respected, the culture discernibly shifted in their organization and people felt able to be more open and authentic. Annie Bliss shared that knowing there was an LGBTQ+ staff network would influence her decision to join organizations in future: 'I have found it really valuable in my current organization that the staff network is genuinely involved in the work of the wider organization – influencing the policy of the organization. It's not just some LGBTQ+ thing that happens in the fringes – it feels like we're trusted as experts by experience.'

Many leaders described how joining their LGBTQ+ staff network or employee resource group also created development opportunities for them. Ralph Breuer reflected on his experience with 'GLAM', the LGBTQ+ staff network he joined at McKinsey: 'I had the opportunity because of being gay and because of the GLAM community to get to know colleagues from all over the world – I got to attend a conference in New York. It was a very hierarchy-free environment, because there's a shared experience of outing, of the conversations with yourself about what it is that you really are. It helped me build my global network, and very early on it helped me learn how to lead.

When I had been with the firm for three years I was one of the most senior "GLAMMIEs" in our firm so very early on I was finding myself in this leadership role, learning skills, interacting with the media, mixing with people from politics, from public institutions – I got to know some very interesting people. It influenced my trajectory.'

To be successful, these groups should have an executive sponsor and a direct line through to senior management, members should be given protected time to attend and the people who run them should be given suitable time and resources and recognition that formally acknowledges the value of the role, and where possible should seek partnership on activities with other staff groups to help widen people's social and support circles and respect the intersectionality in people's identities.

Educate and communicate

Having a strong knowledge base is an important place from which all staff can be more inclusive. Pips Bunce said: 'The more you can educate about the different diversities helps people from these communities feel more understood.' But many leaders reflected that LGBTQ+ experiences, challenges and needs are often poorly reflected in standard diversity training. Becks Buckingham said: 'Make sure you have in place proper LGBT inclusion as part of your diversity training – don't just play lip service to it.' Pips Bunce suggested this can include: 'talking about identities, challenges, communities and real staff stories. Giving that lived experience to allies really helps them understand what that identity means and what they've had to deal with.' This includes keeping up to date with terminology; younger people in particular may talk about their identities in new ways, including being comfortable with fluidity in their sexuality or gender rather than identifying with specific labels. Education is particularly important for senior leaders, given their opportunity to have inclusion impact across the organization. As

Pips reflected: 'A lot of senior people want to do the right thing but don't know how to help. Give them bite-sized help about what they can do to make a difference.'

Sivan Kaniel advises companies who tell her they want to communicate about LGBTQ+ inclusion to their staff, but worry they are not yet doing well enough to showcase their successes. She tells them: 'Why don't you communicate that you want to work on it, ask them if you are doing enough. Send a survey: "Do you think we need an employee resource group?" You can't talk at people, you need to talk *with* them.' She also advises that in developing communications about workplace policy that relates to LGBTQ+ people, as well as involving HR and marketing or communications colleagues, 'have at least one LGBTQ+ person in the room. It's a game changer.'

And of course, individuals can practise inclusive communication. Rosalind Campion said: 'Listen out for what your staff are saying. If they call someone their wife, don't devalue their relationship by asking about their "partner" and then pretend you call everyone's spouses "partners".' It's also important to respect the parity of importance of staff's loved ones when there are issues like health problems or relationship breakups – Judith Gough described the end of her relationship being treated 'like it's two friends breaking up – there isn't that same sense of "how can we support you?" It's like your relationship isn't quite the same as theirs.' And Leng Montgomery said that when it comes to LGBTQ+ people feeling included in the workplace, keep it simple: 'I think having friendly colleagues is really, really nice – some of them won't recognize what they're doing, they just want to chat and see you as a person, invite you into things.'

Provide talent management that helps LGBTQ+ staff fulfil our potential

When it comes to talent management, Nancy Schlichting said: 'It's a matter of being clear about your values: how you value each person, you believe in their potential, and you create an environment where people know how to progress in their careers, continuing to advance so they don't get stuck.' Karen Teo reflected: 'We're not doing enough to uplift each other, to be very intentional in making sure LGBTQ+ people don't fall through the cracks when we are looking at the next leaders, developing talent. In order to counter unconscious bias we need to be very conscious in our programmes in uplifting minorities.'

Knowing that LGBTQ+ people are likely to encounter a rainbow ceiling that affects our opportunities to ascend to the highest rungs of the career ladder should be a call to action for more targeted talent management designed around the specific challenges that hold us back. Pips Bunce said: 'So many firms have gender and ethnicity-focused talent targets which is great; however, very few firms have LGBTQI+, neurodiversity and other focused targets where the levels of representation need more support. While targets are not a silver bullet to fix culture or inclusion, they do drive the right behaviour and ensure that a community are considered, are represented and have a voice. To address this in a truly diverse and holistic manner, firms need to look at the recruitment pipeline, how many of a given community are being hired, how many are being fired, what is their career progression like, how much representation do they have and where do they need support.'

Dame Jackie Daniel described some of the benefits she experienced from proactive talent management: 'I was really lucky as soon as I became a director to be supported with some pretty deep self-development. It was a really expensive programme. The Chief Exec said: "Go and do it." It was a gift. I'd never have been able to do it on my own. The course was mainly around personal development and was really, really important.' But many LGBTQ+ leaders have found that these opportunities tend to be generic or focus on specific challenges for women or people from race or ethnic minorities; few had encountered a development programme that focused explicitly on the challenges of LGBTQ+ people – but many said how helpful that would have been.

Another opportunity is to support LGBTQ+ people to have mentors and sponsors as part of our career journey – because we seem uniquely poor at securing them for ourselves. LGBTQ+ leaders have described many reasons for this, like imposter syndrome and low self-esteem and concerns about homophobia, biphobia or transphobia (including stories of some mentors declining to be seen in public with LGBTQ+ mentees for fear someone assumes they're on a date). Perhaps most commonly, and harking back to Chapter 3, on childhood, LGBTQ+ people seem more likely to have a feeling of staunch independence. Matt Burney, who did not seek a mentor in his career, articulated well what many other LGBTQ+ leaders shared: 'I am a bit too self-sufficient for my own good. I think that definitely stems from my sexuality and the othering I've experienced. Sometimes my tendency is to do things on my own.' Peter Molyneux said: 'My perception would be that people who fitted better were more likely to get that kind of support.' Rick Suarez remembered wryly: 'I had mentors who said they were against LGBT rights. I thought – "Are you fully committed to being my mentor?"' But many of the LGBTQ+ people who made it to become senior leaders did benefit from the support of mentors and recommended it for people at earlier stages of their career.

Be a bold and confidently inclusive leader

Part of the role of any leader is to help LGBTQ+ people thrive in the workplace along with everyone else. Dame Jackie Daniel reflected: 'Leadership does matter. I currently lead an organization with 18,000 employees. The minute I started to talk to staff and groups about what they wanted to see, the idea ignited. There was a big push: how can we drive forward the work on inequalities?' Jim Harra advised: 'You can't do it at the very end of the process – you've got to do it end to end, create a culture in which everybody can thrive. I think sometimes organizations and people can get stressed because we push representation into a culture – you've got to overemphasize its priority to you and repeat that all the time, so the organization learns it genuinely is a priority – show that you mean it.'

Eva Kreienkamp encouraged leaders to: 'Be bold and courageous.' There might be anxiety about negative repercussions from staff, clients or stakeholders or indeed the media or the public – as we have explored in other chapters. As well as homophobia, biphobia and transphobia, LGBTQ+ identities are particularly susceptible to be politicized. But she reflected that: 'Backlash is part of life.' You need to be safe and prepared for it. Keshav Suri said: 'We handle our trolls with a lot of love. You have to have all voices – you can't just be inclusive to a certain extent or to a certain community.'

There are many ways an organization can be more inclusive in how it supports LGBTQ+ staff to succeed. Consciously making those changes is like taking a hammer and starting to chip away at the rainbow ceiling. It's good for business. It's good for people. And it's good for society.

9

Lifting as we climb

'This book is a reality check that the rainbow ceiling exists' – James Devine, Director for Health and Care Workforce, UK

Enabling LGBTQ+ people to achieve our career potential is complex. While equality in the workplace has improved in many parts of the world, the research and stories in this book reveal some of the quirks and obstacles LGBTQ+ people may encounter as we climb the career ladder. They make clear that progress towards inclusion is not universal, nor linear, nor does it reliably flow in one direction. Over their lifetimes, many leaders who shared their stories in this book have seen heartening progress towards equality. That said, most LGBTQ+ people of all ages and levels of seniority are still regularly experiencing and witnessing inadvertent and intentional homophobia, biphobia, transphobia and other types of queer-phobia. This comes from the people we encounter in our lives, as well as from social media, politicians and the wider media and it affects us in all sorts of ways – especially in our careers.

As well as the direct impact of prejudice and discrimination on LGBTQ+ people's career opportunities, the constant barrage to which we are exposed seeps into our own beliefs and can cause us to hold ourselves back, creating further limitations. As theatre director Simon Pollard reflected: 'We're in this rainbow box. It's an important part of our identity but it comes with baggage, internal shame, internal censoring – that ceiling is something that's placed on us, but it's something that we put on ourselves as well.'

All this results in ambitious LGBTQ+ people climbing a career ladder that has slippery rungs towards a rainbow ceiling that holds many of us back; those who break through are often still buffeted by winds and rainbow clouds. The LGBTQ+ leaders we heard from throughout this book are among a minority who successfully made it to the top jobs, but many described feeling alone, unsupported and vulnerable during parts of that climb. Some people felt so precarious in their achievements that they felt unable to participate in this book, fearing that by reaching down to pull up the people beneath, they might tumble back down themselves.

The role of allies

To keep climbing, break through that ceiling, navigate the clouds and achieve career potential, the LGBTQ+ leaders interviewed in this book came back to the transformative role of allies in their lives. These are the friends, families, educators, mentors, colleagues, managers and others who listen, learn and seek to understand. The people who care enough about inequities to take actions and make changes that give LGBTQ+ people a fairer chance of succeeding at work. Those who challenge and reduce prejudice and discrimination in ways that the people affected sometimes cannot do alone. As Chef Allegra McEvedy said: 'There is a rainbow ceiling. I'm chipping away at it. If we're all chipping away, it will give way.'

The role of LGBTQ+ people in increasingly senior positions

For LGBTQ+ people climbing towards the rainbow ceiling and beyond, the opportunities for progress can be encapsulated by two quotes.

The first quote is 'Lift as you climb', coined by Mary Church Terrell, a Tennessee suffragist and first president of the National Association of Colored Women. Just as the people she was originally talking to were held back by their sex and race, LGBTQ+ leaders can also aim to 'lift as we climb'. In other words, as we overcome barriers associated with being LGBTQ+ to achieve our own career success, we can use that hard-won privilege to help reduce those barriers for those who come next. Implicit in this quote is the concept that people don't always feel they can do this. Some senior leaders feel so unable to come out at work and so invested in not being outed that they are afraid to advocate for LGBTQ+ inclusion in case their support gives the game away. Others may feel that they achieved their professional success partly by minimizing attributes associated with being LGBTQ+; they worry that their ascent beyond the rainbow ceiling is somehow conditional on being 'straight-acting' and that drawing attention to this part of their identity could put their own position or future opportunities at risk. Some worry that supporting junior LGBTQ+ people might be criticized as favouritism. Others feel that they had to fight to get to where they are, so why should their successors have it easier? And some LGBTQ+ people simply feel too tired and bruised by the barrage of prejudice and discrimination they experience to make a stand. Unfortunately, rather than 'lifting as we climb', any of these worries (and plenty more) can cause even the most well-meaning leaders to pull up the ladder behind us.

This can manifest in not taking inclusive actions within our gift. Many LGBTQ+ leaders expressed frustration with some of their peers who have amassed a certain amount of privilege but choose to avoid visibility and role model opportunities, or do not champion more inclusive policies or positive changes towards inclusion for LGBTQ+ people. Matt Dabrowski said: 'Lots of execs say, "Oh, I represent the community" but I think: "What have you changed within the company culture?"' Everyone has different circumstances, but when LGBTQ+ leaders do feel able to be role models and strive for inclusion, the impact for the next generations can be uniquely powerful. That's why so many LGBTQ+ leaders talk about their experiences in the media despite personal risk and indeed why they contributed to this book.

Another part of lifting as you climb is supporting peers. Most of the LGBTQ+ leaders who spoke to me said that having friends or networks or staff groups of people with similar experiences was what made the difference in helping them learn from each other about how to overcome self-censorship and prejudice and discrimination and how to build the self-esteem, confidence and competence needed to break that rainbow ceiling.

The second quote is 'You can't be what you can't see', a phrase coined by Marian Wright Edelman, Founder and President of the Children's Defense Fund in the US. Her words describe the power of having role models who share your characteristics in making you believe you can get there too and her words are apt in this context. In a world where so few people have been able to look to senior LGBTQ+ role models in their own careers, just being able to see that these leaders are here, and that they have broken that rainbow ceiling, offers inspiration and encouragement for current and future generations of LGBTQ+ people and those who support them. They show what's possible.

Vice President at the US Chamber of Commerce, Marjorie Chorlins, noted: 'The more you have CEOs out there who are openly gay or lesbian, or trans, or bi, it gives other people a sense of possibility, it creates more space for people to feel like they will be accepted.' And Nesta Lloyd-Jones reflected: 'When I was a policy officer, it was head down. Now as an assistant director, I think there is that responsibility about being open, making others comfortable to be open about their sexuality or anything else.'

These are good reasons for LGBTQ+ leaders who have already achieved success in their career to keep reviewing whether they could now come out or increase their visibility as an LGBTQ+ person. Some leaders reflected that their senior colleagues who have not come out at work may be thinking: 'what's in it for me to come out in this political climate?' Currently in Japan, Loren Fykes said: 'They're not out because they don't think visibility would effect social change; they only see it as causing personal harm. But there has to be some people who do it, otherwise nothing changes.' LGBTQ+ leaders who feel able to be out and open about their sexual orientation or gender identity can consciously use their seniority privilege for good. Of course, LGBTQ+ people do this at every level, but there is a particular power in senior leaders doing so. Darryl Clough reflected: 'Where there's voices you don't hear all the time there's a championing role but it's quite tiring to always be the person to educate others. As a senior leader maybe it's your role to take some of the slack.'

A letter to our younger self

I remember being at that precipice of entering the workplace and starting to progress in my career while navigating the complexities of coming out. I was terrified that being LGBTQ+ would mean I would find it harder to be successful. I worried I wouldn't be considered for certain jobs, that coming out might ruin my chances of making it to the senior roles I dreamed of. My friends and family reinforced these worries, putting in motion the risk of a self-fulfilling prophecy from which it felt hard to disentangle – especially because I couldn't see any LGBTQ+ role models in my career. But it wasn't true. I was eventually able to find those role models, build my confidence and develop a more exciting career than I could have ever imagined back when I was an anxious lesbian teenager – and I am hopefully still climbing.

Many of the leaders I interviewed for this book told me very similar stories – when they realized they were LGBTQ+, they feared that it might not be possible for them to ascend to the highest levels of their chosen profession. But they were wrong. The evidence is here: these senior leaders are breaking that rainbow ceiling around the world. Sharing their experiences so generously is part of their commitment to lifting as they climb and making sure it isn't quite so hard for future generations to find role models. So, I invited them to finish this book with advice for their younger self, and for all LGBTQ+ people with career ambitions who need to see and believe that they are going to be able to break the rainbow ceiling, achieve their ambitions and have a wonderful career.

To my younger self,

You're gay. You're a lesbian. You're bi. You're trans. You're non-binary. You're queer. You're asexual. And it's going to be okay.[*] You're going to figure it out and you're going to do great.[†] Don't be afraid to be yourself.[‡] Your fear is a wasted emotion. I know it feels very real, it's almost tangible, but there's nothing to be fearful of.[§] You are stronger than you can possibly imagine.[¶] I probably should have come out much sooner – I think I'd have put much less stress on myself.[**] Hiding is pretty toxic, it's pretty tiring.[††] Embrace it. Stop hiding. Stop beating yourself up about it. Get on with it.[‡‡] It will take time but things can and will change.[§§] You are not the only person who is feeling this.[¶¶] If you're scared, look around – who are the people you can lean on, how can you

[*]Matt Burney
[†]Ken Ohashi
[‡]Loren Fykes
[§]Matt Burney
[¶]Sarah Weaver
[**]Jim Fitterling
[††]Judith Gough
[‡‡]Dan Farrell
[§§]Judith Gough
[¶¶]Rosanna Andrews

202

make sure people have your back?* It's so liberating being outside of the closet, it's the best feeling ever.† There's no crippling fear or terror anymore.‡ These things that you are the most worried about will never happen.§

The only times I've found it difficult to be LGBTQ+ are when people haven't known.¶ I wish I'd just told them.** Please come out. Now. Don't wait. The earlier the better.†† Just do it, pull off the plaster.‡‡ It's not as big a risk as you thought it was.§§ I wish I had the courage to come out sooner.¶¶ Living that way for so long, that was tough.*** Every year you wait is a waste of time and energy. I'll never know what I've missed because I was not free, I was in the closet, I was not living my truth.††† You'll find yourself quite embarrassed on several occasions by hiding who you are. Make it less gossip-worthy by coming out.‡‡‡ You'll be surprised about the insight and abilities you get from being fully yourself in this world.§§§ And people are more open and inclusive than you might think.¶¶¶ So be bolder sooner.**** Then get used to coming out because you will come out every day – to shopkeepers, to people who answer the phone, all sorts of people. The first hundred times it'll be really traumatic, but you'll get used to it.†††† That sense of ease has consolidated every year since I came out.‡‡‡‡

*Karen Teo
†Sivan Kaniel
‡Judith Gough
§Gautam Raghavan
¶Rosalind Campion
**Nancy Schlichting
††Pedro Pina
‡‡James Devine
§§Peter Molyneux
¶¶James Devine
***Nancy Schlichting
†††Pedro Pina
‡‡‡Rosalind Campion
§§§Gautam Raghavan
¶¶¶Ralph Breuer
****David Quarrey
††††Dan Farrell
‡‡‡‡John Lotherington

Never censor yourself, never apologize for being you. I thought as a teenager: 'oh I don't want people to see me as a gay person, it's just this small part of who I am', but as an adult I'm like: 'no, it's a massive part of my identity and I'm proud of that. It's a fundamental part of who I am'. You've got to be authentic; you've got to be yourself.[*] If I'd not been so obsessed with being straight-acting, would I have been a slightly different person? I sometimes wonder if there's a more flamboyant version of me somewhere inside that was there and I killed it off because I worried being too flamboyant would come back to bite me. I don't know how much is genuinely me and how much I've forced myself to behave.[†]

I think I'm a better human being because I'm queer – I feel it has given me an opportunity to mix in environments with people who think about the world differently, who challenge the status quo. It's a deeply freeing space to be.[‡] Being queer is brilliant, it's like a superpower.[§] Embrace yourself, be yourself, use your whole self as a superpower. Being gay is an intrinsic part of you. If people want to get to know you, they should know the complete you.[¶] Your anxiety about their response is all internalized gay shame that obviously comes from external sources. It's so ingrained in me. I have friends who say 'yes I'm gay but that shouldn't affect how I do something' and now I think 'well it's okay if it does'.[**] The things you think are really different will come round to be your strengths in the end.[††]

From a career perspective, just relentlessly focus on working out what you're passionate about combined with what you're

[*]Judith Gough
[†]Omar Daair
[‡]Mitch Mitchinson
[§]Simon Pollard
[¶]Darryl Clough
[**]Simon Pollard
[††]Mitch Mitchinson

good at. When those two realities overlap is when successful careers happen.* And part of being good at what you do is being comfortable in your own skin.† Just be yourself.‡ It's not going to limit you in your career.§ The quality of your work speaks volumes about you – people will see that before they see anything else.¶ I do believe the perception that people are going to be against you is stronger than the reality. I have got on in the organization and I didn't have to fight and battle.** If you told my closeted 18-year-old self I would get to where I am, I'd have been so disbelieving.††

Find yourself role models.‡‡ I was really isolated and sheltered. Meeting another gay person for the first time was huge for me.§§ When I met role models they gave me a sense of confidence.¶¶ Find yourself a LGBT mentor – it would have made a difference if I'd had someone to look up to and say: 'oh, you can be that senior'.***

Really look at yourself and understand who you are as a person. If I had I could have understood myself, I could have made more intentional decisions: what kind of companies do you want to work for, what kind of leaders do you want to put your loyalty behind?††† Think over time how much of your life you're comfortable sharing, find ways to become comfortable, don't wait until you're there to think about it for the first time. Get out and own it. I wish I'd done preparation to think about that.‡‡‡ Surround yourself

*Pedro Pina
†Marjorie Chorlins
‡James Devine
§Gautam Raghavan
¶Jim Fitterling
**Jim Harra
††David Quarrey
‡‡Eva Kreienkamp
§§Ken Ohashi
¶¶Alim Dhanji
***Becks Buckingham
†††Karen Teo
‡‡‡David Quarrey

with good people who are genuine allies, and mentors who can genuinely push you.*

You are as valid as everyone else and your identity doesn't need to impinge negatively on your ability to succeed.† Don't get beaten down by the pressure to conform. Diversity is a strength within any organization. Being different helps you to see and do things differently.‡ If you're not being respected, find a company that respects you and treats you well. And advocate for yourself. If you saw someone else being treated like that, would you stay quiet? No. So when you speak up for yourself, you're also speaking for others. If you feel you're in an environment where you're not being accepted for who you are or you're not getting respect, then walk away – people are lucky to have you working for their organization. Employment is a two-way thing. If you're working for a company where you're not being respected, where you're being misgendered or sidelined, find the organization where you're going to be treated with the respect that you deserve.§ There is no such thing as a perfect place of work.¶ But you can meet people halfway. You need to give people an opportunity to bring their biases, and also to grow. You have to give people second, third chances – we are all human. Let people have their chance to reinvent and reimagine. They may have a lot of baggage you are not aware of.**

It's all too easy to self-limit. Don't feel you have to apologize – be authentic, bring your whole self to work.†† I certainly struggled with imposter syndrome.‡‡ But, you are good enough. Be comfortable in your own skin.§§ Don't be

*James Devine
†Matt Burney
‡Judith Gough
§Simon Pollard
¶Leng Montgomery
**Keshav Suri
††Judith Gough
‡‡James Devine
§§Marjorie Chorlins

afraid because you feel different. Every step in your career, you've got there, you're there because of who you are.* Don't doubt yourself so much. Do the things you love, not the things you think you should be doing. Trust your instincts, lean into your strengths. You'll be more fulfilled as a person if you're authentically yourself.† You have to be bold – you have to be willing to take risks, to be out of your comfort zone.‡ If I'd given myself the licence to be myself, I don't know what doors would have opened. Just be confident and believe in your own ability – I think I held myself back on so many occasions.§ So push the boundaries – I thought I pushed the boundaries pretty hard but I could have had more courage. People have got your back, it's incredibly fulfilling.¶ Be as brave as you feel you can be, but don't be pressured into feeling you have to conform to any particular stereotype or any particular label.**

There's going to be times when it's hard, you're going to face difficulties, people saying things. Don't be in an echo chamber – be with people who are going to help you get the best in life.†† It's going to be really unfair, so just get on with it. We don't live in a society that's going to help you up.‡‡ Be ready for people to not be okay about you, because when they aren't, it won't cut you to the quick.§§ Figure out who you can trust.¶¶ Find your safe space – your allies, your networks, people like you.*** You will eventually find your tribe of people.††† Sometimes it's good to be with people

*Jackie Daniel
†Annie Bliss
‡Marjorie Chorlins
§Inga Beale
¶Jackie Daniel
**Becks Buckingham
††Darryl Clough
‡‡Mitch Mitchinson
§§Allegra McEvedy
¶¶Peter Gordon
***Karen Teo
†††Keshav Suri

from your community who understand. I have found that when work gets tough, I've leant on my LGBTQ+ network of friends – there's an ability to share experiences with people who've experienced exactly the same. You can offload it, then you're stronger to take on the next day.* We're at quite a precarious time in terms of society and future generations – we need to keep pushing through. We could go backwards here. Maintain confidence, maintain hope.†

Everybody takes their own path – some take a long and winding path, some take a very direct path.‡ You've got more time than you think you do, and you've got more friends than you think you do. It's easy to feel that time's running out, that things are getting away from you. You need to give yourself space and time.§ You are going to do amazing things. You will be who you need to be.¶ Love yourself for who you are much earlier.** Do things which are fun, which make you happy.†† Trust your instincts, fall back on your values, fall back on your character.‡‡ Focus on the things you can impact – and impact those things one day at a time.§§ Do good work, and be a good person.¶¶ That space is there to be claimed and you have absolutely every right to be in it, so enjoy it.*** It's a process, feeling comfortable in your own skin.††† I've had a fantastic career.‡‡‡ I've had a lot of queer joy in my journey.§§§

*Inga Beale
†Jackie Daniel
‡Jim Harra
§Rosemary Tickle
¶Sarah Weaver
**Rick Suarez
††Dinesh Bhugra
‡‡Tammy Smith
§§Ken Ohashi
¶¶Gautam Raghavan
***Jackie Daniel
†††Nesta Lloyd-Jones
‡‡‡Nancy Schlichting
§§§Mitch Mitchinson

Building a life from a place of truth is potentially your most important achievement. So focus on that.* Never put on a façade, never hide your true self. You should be so proud of who you are.†

Good luck,
From the future you

*Pedro Pina
†Pips Bunce

Acknowledgements

The biggest thanks must of course go to the many brilliant, brave, inspiring LGBTQ+ people who so generously spoke to me for this book, trusted me to share their personal stories and even in some cases connected me to further participants. Thanks also to the people who supported me in making introductions and arranging some of these interviews, including the wonderful Ima Abdulrahim, Lord Victor Adebowale, Sir Philip Barton and Lisa Schroeter. Thanks to Pragya Agarwal, who gave me good advice at the start of this project. And to my very first readers, Andrew Marshall, John Lotherington, Marie Pritchard, and my lovely parents, John and Sandra McCay, for devoting time to reading in full and sharing their insights from different perspectives about how to improve this book. Thanks to Steven Weeks from NHS Employers, who helped me interpret the NHS Staff Survey results that partly inspired this journey, and to the NHS Confederation LGBTQ+ staff group for giving me moral support throughout.

Thanks to my publisher, Ian Hallsworth, and the lovely editorial team at Bloomsbury Business for believing in the project; to Alexander Highfield, editor of my previous book in Bloomsbury Visual Arts, for making the connection; and to my agent, Abi Fellows, for her genuine enthusiasm and sage advice throughout.

But most of all, thanks to my glorious wife, Rosalind Campion, for being my constant cheerleader, ideas generator, sounding board, connector, interviewee, motivator (and dog walker to help me squeeze much of my interviewing and writing into the pre-work morning hours).

And finally, an acknowledgement to those LGBTQ+ people who wanted to participate but were too afraid of the repercussions for their career or reputation. In many ways, this book is for you.

References

1 Houdart, F. (2022). An exclusive club: a who's who of LGBTQ+ in the boardroom. Out Leadership https://outleadership.com /insights/whos-who-lgbtq-in-boardroom/ accessed 4 August 2022 and Houdart, F. (2023). Who are the most influential gay men and women in Corporate America? (accessed 28 June 2023).

2 Out for America (2021). https://victoryinstitute.org/out-for -america-2021/ (accessed 4 August 2022).

3 HC-deb (2 February 2023). LGBT History Month. Hansard https://hansard.parliament.uk/commons/2023-02-02/ debates/E6B4739B-274A-4B1D-84CD-289624A7504C/ LGBTHistoryMonth (accessed 3 February 2023).

4 Summerskill, B. (2015). Don't Ask Don't Tell: Barriers to career progression for talented LGB & T individuals in the UK Civil Service. UK Cabinet Office. https://assets.publishing.service.gov .uk/government/uploads/system/uploads/attachment_data/file /417577/Ben_Summerskill_DontAskDon_tTell_FINAL__1_ .pdf

5 BBC (2017). 100 Women: Why I invented the 'glass ceiling' phrase. https://www.bbc.co.uk/news/world-42026266 (accessed 24 July 2022).

6 Elacqua, T.C., Beehr, T.A., Hansen, C.P. and Webster, J. (2009). Manager's beliefs about the glass ceiling: interpersonal and organizational factors. *Psychol. Women Q.* 33, 285–294. doi: 10.1111/j.1471-6402.2009.01501.x

7 Babic, A. and Hansez, I. (2021). The Glass Ceiling for Women Managers: Antecedents and Consequences for Work-Family

Interface and Well-Being at Work. Front. Psychol., https://doi
.org/10.3389/fpsyg.2021.618250

8   Lyness, K.S. and Heilman, M.E. (2006). When fit is
    fundamental: evaluations and promotions of upper-level
    female and male managers. *J. Appl. Psychol.* 91, 777–785. doi:
    10.1037/0021-9010.91.4.777

9   Kinsey, A. (1948). Sexual Behavior in the Human Male.

10 Ipsos. (2021). LGBT+ Pride Survey 2021 Global Survey. At:
    https://www.ipsos.com/en/ipsos-lgbt-pride-2021-global
    -survey (accessed 4 August 2022).

11 Brown, A. (2022). About 5 per cent of young adults in the U.S.
    say their gender is different from their sex assigned at birth. Pew
    Research Center. https://www.pewresearch.org/fact-tank/2022
    /06/07/about-5-of-young-adults-in-the-u-s-say-their-gender-is
    -different-from-their-sex-assigned-at-birth/ (accessed 31 August
    2022).

12 Aksoy, C.G., Carpenter, C.S. and Frank, J. (2016). Sexual
    Orientation and Earnings: New Evidence from the UK. EBRD
    Working Paper No. 196, Available at SSRN: https://ssrn.com/
    abstract=3119665 or http://dx.doi.org/10.2139/ssrn.3119665

13 Badgett, M.V., Carpenter, C.S. and Sansone, D. (2021). LGBTQ
    Economics. Journal of Economic Perspectives, 35(2): 141–70.

14 Herek, Gregory M., Aaron T. Norton, Thomas J. Allen and Sims,
    Charles L. (2010). 'Demographic, Psychological, and Social
    Characteristics of Self-Identified Lesbian, Gay, and Bisexual
    Adults in a US Probability Sample'. Sexuality Research and
    Social Policy 7 (3): 176–200.

15 Drydakis, N. (2017). Trans people, well-being, and labor market
    outcomes. IZA World of Labor, 386. doi: 10.15185/izawol.386

16 Williams Institute, UCLA (2021). LGBT People's Experiences
    of Workplace Discrimination and Harassment. https://
    williamsinstitute.law.ucla.edu/publications/lgbt-workplace
    -discrimination/ (accessed 26 July 2022).

17 McKinsey & Company (2021). Women in the Workplace. https://
    www.mckinsey.com/featured-insights/diversity-and-inclusion/
    women-in-the-workplace (accessed 24 July 2022).

18 Klawitter, M. (2015). Meta-Analysis of the Effects of Sexual
    Orientation on Earnings. Industrial Relations 54(1): 4–32.

19 Folch, M. (2022). The LGBTQ+ Gap: Recent Estimates for Young Adults in the United States (1 April 2022). Available at SSRN: https://ssrn.com/abstract=4072893 or http://dx.doi.org/10.2139/ssrn.4072893

20 Drydakis, N. (2019). Sexual orientation and labor market outcomes. IZA World of Labor, 111: doi: 10.15185/izawol.111.v2

21 Schwartz, C.R. and Graf, N.L. (2009). Assortative matching among same-sex and different-sex couples in the United States, 1990–2000. *Demographic Research*, 21, 843–878. https://doi.org/10.4054/demres.2009.21.28

22 Shamloo, S., De Cristofaro, V., Pellegrini, V. and Salvati, M. (2022). Masculinity and Leadership Effectiveness (Self-)Perceptions. The Case of Lesbian Leaders. *International Journal of Environmental Research and Public Health*. 19. 1–14. 10.3390/ijerph192417026.

23 Freeman, J.B. (2020). Measuring and Resolving LGBTQ Disparities in STEM. Policy Insights from the Behavioral and Brain Sciences 2020, 7(2) 141–148.

24 Hughes, B.E. (2018). Coming out in STEM: Factors affecting retention of sexual minority STEM students. 4(3) DOI: 10.1126/sciadv.aao6373

25 Wolchover, N. (25 July 2012). Why aren't there any openly gay astronauts? *Scientific American*. https://www.scientificamerican.com/article/why-arent-there-any-openly-gay-astronauts/ (accessed 10 September 2022).

26 Vieira, H. (2016). There may be some truth to the 'gay jobs' stereotype. LSE Blogs. https://blogs.lse.ac.uk/businessreview/2016/01/18/there-may-be-some-truth-to-the-gay-jobs-stereotype/ (accessed 10 September 2022).

27 Tilcsik, A., Anteby, M. and Knight, C.R. (2015). Concealable Stigma and Occupational Segregation: Toward a Theory of Gay and Lesbian Occupations. *Administrative Science Quarterly*, 60(3), 446–481. https://doi.org/10.1177/0001839215576401

28 HRC. (2022). The Wage Gap Among LGBTQ+ Workers in the United States. https://www.hrc.org/resources/the-wage-gap-among-lgbtq-workers-in-the-united-states (accessed 9 April 2023).

29 OHCHR (2019). The inclusion of LGBT people in education settings; of paramount importance to "leaving no one behind".

UN. https://www.ohchr.org/en/statements/2019/10/inclusion-lgbt-people-education-settingsof-paramount-importance-leaving-no-one#_ftn5 (accessed 5 September 2022).

30   Mittleman, J. (2022). Intersecting the Academic Gender Gap: The Education of Lesbian, Gay, and Bisexual America. *American Sociological Review*, 87(2): 303–335.

31   AKT (2020). The LGBTQ+ Youth Homelessness Report. https://www.akt.org.uk/report (accessed 28 July 2022).

32   HRC. (2018). A Workplace Divided: Understanding the Climate for LGBTQ Workers Nationwide. https://hrc-prod-requests.s3-us-west-2.amazonaws.com/files/assets/resources/AWorkplaceDivided-2018.pdf (accessed 4 May 2023).

33   Bachmann, C.L. and Gooch, B. (2018). LGBT in Britain: Work Report. Stonewall. https://www.stonewall.org.uk/system/files/lgbt_in_britain_work_report.pdf (accessed 4 May 2023).

34   Suen, Y., Chan, R. and Badgett, M. (2021). The Experiences of Sexual and Gender Minorities in Employment: Evidence from a Large-scale Survey of Lesbian, Gay, Bisexual, Transgender and Intersex People in China. *The China Quarterly*, 245, 142–164. doi:10.1017/S0305741020000429

35   Collins, J.C., McFadden, C., Rocco, T.S. and Mathis, M.K. (2015). The problem of transgender marginalization and exclusion: Critical actions for human resource development. Human Resource Development Review, *14*(2), 205–226.

36   United States Census Bureau (2019). Current Population Survey (CPS). https://www.census.gov/programs-surveys/cps/technical-documentation/complete.html (accessed 9 September 2022).

37   TransActual (2022). Transition Access Survey 2022. https://static1.squarespace.com/static/5e8a0a6bb02c73725b24dc9d/t/637284ceea977434a718dd26/1668449552251/Transition+Access+Survey+2022.pdf (accessed 17 November 2022).

38   International Labour Organization (ILO) 2022. Inclusion of lesbian, gay, bisexual, transgender, intersex and queer (LGBTIQ+) persons in the world of work: A learning guide. https://www.ilo.org/wcmsp5/groups/public/---dgreports/---gender/documents/publication/wcms_846108.pdf (accessed 4 May 2023).

39   European Union Agency for Fundamental Rights (2020). A long way to go for LGBTI equality. https://fra.europa.eu/sites/default/files/fra_uploads/fra-2020-lgbti-equality-1_en.pdf

40   Trades Union Congress (TUC) (2019). Sexual harassment of LGBT people in the workplace. https://www.tuc.org.uk/sites/default/files/LGBT_Sexual_Harassment_Report_0.pdf

41   Drydakis, N. (2015). Sexual orientation discrimination in the United Kingdom's labour market: a field experiment. *Hum. Relat.* 68, 1–28. doi: 10.1177/0018726715569855

42   Gagnon, J.H, Nardi, P.M. Levine, M.P. (1997). Introduction, In changing times: Gay men and lesbians encounter HIV/AIDS, Chicago, The University of Chicago Press: 1–22.

43   Clarke, H.M. and Arnold, K.A. (2018). The Influence of Sexual Orientation on the Perceived Fit of Male Applicants for Both Male- and Female-Typed Jobs. *Front. Psychol.*, 3 May 2018. https://doi.org/10.3389/fpsyg.2018.00656

44   Eagly, A.H. and Karau, S.J. (2002). Role congruity theory of prejudice toward female leaders. *Psychol. Rev.* 109, 573–598. doi: 10.1037/0033-295X.109.3.573

45   Heilman, M.E. (1983). Sex bias in work settings: the lack of fit model. *Res. Organiz. Behav.* 5, 269–298.

46   Heilman, M.E. and Wallen, A.S. (2010). Wimpy and undeserving of respect: Penalties for men's gender-inconsistent success. *J. Exp. Soc. Psychol.* 46, 664–667. doi: 10.1016/j.jesp.2010.01.008

47   Heilman, M.E., Wallen, A.S., Fuchs, D. and Tamkins, M.M. (2004). Penalties for success: reactions to women who succeed at male gender-typed tasks. *J. Appl. Psychol.* 89, 416–427. doi: 10.1037/0021-9010.89.3.416

48   Ueno, K., Roach, T. and Peña-Talamantes, A.E. (2013). Sexual orientation and gender typicality of the occupation in young adulthood. *Soc. Forces* 92, 81–108. doi: 10.1093/sf/sot067

49   Flage, A. (2020). 'Discrimination against gays and lesbians in hiring decisions: a meta-analysis', *International Journal of Manpower*, Vol. 41 No. 6, pp. 671–691. https://doi.org/10.1108/IJM-08-2018-0239

50   Sears, B. and Mallory, C. (2011). Documented evidence of employment discrimination and its effects on LGBT people. The Williams Institute, UCLA Law School. https://escholarship.org/uc/item/03m1g5sg per cent20 (accessed 28 February 2023).

51 Home Office, UK Government (2022). Hate crime, England and Wales, 2021 to 2022. https://www.gov.uk/government/statistics/hate-crime-england-and-wales-2021-to-2022/hate-crime-england-and-wales-2021-to-2022 (accessed 20 February 2022).

52 Stonewall (2017). LGBT in Britain: Hate Crime and Discrimination. https://www.stonewall.org.uk/system/files/lgbt_in_britain_hate_crime.pdf (accessed 20 February 2023).

53 CCDH (2022). Digital hate. Social Media's Role in Amplifying Dangerous Lies About LGBTQ+ People. https://counterhate.com/research/digital-hate-lgbtq/ (accessed 20 February 2023).

54 Mijatovic, D. (2021). Pride vs. indignity: political manipulation of homophobia and transphobia in Europe. Council of Europe. (accessed 20 February 2023).

55 Bachman, C.L. and Gooch, B. (2018). LGBT in Britain Health Report. Stonewall. https://www.stonewall.org.uk/lgbt-britain-health (accessed 6 July 2023).

56 LGBT Foundation (2018). Hidden figures: LGBT health inequalities in the UK. https://dxfy8lrzbpywr.cloudfront.net/Files/b9398153-0cca-40ea-abeb-f7d7c54d43af/Hidden per cent2520Figures per cent2520FULL per cent2520REPORT per cent2520Web per cent2520Version per cent2520Smaller.pdf (accessed 17 February 2023).

57 Hodson, K., Meads, C. and Bewley, S. (2017). Lesbian and bisexual women's likelihood of becoming pregnant: a systematic review and meta-analysis. BJOG; 124: 393–402.

58 Croll, J., Sanapo, L. and Bourjeily, G. (2022). LGBTQ+ individuals and pregnancy outcomes: A commentary. *International Journal of Obstetrics and Gynaecology*, 129(10): 1625–1629.

59 Census Bureau (2020). Census Bureau Implements Improved Measurement of Same-Sex Couples. https://www.census.gov/library/stories/2020/09/same-sex-married-couples-have-higher-income-than-opposite-sex-married-couples.html (accessed 21 February 2023).

60 European Institute for Gender Equality (2021). EIGE-2021 Gender Equality Index 2021 Report: Health. https://eige.europa.eu/publications/gender-equality-index-2021-report/gender-differences-household-chores (accessed 31 August 2022).

61 Ipsos. (2022). Who Cares? Business in the Community & Ipsos research reveals the great workplace divide. https://www.ipsos .com/en-uk/who-cares-business-community-ipsos-research -reveals-great-workplace-divide (accessed 31 August 2022).

62 Syrda, J. (2022). Gendered Housework: Spousal Relative Income, Parenthood and Traditional Gender Identity Norms. Work, Employment and Society (1–20).

63 Slaughter, A.M. (2012). Why Women Can't Have It All. *The Atlantic.* July/August. https://www.theatlantic.com/magazine /archive/2012/07/why-women-still-cant-have-it-all/309020/ (accessed 4 September 2022).

64 van der Vleuten, M., Jaspers, E. and van der Lippe, T. (2021). Same-Sex Couples' Division of Labor from a Cross-National Perspective, *Journal of GLBT Family Studies*, 17:2, 150–167, DOI : 10.1080/1550428X.2020.1862012

65 Brewster, M.E. (2016). Lesbian women and household labor division: A systematic review of scholarly research from 2000 to 2015. *Journal of Lesbian Studies*; 21(1): 47–69.

66 Moberg, Ylva, 2016. 'Does the gender composition in Couples matter for the division of labor after childbirth?,' Working Paper Series 2016:8, IFAU – Institute for Evaluation of Labour Market and Education Policy.

67 Jaspers, E. and Verbakel, E. (2013). The division of paid labor in same-sex couples in the Netherlands. *Sex Roles, 68*(5-6), 335–348. https://doi.org/10.1007/s11199-012-0235-2

68 Moors, A.C., Gesselman, A.N. and Garcia, J.R. Desire, Familiarity, and Engagement in Polyamory (2021). Results From a National Sample of Single Adults in the United States. Front Psychol; 12:619640.

69 Research and Markets (2022). Diversity and Inclusion (D&I) – Global Market Trajectory & Analytics.

70 Subramanian, R. (2021). Lessons from the Pandemic: Board Diversity and Performance. Board Ready. https://uploads-ssl.webflow .com/61d633fd6b59246c2dc62e98/6271a21dc04d2e13529daa84 _BoardReady_Report_Final.pdf (accessed 5 March 2023).

71 Rudin, J., Billing, T., Farro, A. and Yang, Y. (2020). Bigenderism at work? Organizational responses to trans men and trans women employees. *Organization Management Journal, 17*(2), 63–81.

Index

drug/alcohol abuse 148
Dubai 73

Eisenhower, Dwight D. 4–5
empathy 94–5
employer support
advantages of a diverse
workforce 165–6
childcare and child-centric
policies 187–8
default inclusive policies 184–7
demonstrating inclusivity in the
workplace 169–73, 175–8
educating/mentoring
management 168–9
employee benefits equality 184–7
helping LGBTQ+ staff fulfil
potential 192–4
including LGBTQ+ in the
diversity fold 166–8
inclusive recruitment 173–6
LGBTQ+ staff network
and employee resource
groups 190–1
need for a bold and confident
approach to 194–5
practical changes to improve
inclusivity 181–4
rainbow washing/virtue
signalling 170–1
staff diversity education and
awareness 191–2
travelling and working
abroad 174–5
visibility of LGBTQ+
leadership 175–8, 200–1
the workplace as a safe
haven 178–80
Europe 23, 46, 64, 104, 114, 118, 123,
144, 145, 146, 147
European Court of Human
Rights 8

family/carers, ties with 51–2, 161–2
family life see social/day-to-day life
influences
Farrell, Dan 107, 126
Fitterling, Jim 76, 79, 85–6, 90, 95,
165, 172, 179, 180, 183–4, 188
Flage, Alexandre 123
flexibility and opportunities 102–3
Folch, Mark 30, 31, 34
Foreign, Commonwealth and
Development Office, UK 8,
120–1, 137–8, 174
forms and documentation,
inclusive 181–2
France 8
Frost, Meryll 155
Fruits in Suits mixer events 98–9
Fykes, Loren 69, 98–9, 100, 126,
132, 201

Generation Z 26, 65
glass ceiling 10–12, 14, 155
Gordon, Peter 90, 111, 131–2, 171
Gough, Judith 67, 82–3, 89, 94–5,
120–1, 126, 132, 133, 135, 154,
177–8, 192
'gross indecency' charges, UK 8

Harra, Jim 39, 77–8, 80, 83–4, 86,
95, 102, 107, 134–5, 179, 194–5
heads of state, LGBTQ+ 3–4
health and healthcare
staff benefit equality 184–7
health issues and healthcare
access to healthcare 149
addiction 148
gender care waiting lists 149
HIV and AIDS
mental health and wellbeing 148–9
pregnancy and parenthood
150–1, 152
Heilman, Madeline 121–2

marriage, same-sex   36, 37, 154–8,
    162–3, 185–7
maternity/paternity/caregiver
    commitments   103
Maupin, Armistead   162
Mauritania   6
McEvedy, Allegra   46, 62, 78, 107,
    112, 132, 198
mental health and wellbeing   42, 44,
    67, 148–9
mentors and sponsors   58–9, 168–9,
    194
#metoo   141
microaggressions and
    assumptions   105–10
Mijatović, Dunja   145–6
Mitchinson, Mitch   44, 48–9, 51, 94,
    117, 133, 134, 168
Mittleman, Joel   45
Molyneux, Peter   46–7, 61, 69, 94,
    98, 109, 110, 117, 124, 194
'Monday syndrome'   67, 161
Montgomery, Leng   29–30, 59, 86,
    99–100, 104, 109, 128, 131, 144,
    146–7, 149, 171, 175, 188, 192
Motion Picture Production Code/
    Hays Code   55

Nazi Germany   7, 24
networking   96–9, 101, 132, 190–1
Nigeria   6, 7
Nikkei newspaper   83

Ohashi, Ken   44, 49, 93–4, 95, 108,
    115, 153

pay inequality   29–31, 33–4, 71
Pina, Pedro   43, 48, 49, 54, 67, 79, 98,
    101–2, 123, 128, 136–7, 143, 170
Poland   23
Pollard, Simon   54–5, 57, 78, 130,
    151–2, 168, 175

polyamorous lifestyle choice
    160–1
pregnancy and parenthood   149–54,
    156, 161–2, 187–8
press and social media, abuse in   81,
    82–3, 144–5, 147
Pride month   20, 170–1
pronoun diversity   108–9, 172

Quarrey, David   98, 137, 138, 168

racial inequality   33, 90, 100, 110,
    118, 129, 179, 193, 199
Raghavan, Gautam   72, 85, 87,
    88, 89, 95, 120, 121, 125,
    173–4, 177
rainbow ceiling   viii, 2, 13–15, 25
    author's experience   9–10, 127
    awareness and denial of   2–3
    company reputational
        concerns   19–20, 23, 124, 135
    and the glass ceiling   10–12, 14,
        28–9
    letters to younger selves, senior
        LGBTQ+ leaders'   202–9
    LGBTQ+ representation in
        senior roles   1–2, 20, 28–9,
        76–81, 118–19, 133, 134–7,
        175–8, 198–201
    pay gaps   29–31, 33–4
    reasons barriers are
        downplayed   17–23
    through history   4–8, 32
    see also coming out in the
        workplace; employer support;
        hiring and firing; LGBTQ+
        community; travel and work
        abroad; workplace, being
        LGBTQ+ in the
'rainbow washing'/virtue
    signalling   20, 170–1
recruitment, inclusive   173–6

references, job 124–5, 174
Ride, Sally 32
role models, LGBTQ+ 54–6, 57, 66,
    126, 176–7, 200

Saudi Arabia 6
Schlichting, Nancy 54, 66, 67, 70,
    82, 131, 133, 141, 190, 192–3
school education *see* childhood and
    adolescent influences
Scientific American 32
'second adolescence' 56–8
Section 28 (1988), UK Local
    Government Act 8, 39–41
security checks/risks,
    government 5, 120, 137
sexual discrimination 11–12, 71
sexual harassment and assault 112–14,
    141–2
Sharia Law 73
Singapore 7
Slaughter, Anne Marie 157
Smith, Major General Tammy 5–6,
    49, 61, 72, 87, 88, 94, 96–7, 184,
    185–6
social/day-to-day life
    influences 143
    division of domestic
        chores 156–9
    family life and professional
        attainment 154–9
    insecurity and bureaucracy 162–3
    mental health and
        wellbeing 148–9
    polyamorous lifestyle
        choice 160–1
    pregnancy and parenthood
        149–54, 161–2
    public abuse and
        harassment 143–8
    see also childhood adolescent
        influence

social media and press, abuse in 81,
    82–3, 144–5, 147
staff network and resource groups,
    LGBTQ+ 190–1
STEM career paths 31–2
stereotypes, job 32–3, 121–2
Stonewall Riots (1969) 38
Suarez, Rick 79, 93, 109, 144–5,
    173, 182, 194
suicide rates and suicidal
    ideation 42, 148
Suri, Keshav 47, 73, 90–1, 162–3,
    170–1, 172–3, 179–80, 183,
    186, 195
surveys of sexual orientation and
    gender identity 21–6

talent management,
    LGBTQ+ 192–4
Teo, Karen 17, 43, 67, 70, 129, 169,
    173, 176, 184–5, 188, 193
Thatcher, Margaret 39–40
Tickle, Rosemary 37–8, 40, 48,
    49–50, 58, 101, 104, 109, 131, 189
trans and non-binary issues 26,
    27–8, 29, 33, 43, 89, 103–4, 105,
    108–9, 112, 113, 114, 118, 124–5,
    128, 131, 144, 145, 146, 147, 148,
    149, 150–1, 152, 155, 172, 175,
    178–9, 181–3, 188
travel and work abroad 73–5,
    137–40, 153, 174–5
Turing, Alan 32

Uganda 7
United Arab Emirates 73
United Kingdom
    anti-discrimination laws 8
    armed forces 8
    bullying and harassment in the
        workplace 111–12, 114
    colonialization 6